WORLD WAR III
STRATEGIES TACTICS AND WEAPONS

WORLD WAR III
STRATEGIES TACTICS AND WEAPONS

JOHN BRADLEY

CRESCENT

© 1982 by Omega Books Limited

ISBN 0 517 385317

Library of Congress Cataloging in Publication Data
Bradley. J. F. N. (John Francis Nejez). 1930–
    The illustrated history of World War III.

    1. World War III.   2. World politics – 1945–
I. Title.
U313.B73   355.4'8'09048   82-2551
                                  `AACR2

First published in the United States of America in 1982 by
Cresent Books
distributed by Crown Publishers Inc
One Park Avenue New York
NY 10016 USA

Produced by Winchmore Publishing Services Limited.
48. Lancaster Avenue.
Hadley Wood.
Herts. England.

House editor: Catherine Bradley
Designer: Roy Williams
Picture research: Nicholas Bradley
Maps and Charts: Roy Williams and Marie-Helene Bradley
Index and Translations: Don Slater
Typesetting: SX Composing Limited. Rayleigh. Essex
Color separation: Capricorn Reproductions. London and
Lee Fung Asco Limited. Hong Kong.

Printed in Hong Kong by Lee Fung Asco Limited.

CONTENTS

PREFACE

J. B. Duroselle

By profession, the historian is entrusted not with the future but with the past. It is only the more remarkable, therefore, to find an excellent historian, author of several important books and principally interested in relations between the West and the communist world, resolutely moving on from the well-reconstructed past to the possible future. In his remarkable introduction, General Buis has been able to extract from all the technical aspects of the book several precise and sober reflections. I would like to take up a more abstract perspective and speculate on some of the basic characteristics of the future.

First of all the future is a source of *terror*. Man hates uncertainty. As there is no absolute certainty, even concerning the present moment, man falls back on the past. Or he looks for precedents — though history never repeats itself; or he does his best to believe — if he is reasonably content — that things will always continue the same. Or he suffers, he hopes for a return to a past which is considered normal: "Back to Normalcy," said the future American president Warren G. Harding in 1920, after the Great War.

Concerning the war, John Bradley has been able to demonstrate in a striking manner one of the paths between the past, "the balance of terror," and a possible outcome: the appearance of a "vital" concern for the Soviets, the disintegration before our eyes of the bases of their ideology, of their faith, their religion. In a recent book, I have referred to this constant historical given: the emergence of the "insupportable" in an immobile, rigid, blocked society. Nothing changes, except the consciousness of men, who begin no longer to tolerate the status quo.

The future is also *unforeseeable*, not in the case of nature, where one can know in advance, for example, the movements of the stars, but when we are dealing with human societies. There is a tangible reality which we call human freedom or, better still, ingenuity, creativity. Creation, the discovery of hitherto unperceived relations, cannot by definition be predicted. Bismarck once said that although he could reasonably foresee Europe's diplomatic future two years in advance, he could see no further than that. But even this was dependent on the fact that he held the keys to this diplomacy himself, and knew clearly what he at least was going to do. Thus one must give John Bradley credit for having carefully avoided presenting the third world war as if it were inevitable. His method is to continue the narrative as if the past was stretched out before us, at once a pleasant and prudent form of presentation.

The future is *serious*. By this I mean that, when one speaks of it and intends some educational value, one must avoid palpable nonsense. Our children manifest a great enthusiasm for animated science fiction on television. All of these, despite always presenting wars between worlds, are totally incoherent in matters of space, time and speed. Oh, Einstein! One no longer travels from planet to planet, nor even from solar system to solar system, but from galaxy to galaxy. I also remember reading, in 1951, a special edition of the American magazine *Collier's* about World War III, with "reports" and "photos" as evidence. It began with the assassination of Tito and ended, of course, with a brilliant American victory. The last photo portrayed Red Square with a newspaper kiosk in which one could freely purchase *Collier's*, a symbol among symbols of liberty regained.

It is therefore good to read here the very detailed studies of the period since 1945, with supporting statistics and analyses of the events, allowing one to extrapolate in the direction of the probable rather than the absurd. The real conclusions are those concerning the ruinous state of the "American umbrella," the essentially national character of all deterence — as de Gaulle indeed had seen — and those regarding the interest there might be in making Europe one great Nation — for a European Community of separate national defense systems, even independent of the United States, unlike the old CED, would not be capable of establishing that unique response which at the time of crisis the Nation could eventually create.

Finally, John Bradley maintains a certain optimism, which is not surprising when one knows him. And I will join with him in attributing to the future a fourth quality: The future is moldable. Though from the present moment the past definitively fixes the unrolling of events and causes them to disappear, with the exception of some rare traces which the historian gathers up, it does not follow that the future is equally fixed. Such a determinism might satisfy our most abstract reason. But it flies in the face of all our life, all our actions, of our most profound intentions. The most fatalistic Jansenist, the most mechanistic physicist acts as if he were a free man. That I on my own can do little to prevent the third world war does not prejudice the action of many men together applying themselves to preventing it. And I would say, to conclude, that with this excellent book, should be read attentively by those in power, John Bradley has himself contributed, through the subtlety and solidity of his reasoning, to the cause of peace which, as Pascal said, "is the greatest of goods."

A nuclear mushroom balloons from the Nevada Test Site after a successful test of a 37 kiloton nuclear device.

INTRODUCTION

The era in which the atom first made its shattering appearance is over. During the present period, massive systems of nuclear weapons have been developed and deployed — especially by the Super Powers — while general military strategies, gradually evolved, have not yet managed to disengage themselves from superseded forms of warfare, which were based on the relative number and quality of personnel and weaponry. If one takes into account the fact that during this period military confrontation has not only changed in degree, but in its very *nature*, the reality of overwhelming military strength is seen to be so incalculable that assessing the relative balance of forces between the Super Powers loses its point. Despite the continually more ostentatious flaunting of strategic hardware, the old adage — "show force in order not to have to use it" — which backward-looking people endlessly repeat (as if to demonstrate decisively that there is nothing new under the sun and that nuclear deterrence certainly holds no surprises) in reality no longer makes sense. Indeed, strategy is no longer a matter of ascertaining and making known that one's army can conquer the enemy's as well as convincing him of that: it is rather a question of being in a position to penetrate the enemy's defenses and of clearly proving to him that, if he attacks, his own country will inevitably be destroyed or mutilated. This must be made equally clear whether it is a matter of an enemy who is prepared for an unlimited confrontation or one who simply dares to take the first step toward an escalating conflict.

This inability to "contain" another nuclear power by force — to dictate its conduct — will remain an absolute limiting condition so long as no "technological breakthrough" appears which could transform the fundamental premises of the situation: in other words, as long as "mutually assured destruction" remains a fact of life, Soviet bravado notwithstanding. Moreover, though of secondary importance, this face-off of excessive but impotent power complicates the task of evolving strategies which can project not only what form a third world war will take, but which can, above all, construct an unfolding scenario from credible premises. How could a war between the two Super Powers arise when both incessantly and deliberately arm any country whatsoever to fight whosoever suits them and when each is fiercely determined not, at any price, to attack the other directly?

Aside from the subtle commentary, analyses of detail and descriptions of movements which John Bradley presents throughout the unfolding of his "Great War," his considerable achievement — and it is the most difficult thing — has been above all to give this direct confrontation a plausible origin.

He has, in addition, managed to posit an outcome which is neither an apocalypse nor a failure of nerve in the face of the atom, that is, a surrender pure and simple. Finally, and above all, he has furnished the conflict with a pivotal factor, a point of inflection — unforeseen by commentators — which will prove to be decisive: the coming into play of a second-order power which possesses a *national* system of strategic arms.

Thus the second of John Bradley's achievements has been to forge an unforeseen link between the threat to employ nuclear weapons and their actual employment. It is no longer credible to think that nuclear weapons will be employed in the form of a more or less mild warning shot: the idea of gradual and controlled escalation gathers few supporters any longer. The key is in deterrence based on the possibility of reciprocal use, but not in just any form: it is in strategic weapons used "in proportion to the crisis," that is, used to a degree which is unsupportable but which still allows for the possibility of recovery with time and international aid, and which holds up to the terrified eyes of its participants a respectable model of survivable apocalypse. Precisely targetted megatons will inflict atrocious damage and prove irrefutably what the little bomb of Hiroshims could not: that modern nuclear weapons are of an entirely different order.

In order to construct his scenario away from the tangled jungle of hypothesis, John Bradley first clears the underbrush. Those eccentric flash points which are often considered capable of starting the brush fire which could threaten the two mansions at the edge of the woods are first eliminated from the range of possibilities. What has recently been conveniently dubbed, "horizontal escalation" will thus not begin either in the North Pacific or in Asia or in the Gulf or Indian Ocean, and still less in Africa, the Caribbean or Central or South America.

This leaves Europe, rich in formidable complexities. There, the balance of "theater nuclear weapons" clearly leans in favor of the USSR. A wave of pro-neutrality sentiment sweeps the western tip of the Eurasian peninsula. Spread by the Scandinavian countries, this wave has won over the states of ancient Lotharingia: Germany, Benelux, Italy. Great Britain is also affected by it. France is only lightly touched, its citizens feeling, perhaps confusedly, that their own strategy — based on that noble weapon, the nuclear bomb — is right for them. They thus have something to rely on which is independent of America's improbable — because lunatic — offer of suicide. NATO, crumbling of late, seems on the path to disintegration.

The Warsaw Pact, like an arch which can only

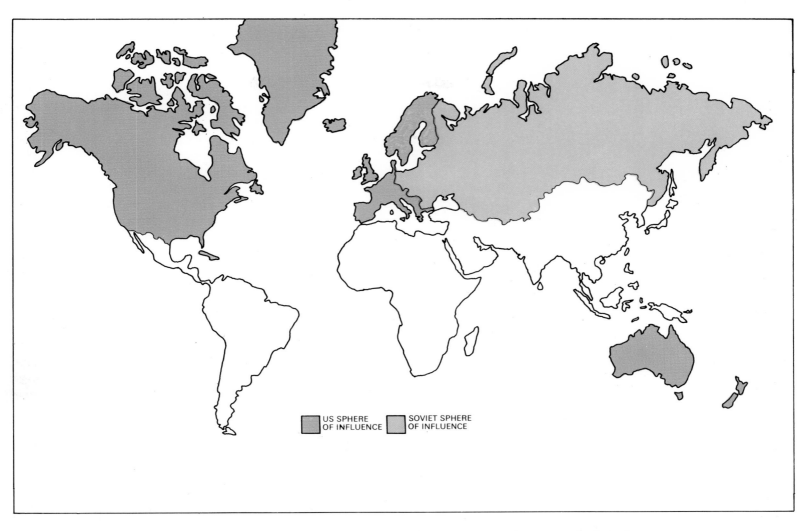

US SPHERE OF INFLUENCE   SOVIET SPHERE OF INFLUENCE

maintain its rigid structure when faced with a symmetrical arch placed in opposition, only exists because of NATO. While NATO is giving way, the nations of the Pact are facing the same economic and food supply problems which led Poland to turn on its leaders, the communist regime obedient to Moscow, in 1980.

Thus, at the end of the 1980s, Eastern Europe begins to stir. Rumania is the first to rise up against COMECON, refusing to participate either militarily or financially in the Pact and demanding the creation of a nuclear-free zone in Europe. Although less dramatic, the economic situations of East Germany, Czechoslovakia, and Hungary inspire groups of communist dissidents to appeal to the Polish example. As to outlying Yugoslavia, it comes apart under the pressure of the Slovenes and Croats, who lose all patience with carrying the burden of the other federated provinces and districts. We can add to this the reawakening of diverse nationalisms, of which Kossovo has already given us such a forceful glimpse in 1980.

All these potential dissidences carry with them the short or medium-term threat of bringing into question the irreversibility of communism. Now, under what conditions would a nuclear Super Power decide to use force to resolve a problem? Only one: this problem must be *vital*.

— not to be forced into exchange of nuclear weapons

— not to cross the threshold beyond which lack of proteins directly threatens the survival of its citizens
— not to allow its satellites to reject marxist ideology, as defined and made into a religion by the Communist Party of the Soviet Union (CPSU), as a scapegoat for all their hardships.

Now, all the signs that Moscow reads in the domestic unrest of the socialist republics converge on one intolerable point: a steady progress

Below:
Soviet armored infantry fighting vehicles during a sea landing on the Polish Baltic sea coast which was part of maneuvers designed to intimidate the Polish leadership and people.

Above:
Soviet APCs in Afghanistan seen with Afghan military personnel. Soviet support has been massive and seemingly unproductive.

categories in a state of operational readiness, of massive exercises along the Polish coasts on the Baltic.

However, it is not the purpose of the introduction to reveal the story of the specific military operations involving confrontation between conventional forces of NATO and the Warsaw Pact, nor to describe and appraise the psychological and material preparations for war carried out by the aggressor nation. To recount those parts of the book which concern the details of military action might lessen the enjoyment of the reader who is interested more in the vicissitudes of the sword play than in the result of the attack. In this part, the author takes risks not as a theoretician, but as a narrator. In the event, however, we may say that he takes all these risks, for he presents not only the machinations which are put into play, but also their "how" and "why." The two first chapters thus constitute a remarkable academic work — but the work of an involved academic. The first deals with East-West relations from 1945 to 1982: the Cold War and its limited conflicts in the form of brinkmanship; the sham of *détente*; the neo-Cold War which is still in progress. The second establishes in detail the relations of forces and doctrines on the two opposing sides. Together these two parts render the book a most pertinent

toward the rejection of orthodox ideology. Here then is the third vital threat.

When it withdrew from China in 1960, Moscow had had to yield. The USSR would no more make war on the China of Mao than it would proselytize for a question of orthodoxy. It is a different matter with the socialist republics. When the time comes, the USSR can and must try to reestablish by force a *status quo* whose deterioration COMECON and the apparatchiks have been powerless to prevent over the past 30 years. It is no longer a question of attacking the schismatics directly, as in the case of Afghanistan. The USSR did not consider this a possibility even when it was a matter of Poland alone: it foresees that the consequences would be dire in the event of directly attacking nations which are officially not just friends but sisters.

In the event, the USSR decides on an Israeli-style operation, but on its own scale. If possible with their help, Russia first surrounds the European socialist republics with a military buffer zone. Having isolated them, it forces them back into line either through occupation or straightforward annexation. In this case, NATO supplies the bad examples to be punished. What remains of it is still considerable. It is not entirely impossible that the United States could be dissuaded from a "strategic exchange" by being convinced that the USSR is only engaged in a limited punitive operation against Scandinavia, Germany, and a few other members of NATO which lie along the demarcation line, or even — circumstances permitting — against parts of France. It is an enormous gamble, but we are talking about vital interests. There is no choice: military action must be undertaken.

The Soviet general staff has long since prepared plans for a global attack which employs only conventional arms. They have been the object of numerous war-games, of mobilization exercises required to put Soviet divisions of two and three

vade mecum (reference work), a basic text for all those (and this should include everyone) who are concerned about their chances for survival or for the survival of even a humble cryptogam on the surface of this planet.

So let us leave the reader to follow the complicated advance of the Soviet conventional forces, to evaluate the manelvers of the North, Central, and Southern army groups of the Pact and the quality and condition of the resistance which they encounter. Let us only note that so well-informed an author has obviously not omitted to investigate all the ways and means by which Western Europeans might be psychologically prepared so as to demobilize them. A number of things happen: clandestine activity, misinformation, rumors, and also an obsolete practice which one thought had died long ago — Soviet ambassadors visiting the governments to which they are accredited with the aim of convincing them not to trouble themselves about the sound of marching armies which are not aimed at them but are only out to punish West Germany for feeding the general state of disorder and the particular disorder which reigns in Poland.

In outer space, a series of collisions and narrow misses between American and Soviet satellites mysteriously arises. On the ground, the Iron Cur-

Above:
An artist's impression of two satellites above the earth. The war in space can only become more sophisticated.

Left:
The underground Headquarters of the Civil Defense ·in Washington. Here members are seen taking part in a bomb defense drill.

13

Above: Russian Alpine troops sweep through the forests of Bavaria.

tain is effectively raised by the Soviets and some incursions of Red Army units onto the territory of NATO countries occur "by accident." Russia's high seas fleet, built with so much love, determination and fanfare, does not move from its bases. Thus, all is set for the West to believe that the USSR will carry out a military operation in the sphere of influence allotted to it by Yalta and confirmed by Helsinki.

The American President firmly believes this. Europe is uneasy.

It is summer. Soldiers on leave are sun-bathing on far-off beaches or carrying out non-military work far from the countries in which their units are to be operationally deployed according to plans. The staffs of major NATO governments are skeletal.

Thus, on D-day, the surprise for the West is

total. Moreover, from the start, aerial bombing, infiltrated commandos and collaborators succeed in destroying all communications centers and in cutting off all the large advance units from their subordinate units as well as from their overall command. Each reacts in its own way and according to its rank, courageously but in disorder, without any logistical support. The author even goes on to imagine the unimaginable: acting on their own authority, commanders of French divisions stationed in Germany engage with dislocated NATO forces nearby.

infiltrated commandos, and collaborators succeed

While the conventional battle described by John Bradley unfolds, the American President is continually confronted with "terrible dilemmas" on the question of nuclear war, which he compounds by considering alternatives which simply permit him to remain in a state of indecision. The Europeans are aware that the US will confine itself to "theater nuclear weapons" (tactical) and that it will not bring to bear on the enemy the full weight of its central strategic arsenal, which is the only effective deterrent. The American President eventually decides on precisely this immediate engagement of tactical nuclear arms, an "agonizing" decision. Moreover, the Europeans are astounded to find that the American—Soviet discussions which vitally concern them are being carried on well over their heads and that they are being informed only vaguely of their content. To add to the debacle, the American President decides that the use of tactical nuclear warheads would be envisioned only after D+12, if no "peaceful" solution has emerged from the discussions on the Hot Line.

A Pershing 2 intermediate nuclear missile streaks away from its launcher.

While Soviet army units pursue their various offensives, the governments of NATO find themselves in exile. Thus the Bonn government is installed in Paris where it has been offered refuge.

At this point in the scenario, John Bradley's vision acquires a prophetic value in my eyes and should do so in the eyes of Europeans and Americans. John Bradley shows that due to the force of circumstances, the Atlantic Alliance is unable to act as the axis of European defense. It is urged that this axis cannot be other than Franco–German: in the nuclear age, defense must be national. Let us note, as an aside, that this important consideration (which will lead the current conflict to the "zero option" and could open the door to a disarmament which is ardently desired on both sides) has been put forward, in fictional form, not by a French strategist who has long held this conviction, but by British intellectual and academic, and moreover in a book published in the United States.

At this point in the chain of events, and before the entirely comprehensible and justified default on its obligations by the United States, the French and German governments raise among themselves for the first time the possibility of a French nuclear intervention. This step is an obvious one to West Germany, which is aware that an American–Russian deal is being made behind its back, in which the only remaining point of difference is whether Germany will be occupied permanently or for a limited time. West Germany also knows that tomorrow, on D+12, the Russo–American exchange of tactical nuclear arms will make a smoldering waste of its country. The step toward independent intervention equally forces itself on France, to whom a permanent Russian presence on German soil would be a "political" blow at its

critical "vital threshold." Moreover, intelligence is reaching Paris that powerful Soviet forces are penetrating the Black Forest. France sees the "geographical" threat to its critical "vital threshold" taking material form. France maintains that its very life is doubly threatened along two approaches. No hesitation is now possible. It is the hour of the nuclear warhead.

The general staff proposes to the French president the firing of a nuclear warning shot. With his superior overview of defense, the president rejects this solution. The German and French government come together again for a new debate on the possibility and means of carrying out a nuclear strike. Deliberately, the United States is neither informed of the object of the discussions nor even of the decisions finally arrived at. Two European countries, one especially, take into their hands the destiny of Europe.

Just as Generals Patton and Leclerc revolutionized mobile war by taking the initiative in using armored divisions to spearhead attacks, the French president already understands that to open with a mild warning shot would be to fuel a nuclear war. It would be necessary at the outset to strike first and to the very limit of the unendurable, and yet with the certainty that one was offering oneself up to a horrifying retaliatory strike. I leave it to the reader to discover which major Russian city was struck with a force of the order of megatons and which French metropolis suffered within the hour an equivalent retaliatory strike from an enemy who had thoroughly analyzed and understood the options and had tailored its response accordingly. I also leave it to the reader to discover what French proposals were made to the Russians after the French strike, even before suffering the Russian counter blast. In so doing I am leaving it to the reader to discover the trauma wreaked on the Kremlin by the nuclear exchange and its effect on the nature of its response to the French proposals.

Readers of John Bradley's *hypothetical account* may be provoked by the section which enumerates the conditions which would permit an aggressor to launch a surprise attack against the West, which is presented as overly naive and negligent. If one accepts certain conventions in this matter, the criticism on this point will be light while the core of the book demonstrates — in a masterly fashion, and in opposition to complacent faith in the Atlantic Alliance — that a hot war between nuclear powers can only take place if what is at stake is the very survival of its initiator: no other reason whatsoever would impel any power to nuclear war. Moreover, the book demonstrates that deterrence can be situated at a level of strategy which is beyond considering its actual em-

Below:
Soviet penetration in the Black Forest is seen as a threat to the French "vital threshold."

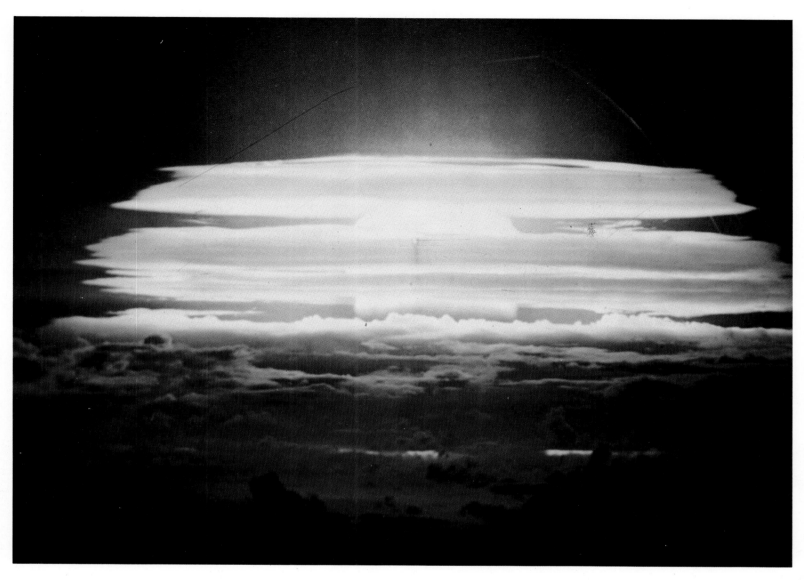

ployment.

The book adheres to a literary rule which demands such skill: the rule that the author must not explain or theorize, but let his narrative speak for him as it unfolds. This is certainly the case with this account of a third world war, and it is what makes it a book which will shock its public: whether an informed public or not, certainly a public which is anxious, alarmed, and eager for a careful evaluation of its chances for survival.

I myself will particularly retain two points from this inspiring book — its discrediting of the taboo against the idea of necessary escalation and its portrayal of national defense in all its majesty.

As far back as 1965, General de Gaulle assumed and proclaimed his choice of a policy of national defense, based on the certainty that no great nuclear power would ever risk its life for an ally, however close. More recently, on September 3, 1979, former Secretary of State, Dr. Henry Kissinger coldly announced at Brussels that "during the 1980s, the growth of the Soviet arsenal will surely render the United States vulnerable" and that consequently "the allies should not continually ask us to multiply strategic assurances which we are unable to give." General Haig, then ex-commander of the NATO forces in Europe and latterly

Secretary of State, echoed this sentiment. Ex-president Nixon has recently expanded on this same theme, with good sense but also with perfect

Above: A Nuclear explosion.

Below: Ex-President Richard Nixon.

17

Ex-French President Valéry
Giscard d'Estaing forged close
links with his German counterpart
Helmut Schmit which have been
sustained since.

reign of SAC and the choice of a strategy of flexible response for NATO, this same NATO (which surely does not lack certain qualities) has proved itself to be — volens nolens and by the same token — the principal obstacle to the realization of a European entity with decision-making capability. It is the same as with the Warsaw Pact. In saying this I am in no wise prejudging either the feasability or the usefulness of creating a united Europe (and, in any case, which Europe?). I simply state a fact.

In his narrative, as I have said, the author does not theoretically elaborate on this critical point. Rather he lets the matter rest with the observation — which bodes ill for Europeans — that the Americans and the Soviets, talking directly to each other in the middle of a full-scale battle for Europe, will carry on as many French people have argued throughout the postwar period that they necessarily must: they will sever their respective strategic arms systems from the conflict and regard Europe as a shooting gallery for their tactical nuclear weapons.

The author is able to demonstrate that only a *national* strategic nuclear capability has value as a deterrent. The firing of the French missile is like the cannonade at Valmy: certainly a Valmy whose cost will be horribly dear; a Valmy on the scale of our nuclear age, but a Valmy nonetheless. It would be a Valmy which annihilates a prosperous region for 30 years but which saves France and Europe.

At the same time, John Bradley has the German government withdraw to Paris and not somewhere else. It is in the course of Franco—German councils of war that the decision is taken to employ a certain French strategic weapon after its fashion.

This leads us to two important qualifications. The first is that Europe can have no defense other than its own nuclear deterrent, and that the more powerful its nuclear capability the more deterrent it will be. Moreover, only overwhelming power would allow us to escape the "Valmy phase." For this to happen it is essential that France should fundamentally reorganize its military structures, putting the emphasis on its nuclear effort and that Europeans should participate in this effort. As it is impossible to carry on such discussions in any form with the British, and since France and Germany together constitute the spine of continental Europe, the development of a European deterrent must begin with the conjunction of these two nations. Unfortunately, nuclear systems require a single authority: the minimum political entity corresponding to this requirement being the federation, it does not therefore seem that the objective would be realizable, barring an overriding threat, in the short or medium term. It will probably come

cynicism when one considers the contrary assurances he lavished on Europeans during his time in active politics.

Despite these remarks and the additional warnings of wellknown specialists, many Europeans still believe — or wish to believe — in the existence of the American nuclear umbrella. In public remarks made during the first years of his period of office (1974–81), the French president himself, Giscard d'Estaing, toyed with the possibility of returning France to the NATO fold, by indirect means. He also played down the notion of "battle" on which the nuclear strategy of national deterrence is correctly founded.

After having read John Bradley's account of a third world war, one rationally comprehends that the American umbrella does not exist. It existed during those years (1948–62) which stretched from the Berlin blockade to physical establishment of the Iron Curtain and the construction of the disgraceful Berlin Wall. At this time, American support took the form, not of NATO (1949), but of the American Strategic Air Command (SAC) whose missiles and bombers had no credible counterparts in the East. Since the end of the unopposed

too late and we will be led through the scenario of this third world war.

Moreover, just as until Patton and Leclerc, combat between land army armored divisions continued to resemble naval combat, with small craft giving cover to ships of the line who engaged in combat at a distance, so the military establishments of nuclear powers continue to be stuck in old ruts: warning shot, use of tactical nuclear weapons, controlled escalation. Perhaps they hold onto these simply in order to justify their possession of certain weapons.

John Bradley, innovating in the style of Patton, grants the French president the intelligence to refuse escalation (one does not play "one for you, one for me" with a nuclear Super Power) and to proceed immediately to an insupportable level of nuclear destruction.

This takes us a long way and should give those who are preparing to create and deploy a new generation of tactical nuclear arms good cause for reflection. These considerations sweep away the old theories (12 years) which involve employing tactical blasts in combination with conventional forces. Napoleon's inspired and concise formula, "the artillery conquers, the infantry occupies" has served as a feeble apology. Nothing can be extrapolated from conventional explosives to nuclear explosions. The former is one element of

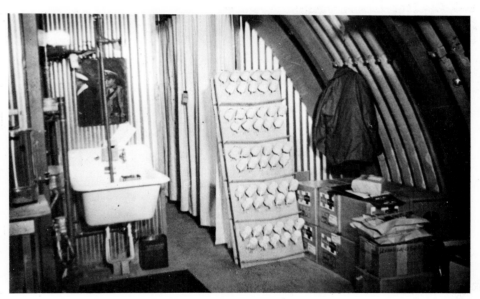

military action, the latter is a grand finale.

By way of a closing remark on this new vision of warfare, let us add that John Bradley has managed to integrate nuclear strategy and deterrence, the threat to use nuclear weapons and their actual employment. This is not a fixed law: it is an open path to be explored.

Paris 1982

General Georges Buis

Top:
A giant Soviet military hovercraft on the move. The sheer size and numbers of their equipment is the key to the conventional superiority of the Soviet forces.

Above:
A nuclear shelter. Civil Defense has been a matter which the Western powers have neglected, and the West would be virtually unprotected in the occurence of a nuclear conflict.

Teheran conference in 1943 where Stalin. Roosevelt and Churchill discussed strategy for World War II.

CHAPTER ONE

INTERNATIONAL POLITICS OF A THIRD WORLD WAR

THE POSTWAR SUPER POWERS AND ARMS LIMITATION

Right:
Harry S. Truman was President of the United States of America in 1945 and during the crucial years that followed World War II.

It is almost impossible to pinpoint the basic causes of any world conflict. The examination of causes of past conflicts usually takes us back to the preceding conflict: thus, for example, World War II's root causes are firmly planted in World War I and those of that conflict can without difficulty be traced right back to the Napoleonic Wars. With a third world war the problem seems to be the same, albeit this conflict is only real in its potentiality. Nonetheless ex-US President Richard Nixon claims in his recently published book (*The Real War*, 1980) quite categorically that World War III has already started, and is being fought by the East (chiefly the USSR) and West (reluctantly the USA) all over the planet earth, particularly in Asia, Africa, and Latin America. Nixon traces the origin of this ongoing conflict to World War II.

There is a certain intellectual plausibility in affirming that as soon as World War II was over, another conflict took its place, namely what came to be known as the Cold War. Nonetheless this explanation is an oversimplification. It has now been proved beyond any doubt that during the crucial years 1945–47, there was no state of conflict between the two major victors, the USSR and USA, while the third victor, Great Britain, became absorbed in internal reconstruction, opting out of international politics. It is therefore hardly correct to state that the seeds of the future conflict, World War III, were sown in those crucial postwar years; this view is particularly implausible given that the adversary powers, of which we now begin to speak as super powers, were "jockeying for power positions" in international affairs, (in Zbigniew Brzezinski's words) in order to fill the places left empty by Britain, France, Germany, and Japan, the prewar "Super Powers." Neither of these "new" Super Powers was certain of itself and both were ignorant of the true nature of international politics and its aims: in order to maintain international stability, peace, a balance of power had to be established. The United States was particularly uncertain of itself. Its president, Harry S. Truman, had only just come to power, after the untimely death of President Franklin D. Roosevelt in April 1945, and was in fact learning the business of international politics from scratch, which, incidentally, his predecessor never bothered to do. Nonetheless it is true to say that President Truman had no coherent strategy for international politics in 1945 and that it took him two years before he began to formulate one. Once the strategy was formulated, largely through the State Department, particularly by a federal foreign affairs civil servant, George

E. Kennan, namely that of containment, that policy had to be applied consistently. Of this application we can only speak after June 1948, when the Berlin crisis was sprung on the United States and its allies. Doctrinally the United States was equally unprepared for its role in international politics and had no idea whether and when the balance of power between East and West had been achieved.

During those two crucial years 1945–47 the

United States felt itself supremely secure in the world. It had just emerged from a world conflict with its economy in top shape; in fact its economic preponderance in the world had never been greater. Furthermore its military power was on *a par* with Soviet Russia's, now further enhanced by the atomic weapons which were used for the first time with such devastating effect against Japan in August 1945. Although a precipitate demobilization was immediately launched upon the termination of the conflict, nevertheless, it was thought that the monopoly of atomic weapons more than compensated for the reduction of military forces. When in 1948 the United States' leaders suddenly realized that they had some 1,400,000 men under arms, which in fact meant only some 10 combat divisions to face 175 Soviet divisions and 12 low-yield atomic weapons to square the difference, they were seized by what amounted to panic:

the Red Army could in fact sweep almost un-hindered to the Channel, penetrate into the Middle East and into the Asiatic landmass as it pleased, without the United States being able to oppose it. It is only then that we can speak of the Cold War conflict, and in any case the conflict was far from a real war.

Paradoxically the experienced Soviet leader, Josef Stalin, had neither consistent strategy nor policy. In February 1945, when the three Allied leaders met at Yalta, Premier Stalin and President Roosevelt came to an *understanding* by which they simply divided the world between themselves, without telling Premier Winston Churchill about it. It is not quite clear how far Roosevelt grasped Stalin's logical understanding of the deal; in any case it fell apart with Roosevelt's death just before the war ended. At Potsdam Stalin was prepared to come to terms with President Truman and renew the gentle-men's agreement on the division of the world. The new President would not hear of it. Stalin was quite unprepared to come to such an agreement with Churchill, and particularly with Churchill's socialist successors, for he began to consider Britain as not quite an equal partner. In fact Stalin was not impressed by either Truman or Clement Attlee and did not think they would hinder him as he expanded his power. He thought that most of the world in any case would fall to him, provided he took advant-age of his position as a victor ruling a super power. He also had to take reasonable pre-cautions to reestablish an international balance of power and possibly tilt the balance in his favor by means of military power, given that economically, after the devastation of the war, his country was weak.

Stalin's establishment of the international balance of power was almost instinctive. It is now known that Stalin failed to grasp the strategic implications of the atomic bomb, whose monopoly was that of the United States between 1945–49. Nonetheless Stalin offset his economic weakness and lack of atomic devices by arbitrarily fixing a 3:1 ratio in con-ventional forces. After the war the United States demobilized some 488 rifle and 155 air divisions. Stalin also demobilized some of his 11,365,000 men. By 1948 he still had 2,874,000 men in his 175 divisions: the ratio 3:1 was certainly there. The balance of power was "slightly" in favor of the USSR, for the United States had only 10 combat divisions and a limited number of atomic devices which in a conflict between the USA and the USSR would have had a marginal effect on the course of events. Curiously Stalin's successors also maintained the military ratio

after his death in 1953, even when they had themselves become a nuclear power, possibly because this decision by the old tyrant had political implications for his hegemony. Stalin even devised a military doctrine of "permanent factors" to justify his strategy. His doctrine (freely borrowed from Clausewitz) spoke of the nuclear weapons as a secondary factor, ranking with that of surprise attack. Stalin's strategy and military doctrines envisaged as its aims: (1) deterrence and defense against the USA; (2) strengthening of the defense zone in Eastern Europe; (3) conven-tional rearmament and (4) strategic research (both in nuclear weapons and delivery behicles). There is no doubt that Stalin was successful in the application of his strategy: he was a cautious strategist and was ready to accept failures, which were inevitable considering that his strategy embraced the whole world. However, instead of achieving international balance and peace, which it almost did, Stalin's actions in two instances almost produced wars: in 1948 over Berlin, and in 1950 with the invasion by the North of South Korea.

The crisis over Berlin finally opened the eyes of the USSR's erstwhile allies and provoked instant defensive measures. The Americans almost panicked: ex-Premier Churchill urged them to use the few atomic devices against the USSR to force it to abandon, not only Berlin, but occupied Eastern Europe. Though the Americans rejected Churchill's advice, the Foreign Office issued its envoys with "war" instructions: the treaty of Brussels was renegotiated and when the United States finally agreed to join it, the result was the North Atlantic Treaty (NATO) signed in April 1949. Berlin was Stalin's major miscalculation which almost provoked a con-flict and ended with a solid defense organization of the West against the Soviet "threat," both of which were unforeseen consequences of his strategy.

In June 1950 the invasion of South Korea enlarged the Soviet "threat" worldwide and the Western response proved to be accelerated re-armament and construction of world-wide alliances, such as the Baghdad Pact or South East Asia Treaty Organization (SEATO). During the actual fighting, which was done under the auspices of the UNO, the Super Powers again came close to a conflict, which was only avoided thanks to Stalin's flexibility. He was in any case fighting the Korean war by proxy, through the Koreans and Chinese. Nonetheless this political and military miscalculation cost Stalin dear, although a "hot" conflict between the Super Powers was averted. The Soviet Union and her allies were forced into conventional rearma-

ment, though economically they could ill afford such an effort. Communist China, which had intervened on North Korea's behalf, when it looked as if that communist country would be wiped out after its initial success against South Korea, learned a hard political lesson: a super power's own interests were paramount and ideological allies, even if they do the fighting, count for nothing. Despite these two crises, Stalin, while alive, succeeded in maintaining the international balance of power and avoiding a direct super power conflict. Had Soviet Russia taken over Berlin, threatened the Western parts of Germany, occupied the whole of Austria, invaded Yugoslavia and Finland, as the West expected this "aggressive" communist Super Power to do, both a conventional and atomic conflict between the West and East (since September 1949 the USSR seems to have possessed atomic devices) might have taken

Below:
Korea was in fact Stalin's war by proxy.. US Marines advance while refugees flee UN troops fighting for Seoul and facing the heaviest resistance since the Inchon landing.

place in the early 1950s. But while alive Stalin was skillful enough to avert a new war; then in March 1953 he died rather suddenly. His successors had no experience in international affairs and would take time to gain enough to be able to solve their problems. Stalin was an absolute dictator not only at home but also in international politics: paradoxically the world would be unstable without him.

After the power struggle between Nikita S. Khrushchev and the Malenkov-Molotov group, the definite successor of Stalin, Khrushchev, was finally able to formulate his own policies and strategies, and after 1957 began to implement them. To start with, conciliatory moves by the USSR reduced international tensions: in Berlin harassment of Allied aircraft ended; the Korean armistice was signed; normal relations were reestablished with Yugoslavia and even with Israel, Turkey, and Greece. This enabled the West and East to come to an agreement on Austria with which a peace treaty was signed in May 1955. The war in Indochina was also terminated by negotiations and both Super Powers proved to the world that they were determined to avoid conventional conflicts. This relaxation of tension resulted in major switches in political and military strategy. The new leader, Khrushchev, because of economic strains and his belief in mutual *nuclear* deterrence

shifted the emphasis from conventional forces, which under Stalin had dominated Soviet strategy, to strategic offensive forces and air defense. This was the "nuclearmania" of Khrushchev as it became known after his fall from power in 1964. In the meantime he reduced conventional forces, largely to strengthen his economy, developed long-range missiles, which were successfully tested in 1957, and with these new military means tried to maintain the balance of international power, perhaps slightly tilting it in his favor.

Under Khrushchev's leadership, 1957–64, the Soviet Union had two primary targets in international politics. Since it had failed to neutralize Germany as a whole, it attempted to neutralize Berlin, which in the meantime had become the capital of the Eastern zone, which was now called German Democratic Republic (DDR). Khrushchev launched his campaign for a change in Berlin in 1958: he wanted to change the divided capital's status into that of a demilitarized free city. In the fall of 1959 President Eisenhower admitted to Khrushchev that Berlin's situation was abnormal, which must have encouraged Khrushchev so much that, after meeting the new President, John F. Kennedy, in Vienna, he issued a whole series of ultimata and deadlines on Berlin. However the West was prepared to resist this Soviet political

Below:
Nikita Khrushchev tried to use the Cuban missile crisis to test American determination and win international respect for USSR.

MISSILE EQUIPMENT
MARIEL PORT FACILITY

4 MISSILE TRANSPORTERS

OXIDIZER TRAILERS

FUEL TRAILERS

LAUNCH STANDS

17 MISSILE ERECTORS

2

(APPROX. 3.5 NM NORTH OF MAIN PORT FACILITY)

blustering and military threat, so that the long drawn-out crisis was ultimately resolved by a compromise. Throughout early 1961, 20 to 30,000 refugees succeeded in escaping from the DDR through Berlin to West Germany. Since Khrushchev could not score a political victory in Berlin, he at least covered the failure by a "physical solution": on August 13, 1961 the Berlin Wall was constructed and the flow of refugees checked. However, the Berlin problem itself was solved politically only some 10 years later, in a different international context.

As early as 1956 the Soviet Union asserted its hegemonial rights over Eastern Europe, when it intervened in Hungary, in November 1956, after the collapse of the indigenous communist system. The emerging system was destroyed by force of arms and the Hungarian Communists who preferred the native alternative, were wiped out with it. At the time the United States felt compelled to let the Russians sort out their hegemonial problems freely without interference, particularly because the American allies, France and Britain together with Israel, were engaged in a similar hegemonial exercise over the Suez canal. Only when the Soviets had issued a missile threat against France and

Britain, did the United States put its "nuclear umbrella" round its allies, but at the same time compelled them to abandon their attempts at reestablishing their colonial hegemonies in North Africa, of which it had disapproved from the very beginning. However, the Russians were able to draw the lesson in 1956 that within their hegemony, they were free to exercise military power solutions, without the

Above:
Nikita Khrushchev, 1st Secretary of the Soviet Communist Party. His poor performance during the Cuban missile crisis led to his fall from power in 1964.

Top:
Cuban Missile Crisis; Mariel Port and the missile transporters at start of the crisis.

peace of the world being threatened in any way. This "false" lesson inevitably led to the first nuclear confrontation between the Super Powers over Cuba, which in fact proved to be the most serious threat to peace in the 1960s.

The Cuban nuclear crisis started inconspicuously enough in 1959 when Fidel Castro, who was not even a communist, surprisingly wrested power from General Batista. When Castro's regime outraged American public opinion by public executions of Cubans and by harming American economic interests, the United States retaliated. This meant Cuba had no option but to turn to the USSR for political, military and economic aid. Soviet leaders began to think of Cuba as a member of their hegemony, shipped arms and economic aid there, and also began to plan a strategic "short cut" to achieve

nuclear parity with the United States. The Soviets thought that by basing their ICBMs in Cuba, American foreign-based missiles would thus be neutralized and the balance of international power definitely tilted in favor of the USSR. The Americans who surveilled Cuba with their U-2 aircraft soon discovered the construction of missile ramps and the first nuclear confrontation between the Super Powers began.

President Kennedy took personal charge of the management of this nuclear crisis. His National Security Council was in continuous session helping the President to resolve the crisis. Conventional forces were concentrated in Florida and nuclear aircraft as well as all available missiles were put on permanent alert. At the same time the United States made known

US Navy patrol plane flies over a Soviet freighter carrying missiles on its deck. The USS destroyer *Barry* is also trailing the ship.

the fact that Soviet missiles were installed in Cuba to threaten American cities. Direct negotiations, in the form of ultimata, with the USSR, which was caught unprepared and obviously in the wrong, continued. Cuba was placed in "quarantine" by the United States Navy, until such time when the USSR withdrew the offensive missiles. During a week, in October 1962, the world hovered on the verge of a nuclear disaster, while the Super Powers faced each other: in the end it appeared that the Soviet challenge was a bluff which had been called by the United States. Premier Khrushchev was forced to withdraw his missiles, and this proved so humiliating that it put the seal on his eventual downfall. Soviet military leaders deserted him, blaming him for this premature challenge: his power colleagues simply voted

him out of the leadership.

This unexpected and unplanned nuclear crisis seems to have frightened not only the Super Powers but the whole world. Everyone perceived clearly how easy it was to provoke a nuclear confrontation and how easily it could escalate into a conflict whose consequences were beyond human imagination and certainly beyond human experience. The most immediate result of this confrontation was that the Super Powers established a direct line of communication between Moscow and Washington, D.C. (the Hot Line). At the same time it was reasoned that since any Cold War confrontation could lead to nuclear holocaust a way had to be found out of the Cold War. International negotiations were to lead the world out of the confrontations of the Cold War to a more relaxed phase of international relations, later termed *detente*. Simultaneously negotiations were initiated between the Super Powers in view of ultimate strategic disarmament: conventional disarmament of the rival blocs, NATO and WPT; and general disarmament through the United Nations.

Attempts at the relaxation of international tensions, and even at the ending of the Cold War, had been made before 1962, and had been periodically renewed since Stalin's death by both East and West, but somehow they had never proved effective. Stalin's successors, Khrushchev, Georgy Malenkov, and Viacheslav Molotov, found themselves in complete international isolation, and since the only way out of it was to make limited concessions which would not harm them, they began to do so, until they could redesign and reformulate their foreign

President Kennedy takes the oath of office in Washington on January 20, 1961 and becomes the 35th President of the United States of America. He dealt firmly with the Cuban missile crisis and brought the world back from the brink of a nuclear war.

Lockheed U-2 was a long-range reconnaissance aircraft. It was one of these aircraft which discovered the construction of the missile sites in Cuba.

Russian T-24 tanks in the streets of Berlin, break up violent anti-communist riots in June 1953.

policy. Thus it was relatively easy to reestablish diplomatic relations with a great number of countries, with whom Stalin had broken, and conclude an armistice in Korea. However the hesitations and vague attempts to relax tension had a predictable effect within the Soviet hegemony: first Eastern Germany rose in revolt in June 1953 and then all the other satellite nations in Eastern Europe were shaken by waves of unrest and disturbances. This then became the limit of the Soviet detente attempts: diplomatic rapprochement, but no other moves which would endanger Soviet hegemony.

After the USSR had greatly reduced tensions in 1954 and particularly in 1955 following a summit meeting in Geneva, it became clear in 1956 that any further moves toward detente would upset rather than advance Soviet interests. The USSR had to resort to naked power in Hungary to reestablish the communist state which had collapsed; in Poland this was only just avoided. In the aftermath of 1956 the USSR dissolved the Cominform, founded by Stalin in 1947, which had become a hindrance to Soviet international policies, and in the summer of 1957 when the new leader Khrushchev emerged; he brought with him finally the new policy, the so-called "atomic diplomacy" at which the USSR had been aiming in the past four years. This policy differed from the one personalized by Stalin in that it actually took into account the power political circumstances of the late 1950s, above all it considered the problem of strategic weapons. While Stalin was alive, no discussion of strategic weapons was possible, and the Soviet Union relied on a political and military strategy evolved by Stalin during World War II. In the fall of 1953, after the USSR had exploded its first hydrogen device, the successors of Stalin decided to tackle the strategic problems in three ways: (1) bilaterally with the USA, which originally was not very successful; (2) multilaterally, through the Warsaw Pact, with the states either in possession or about to become nuclear powers, and (3) in the UNO. The last approach was initially the most important.

Late in 1953, on Soviet initiative, the two UN commissions for Atomic Control and Conventional Arms Control were merged into the UN Disarmament Commission and in April 1954 a five-nation subcommittee (the USA, USSR, UK, France, and Canada) was set up to review the whole issue of disarmament. On June 11, 1954 Britain and France presented their memorandum on the timing and phasing of a disarmament program, while on May 10, 1955 the Soviet Union presented its own proposals. For the first time the Soviets departed from a total disarmament program and indicated that a partial and gradual reduction of armaments would be a good starting point for negotiations. When, however, the Western Powers presented their comprehensive disarmament plan and had

it sanctioned by the UN General Assembly, the Soviet Union rejected it and withdrew from the disarmament talks.

Curiously enough it was at this stage that the Soviet Union accepted American test ban proposals and initiated bilateral talks with the USA which rather quickly resulted in a bilateral moratorium on the suspension of nuclear tests. Then a test ban conference opened in Geneva in 1958, but in March 1960 the talks were extended to include 10 other nations and began to aim at a general and complete disarmament. The result of the bilateral, super power negotiations was the first strategic treaty on the Antarctic: it was signed on December 1, 1959 in Washington and after its ratification by the US Congress and the Supreme Soviet in June 1961, it guaranteed the demilitarization of that continent. Unfortunately, nothing else was achieved, either in the United Nations or bilaterally between the Super Powers: in May 1960 in fact international tensions sharply increased after the Russians had shot down Gary Powers' U-2

aircraft over Soviet territory, and Premier Khrushchev scuttled the Paris summit conference. Negotiations were resumed in March 1962, in a disarmament committee of 18, some seven months before the nuclear confrontation over Cuba. In the wake of it both Super Powers exhibited renewed interest in general disarmament. However the Super Powers made it their business to concern themselves above all with strategic problems, leaving general questions of disarmament to the UN committee.

After the Cuban crisis, on June 20, 1963, the USA agreed with the USSR to the establishment of the Hot Line between Moscow and Washington, (in 1971 the Hot Line connection was linked to communication satellites). The series of partial disarmament agreements that followed could and did sometimes apply to other powers, but their main purpose was to achieve overall strategic agreement between the two Super Powers. Thus in 1963 the treaty banning nuclear tests in the atmosphere, cosmic space and underwater, became effective, while in 1968 the non-proliferation treaty was signed, but not by all nuclear powers (France, China did not sign). The invasion of Czechoslovakia in 1968 by the Soviet forces impressed the European powers more than the United States, which continued its bilateral negotiations regardless. In fact, in November 1969, three years after President Lyndon Johnson made his proposals, the Super Powers opened strategic arms limitation talks.

On November 17, 1969 bilateral talks were launched at Helsinki and their initial aim was to eliminate an accidental nuclear conflict and limit strategic arms (ICBMs, long-range nuclear bombers, MIRVed missiles, and anti-missile systems.) Politically the Soviets were keen to come to an agreement which for them and the West would pave the way for a formal detente, namely the conference on European Security. Strategically it was also in the interest of the USSR to come to a formal agreement with the USA, for such an agreement would acknowledge internationally the strategic parity between the Super Powers. Negotiations proceeded for almost

The Strategic Arms Limitation Treaty SALT I being signed in Moscow 1972.

The *Kiev*, the Soviet hybrid cruiser which serves as an aircraft carrier. It was greeted with great curiosity by Western observers when it first appeared in exercises during the late 1970s.

two years, the delegations meeting twice yearly, alternatively in Helsinki and Vienna, with the American delegation always ready to sign an agreement. However, it seemed that the Soviet delegation was unwilling or unauthorized to come to a real strategic agreement. At first the cause of this Soviet unwillingness was the relative ignorance of strategic problems by the head of the Soviet delegation, V. S. Semenov, Vice-Foreign Minister. Another cause was the obvious reluctance of the number two of the Soviet delegation, Colonel General Ogarkov, to make final decisions on the spot. Obviously the military leaders were not keen on such an agreement. However on September 30, 1971, two agreements were signed: one on the prevention of accidental conflicts and the other concerning improvements to the Hot Line. Subsequently, on May 26, 1972, President Richard Nixon and Mr. Leonid Brezhnev, then constitutionally only secretary-general of the Soviet Communist Party, signed in Moscow a concrete strategic agreement, SALT I: both offensive and defense missile systems were temporarily frozen and these limitations were to last until 1977, when a new agreement would be negotiated. This agreement was in fact a great turning point in American-Soviet relations: the ceiling imposed on the USSR was 1,618 ICBMs and 650 SLBMs; on the US 1,054 ICBMs and 656 SLBMs. The numerical disparity was due to the American missiles being MIRVed (Mutually Independently Targetted Vehicles). On July 3, 1974 the Moscow protocol dealing with the limitation of defensive systems, was signed. While previously the ABM systems could be placed anywhere, the Super Powers now agreed that they should not build any more of these systems, and the USSR undertook not to place its ABMs round the ICBM silos, while the USA promised not to place them round Washington, D.C. All the other agreements of SALT I were for a limited period of five years (1977), but there was no time limit imposed on the ABM agreement. Immediately after the SALT I became effective on October 3, 1972, the Super Powers started a new round of talks which were to result in SALT II. These started in Geneva on November 21, 1972. Optimists began to talk of a real detente and permanent peace in the 1970s. However, SALT II negotiations soon proved much more difficult and protracted. One reason was that before they were concluded the United States had three presidents in quick succession: President Nixon who had to resign; President Gerald Ford who was defeated in an election; and President Jimmy Carter who won the election but did not seem to command the same consensus in foreign affairs as Nixon had. Already President Ford's signing of the additional Vladivostok protocol which spelled out concretely the ceilings of missile and strategic bomber numbers (2,400 on both sides), without touching on the qualitative problems involved (throw weight), was causing misgivings in the United States. President Carter decided to concentrate on these problems exclusively and this seemed to be the reason for the delay in negotiations. In the end SALT I's time limit was overrun by two years and it was only on June 18, 1979 that President Carter and President Brezhnev were able to sign SALT II in Vienna. According to this agreement the 2,400 vehicles of delivery on each side, included all the ICBMs, SLBMs,

Left:
A Minuteman III intercontinental ballistic missile being launched from its underground site.

ASALMs, and strategic bombers; by December 31, 1981 they should be reduced to 2,250. Thus each side undertook to limit itself to 1,220 ICBMs, SLBMs, and ASALMs (820 ICBMs with MIRVs only). However it was the qualitative undertakings that were of interest in this agreement: both sides promised not to build new ICBM silos; transfer or displace these same; rebuild and improve silos built before 1964; adapt silos of light ICBMs for the heavy ones; develop any heavier ICBMs than those operational during SALT II; each ICBM, SLBM, and ASALM could only have 10, 14, and 10 MIRVs respectively.

By 1979 the Americans were full of doubts about Soviet strategic intentions. Since 1965, when Secretary of Defense, Robert McNamara, imposed on the US unilateral strategic restraint, there had not been any competitive development of strategic forces, so that it appeared that the Russians had not only achieved strategic parity with the USA, but would soon achieve superior-

Top left:
The SS-18 super missile seen in the silo ready to be fired. It is roughly 20 times as powerful as any of its American counterparts.

Above:
A Minuteman III being fired.
Notice the way the exhaust escapes from vents at the sides of the silo.

ity: thus prior to SALT I their ICBMs were of three types, SS-17, SS-18 and SS-19; the SS-18, a sort of supermissile, was estimated to be 16 to 40 times more powerful than the US counterpart, Minuteman III. After SALT I the Soviets put into service four new types of missiles including the SS-11, a light missile, which was an innovation, and the SS-20, a mobile missile, which was extremely important for the strategic balance of power, particularly in Europe, where it was currently deployed at 20 missiles per year. The Soviets also added three new types of SLBMs, three types of strategic submarines and the strategic Backfire bomber to their strategic arsenal, all permitted under the SALT II agreement. On the American side it was thought that the new development of the land-based MX missile, at sea the Trident system and the B-1 aircraft would restore the balance and keep parity despite Soviet developments. However, the new President Carter canceled the B-1 aircraft, deferred the decision on the MX missile and slowed down the production of Trident I, which caused even greater misgivings concerning strategic parity.

The Carter administration, nevertheless, continued with SALT II negotiations and in its defense invoked the so-called MAD factor (Mutually Assured Destruction). However, it was a shock for the US when they realized that Soviet strategic thinking most resolutely refused even to acknowledge the existence of the MAD factor in its theories. Thus the USA, where the factor was part and parcel of strategic thinking, found itself in the unenviable position of having no other strategic options left in case of a

strategic conflict between the Super Powers. In addition the MAD factor was considered by many US politicians morally wrong, since it envisaged the wholesale slaughter of civilian populations. Consequently as the factor became inoperative, a new strategic doctrine had to be adopted, which would make possible further maintenance of the strategic balance of power from which the whole world would benefit. However the suspicions and misgivings of US military leaders toward the Soviet Union had spread to the Senate which had to ratify the SALT II agreement before it could become effective. The Senate was dealing with the treaty rather slowly, when in December 1979, suddenly and unexpectedly, the Soviet armies invaded Afghani-

Above:
President Ronald Reagan seen here when he was governor of California. As President he has decided to take a tough line in negotiating any arms limitation deal with the Soviets.

Top:
A Soviet Navy Yankee class ballistic missile submarine which carries 16 SS N-6 missiles.

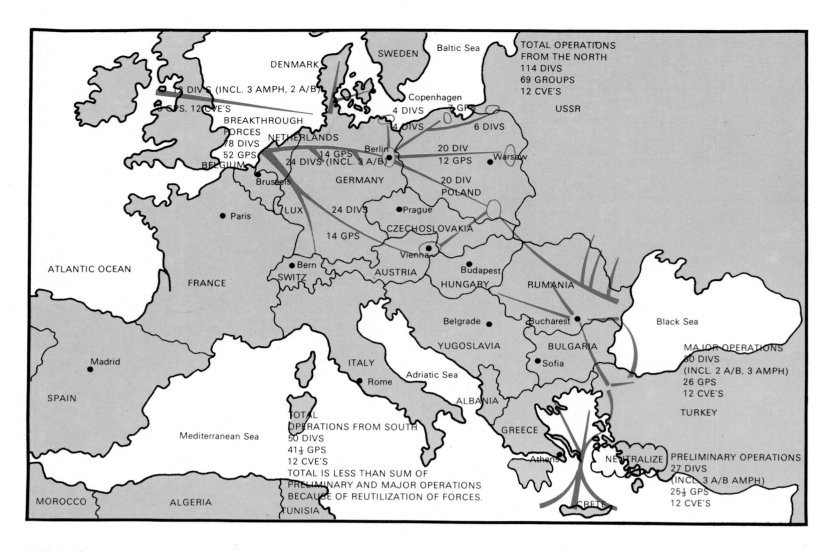

Map labels (as shown): SWEDEN, Baltic Sea, DENMARK, Copenhagen, TOTAL OPERATIONS FROM THE NORTH 114 DIVS 69 GROUPS 12 CVE'S, USSR, ... DIV'S (INCL. 3 AMPH, 2 A/B), ...PS, 12 CVE'S, BREAKTHROUGH FORCES 78 DIVS 52 GPS, NETHERLANDS, 4 DIVS, 4 DIVS, 6 DIVS, Berlin, 20 DIV, 12 GPS, Warsaw, BELGIUM, 14 GPS, 24 DIVS (INCL. 3 A/B), GERMANY, 20 DIV, POLAND, Brussels, LUX, 24 DIVS, Prague, Paris, 14 GPS, CZECHOSLOVAKIA, Vienna, Bern, SWITZ, AUSTRIA, Budapest, ATLANTIC OCEAN, FRANCE, HUNGARY, RUMANIA, Belgrade, Bucharest, Black Sea, Madrid, ITALY, YUGOSLAVIA, BULGARIA, Sofia, MAJOR OPERATIONS 30 DIVS (INCL. 2 A/B, 3 AMPH) 26 GPS 12 CVE'S, SPAIN, Rome, Adriatic Sea, ALBANIA, TURKEY, Mediterranean Sea, TOTAL OPERATIONS FROM SOUTH 50 DIVS 41⅓ GPS 12 CVE'S TOTAL IS LESS THAN SUM OF PRELIMINARY AND MAJOR OPERATIONS BECAUSE OF REUTILIZATION OF FORCES., GREECE, Athens, NEUTRALIZE, PRELIMINARY OPERATIONS 27 DIVS (INCL. 3 A/B AMPH) 25⅓ GPS 12 CVE'S, MOROCCO, ALGERIA, TUNISIA, CRETE

NATO plans drawn up during the Cold War envisaging a major land offensive in Europe.

stan, in order to "help the Afghan revolution." As a result of this intervention in Afghanistan, President Carter suspended the Senate consideration of the SALT II treaty. Thus conventional warfare and revolutionary aid jeopardized a strategic agreement between the Super Powers, upset the process of detente and boded ill for peace in the 1980s.

In the fall of 1980 President Carter was defeated by Ronald Reagan in the presidential election. Already during the presidential campaign, the republican candidate made it clear that he would formulate new policies, particularly in the strategic field. It was obvious to him that Carter's treatment of the USSR as an equal in international politics rebounded on him, to America's disfavor, and Reagan was determined to put the balance right. Throughout the year of 1981 he refused to engage in negotiations with the USSR and instead "continued to build up his position of strength." He seemed to imply that Soviet political expansion during the Carter presidency would cost them dear in the strategic field: thus the President appeared ready for another round of an arms race which apparently "the Soviets could not win."

Politically the President's views were reinforced by his Secretary of State, former General Alexander Haig, who was a follower of Dr. Henry Kissinger's "linkage" detente, but

who had criticized tersely Carter's position of weakness in negotiating with the USSR. However Haig's political position of strength had to be created first, since in the early 1980s even the American public opinion became aware of the fact that in the strategic sphere the USSR was more than equal. Thus in 1981 it was revealed that in a comparative evaluation of US-Soviet research development, test and costs (RDTC) the Soviets had consistently outspent the Americans in the decade 1970–80. In fact in 1982 the Soviet RDTC would be greater than the US RDTC by $20,000,000,000,000. While in the 1970s the Soviets produced twice as many strategic systems as the USA, in the 1980s this quantitative superiority was turned into a qualitative one, and President Reagan, supported by Secretary of State Haig, took decisions to reverse this trend: The Trident program has been accelerated; the MX missile will be developed and the neutron bomb will also become part and parcel of the American strategic posture in the 1980s. It was reasoned that once the adverse trend is reversed, strategic deterrence would be reestablished; SALT II would then be renegotiated from a position of strength. However, these American plans and intentions would take back the Super Powers to the situation in the 1970s which the USSR made such an economic and military effort to escape from.

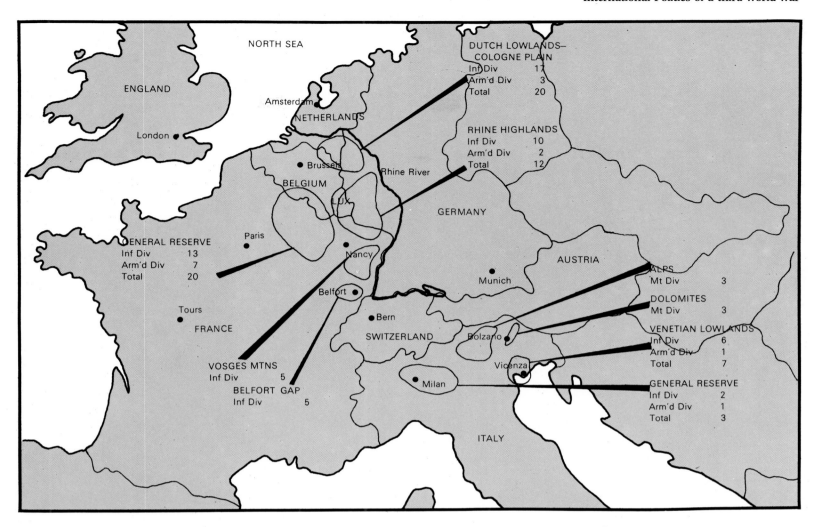

Parallel to the strategic, bilateral negotiations, the Super Powers and their blocs were engaged in political and conventional arms negotiations. Attempts at some sort of conventional understanding in Europe were going as far back as January 1956, when the Warsaw Pact countries proposed a system of collective security to replace the existing alliances, NATO-Warsaw Pact. However, after Soviet interventions in Poland, and particularly in Hungary, this appeal appeared extremely badly timed and consequently fell on deaf ears in the West. Nonetheless, during the year 1956 Western Europe discovered the obvious, namely that the USA had its particular strategic interests to look after, and not those of its allies. Britain and France who had invaded Egypt to consolidate their strategic interests in North Africa, were compelled by their ally to withdraw, with consequent loss of prestige in the area. Thus when in May 1958 the Warsaw Pact offered NATO a non-aggression pact, the Western Europeans, while still suspicious, were willing to listen to and consider these proposals. It is now clear that no practical agreement between the two blocs was possible before a strategic agreement between the Super Powers. In addition the United States began to exhibit its lack of interest in Western Europe by getting heavily involved in the war in Vietnam, particularly after 1965.

Then in May 1966 France reacted by pulling out of the military activity of NATO and in February 1967 Britain announced that it was interested in reducing its commitments in Germany, as well as in the Far and Middle East. Thus both sides of the alliances became amenable to troop reductions and conventional arms agreements, but there was still no consensus as to the way this should come about.

In July 1966, the Warsaw Pact countries issued the so-called Bucharest Declaration which

Above:
The Suez Crisis: British and French troops invade Egypt in December 1956. This was the last effective incursion in the area by Britain and France but could not be sustained in the face of economic and international repercussions.

Top:
NATO plan drawn up during the Cold War to hold the Rhine-Alps-Piave Line.

American troops in Vietnam
supported by Bell-Huey helicopters.
American involvement became
massive after 1965.

Inset:
Troops board a US Chinook
helicopter. The US Army relied on
helicopters to conduct operations
such as troop transport and
casualty evacuation in the jungles
of Vietnam.

appeared as their contribution toward an agreement on reducing international tension and troops in Europe. This declaration of principles, whose many points became part of the Helsinki Final Act, proposed the dissolution of NATO and WPT; abolition of foreign military bases; establishment of non-nuclear zones and convocation of an European Security Conference. With increased US involvement in Vietnam and with NATO allies, including West Germany, urging the reduction of troops, the alliance as a whole began to take Warsaw Pact declarations more seriously, and was prepared to pay the political price for it. Still in 1966 NATO's concrete call for a reduction of forces went unheeded. Only in 1969 did WPT suddenly spell out its own proposals for such reductions: (1) European collective security system should be established and all European countries should renounce force or threat of force in their relations; (2) trade, economic and scientific exchanges should be extended and (3) an international conference should be convoked. Though NATO wanted the talks on reduction of

Far right:
Dr. Henry Kissinger served first as National Secretary Adviser and then became Secretary of State. He conducted most of the SALT I negotiations.

Below:
A strike assault boat on patrol on the Mekong river.

military forces to start immediately, the Warsaw Pact insisted that such talks should rather follow a collective security conference. They repeated their arguments in 1970 (the Budapest Declaration), but by then the USA and NATO linked such a conference with the resolution of the German and especially Berlin problem.

While the East wanted to legitimize internationally its postwar gains in Germany, Berlin and Eastern Europe in general, the West not only desired a mutual reduction of expensive military forces, but also a solution to the German problem which had embittered European relations since 1945. However, when the Americans linked the problem with the SALT I agreement its solution was just round the corner. In 1970 Chancellor Brandt launched his *Ostpolitik* with peace treaties with the USSR and Poland, the two most difficult ones. The latter treaty finally settled the irritating border problem which in turn brought about a limited Soviet concession, the quadripartite agreement on Berlin, concluded late in 1972. In May 1972, together with SALT I, the Super Powers agreed on the Euro-

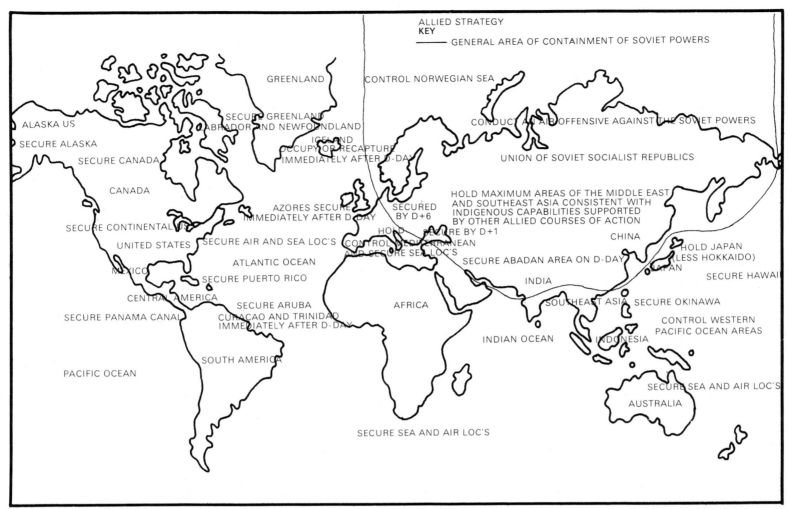

GREENLAND

CONTROL NORWEGIAN SEA

ALASKA US

SECURE ALASKA

SECURE GREENLAND
LABRADOR AND NEWFOUNDLAND

ICELAND
OCCUPY OR RECAPTURE
IMMEDIATELY AFTER D-DAY

CONDUCT AN AIR OFFENSIVE AGAINST THE SOVIET POWERS

SECURE CANADA

UNION OF SOVIET SOCIALIST REPUBLICS

CANADA

AZORES SECURE
IMMEDIATELY AFTER D-DAY

SECURED
BY D+6

HOLD MAXIMUM AREAS OF THE MIDDLE EAST
AND SOUTHEAST ASIA CONSISTENT WITH
INDIGENOUS CAPABILITIES SUPPORTED
BY OTHER ALLIED COURSES OF ACTION

SECURE CONTINENTAL US

UNITED STATES

SECURE AIR AND SEA LOC'S

HOLD
CONTROL MEDITERRANEAN
AND SECURE SEA LOC'S

SECURE BY D+1

CHINA

HOLD JAPAN
(LESS HOKKAIDO)

MEXICO

ATLANTIC OCEAN

SECURE PUERTO RICO

SECURE ABADAN AREA ON D-DAY

JAPAN

SECURE HAWAII

CENTRAL AMERICA

INDIA

SECURE PANAMA CANAL

SECURE ARUBA
CURACAO AND TRINIDAD
IMMEDIATELY AFTER D-DAY

AFRICA

SOUTHEAST ASIA

SECURE OKINAWA

CONTROL WESTERN
PACIFIC OCEAN AREAS

INDIAN OCEAN

INDONESIA

SOUTH AMERICA

SECURE SEA AND AIR LOC'S

PACIFIC OCEAN

AUSTRALIA

SECURE SEA AND AIR LOC'S

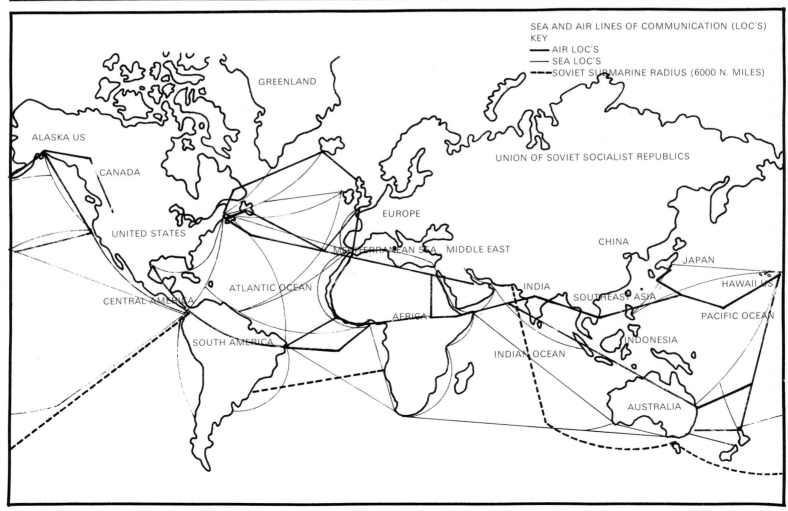

GREENLAND

ALASKA US

CANADA

UNION OF SOVIET SOCIALIST REPUBLICS

UNITED STATES

EUROPE

CHINA

JAPAN

MEDITERRANEAN SEA

MIDDLE EAST

ATLANTIC OCEAN

INDIA

HAWAII US

CENTRAL AMERICA

SOUTHEAST ASIA

PACIFIC OCEAN

AFRICA

SOUTH AMERICA

INDONESIA

INDIAN OCEAN

AUSTRALIA

pean Security Conference and the Mutually Balanced Forces Reduction talks (MBFR). But the Soviets chose to interpret this agreement as between the Super Powers rather than between the blocs, and the then Secretary of State, Dr. Kissinger, had to travel to Moscow once again to make it absolutely clear to the Soviet side that these were bloc negoations. Even after the Soviets had finally conceded this point, there was general pessimism in the United States about the talks, for it was thought that whatever the outcome they would go against NATO.

In the meantime a preparatory conference on European security opened in Helsinki with 35 countries in attendance. The NATO invitation to Poland, USSR, Czechoslovakia, the German Democratic Republic, and Hungary to come to Geneva and open the MBFR talks remained unanswered. Twelve days before the first scheduled session the Warsaw Pact answered by accepting the date only, and suggesting that the talks be held in Vienna and *all interested countries* be invited. NATO's acceptance of Vienna as a place for the talks and rejection for all the European countries to be invited was approved by WPT practically on the eve of January 30, 1973. Bulgaria and Rumania were added to the WP delegation and five NATO countries, from the northern and southern flanks joined in. Thus finally the MBFR talks were opened and it became immediately evident that the Eastern and Western points of view were very different. In the final analysis the difference boiled down to the symmetrical reduction, which was the Warsaw Pact's point of view, and asymmetrical reduction of forces which was NATO's proposition. Since Warsaw Pact forces were numerically superior to NATO's, the symmetrical solution seemed obviously to favor the Warsaw Pact, while the latter solution would, according to Warsaw Pact's interpretation, lead to NATO's military preponderance. However, both sides were prepared for long-term negotiations.

The tendency among the NATO allies was to link MBFR progress with progress on European security. However, it seems clear that as a result of American discomfiture and confusion consequent on the Watergate scandal followed by President Nixon's resignation, NATO's position was not always consistent. Thus NATO agreed (Rejkjavik and Rome declarations) that the "overall capacity of NATO should not be reduced except as part of a pattern of mutual force reductions balanced in scope and timing." To get the talks going NATO had to yield almost immediately and exclude the word balanced from the title of the talks; although the Benelux countries were included in the zone under dis-

cussion, Hungary was excluded on the insistence of WPT countries. On November 8, 1973 Warsaw Pact proposals were tabled: armed forces and weapons should be decreased by 15 percent in the zone of Europe which included the two Germanies, Poland, and Czechoslovakia as well as Benelux. Indigenous and stationed forces (land, air, and strategic) should be included in these reductions. These reductions were to be achieved in three phases starting in 1977. However no controls were built into the proposals and in any case such reductions would have perpetuated the existing imbalance of forces; but NATO's negotiators could obtain no further concessions from the Warsaw Pact. On October 31, 1974, the Warsaw Pact suggested a 10,000-men reduction by both US and Soviet forces in the European Zone, but this was again the old unacceptable symmetrical proposal, which NATO had previously rejected. Only on February 13, 1975 did negotiations result in something positive: all participants in the talks signed a declaration in which they undertook not to increase their forces in the Central European zone while the talks were continuing. Just before the final conference on European Security the Warsaw Pact tabled its latest proposals, no doubt to impress the 35 countries which were going to sign the Helsinki Final Act, thus laying the foundation for permanent peace; it reiterated the symmetrical reduction of 10,000 men on US and Soviet sides, while West Germany, Britain, Belgium, Holland, Luxemburg, Canada, Poland, East Germany, and Czechoslovakia would reduce their forces by 5,000 men each. All these and other proposals were unacceptable to the NATO allies; nevertheless, the final act of the conference on European Security was signed, thus making this foundation for permanent peace in Europe a rather shaky one.

On July 30, 1975 all the current leaders of the 35 countries who had been negotiating during the past three years the treaty on European Security and Co-operation gathered in Helsinki to sign solemnly the treaty. All the participants pledged themselves to maintain peace, reduce international tensions, and practice peaceful cooperation. They also renounced force or threat of force, in their relations and hoped that further controlled disarmament would strengthen security in Europe. Concretely, large-scale military maneuvers were to be notified to all the Helsinki signatories and military observers for such exercises exchanged. Trade and economic relations were to be liberalized and increased, and individual human rights asserted. An international forum would follow up the observance

Left above:
NATO plan drawn up during the Cold War outlining a strategy of containment against the Soviet Union.

Left below:
NATO plan showing air and sea lines of communications and their vulnerability to Soviet submarines.

HMS *Andromeda*, in coastal waters off the Axores, is part of Britain's continuing contribution to NATO presence in the Atlantic.

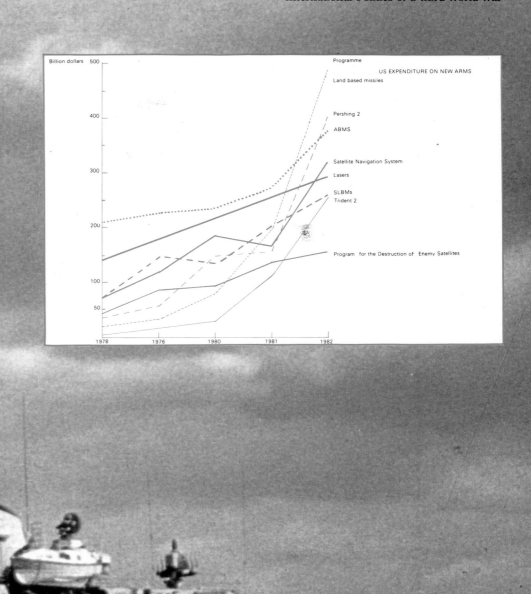

US EXPENDITURE ON NEW ARMS

Billion dollars

Programme
Land based missiles
Pershing 2
ABMS
Satellite Navigation System
Lasers
SLBMs
Trident 2
Program for the Destruction of Enemy Satellites

Above:
A US Navy Tomahawk Cruise
missile in flight.

of this treaty and meet periodically in capitals of the participatory countries (Belgrade in 1978; Madrid in 1981). Politically the conference was a great success for the Soviet Union, while the Americans and the West were either reluctant or pessimistic. To many Westerners it appeared that the resulting detente was only to serve the Warsaw Pact, for it brought about no progress in the MBFR talks, nor reduction of international tension outside Europe.

Six months later, on February 19, 1976, the Warsaw Pact representatives repeated in a different way their previously unacceptable symmetrical proposals: in the first phase American and Soviet forces were to be reduced and in the second, direct participants on both sides. In October 1977, they presented a proposal by which the numerical state of armed forces was to be clearly ascertained, in an obvious maneuver to get around the assymmetrical reduction. In June 1978 both sides finally agreed that after a gradual reduction of forces, NATO and WPT should deploy 900,000 men each in Central Europe; however, five months later, the negotiating countries only agreed not to increase their forces numerically, while negotiations continued, as previously agreed in February 1972. In June 1979 the WPT negotiators proposed a collective reduction of armed forces to 700,000 by both alliances, which proved unacceptable to NATO. After this last abortive effort, both sides became more realistic and agreed on the mutual exchange of troop numbers stationed in Central Europe, so that negotiations for the reduction of these forces could be based on more solid information. In contrast, in the strategic sphere, negotiations suddenly became chaotic: when NATO, in response to the Soviet deployment in West Russia of their latest SS-20 missile, began to discuss placing in Western Europe the more advanced American missiles, Pershing 2 and Cruise, the Soviet Union had recourse to political threats and blackmail, which it had renounced in Helsinki. This Soviet blustering made the Americans and NATO even more determined to restore the tactical theater balance in Europe.

On July 19, 1980 the WPT presented its new proposals in Vienna: as phase one they proposed US-Soviet troop reductions of 13,000 and 20,000 and as phase two all-round reductions of troops by both NATO and WPT. In November 1980 additional proposals envisaged phase one as lasting three years: between the phases a collective freeze on military expenditure by both alliances was envisaged. All these suggestions, while not meeting Western requirements of December 1979, were acceptable compromises provided the WPT accepted in turn the basic Western requirement of verification. However, since this did not seem to be the case, it could therefore be deduced that the WPT compromise proposals did not originate in their desire to come to some valid military agreements, but were the WPT reactions to American and NATO military decisions taken during the MBFR talks.

In April 1978, faced with WPT and Soviet strategic and conventional modernization and proposed increases in military expenses, NATO allies accepted in principle American proposals to modernize their weapon systems, and in particular produce the neutron bomb, replace aging IMBMs with improved Pershing 2 and Cruise missiles; NATO allies then actually voted for a three percent increase in defense budgets over the inflation increases. It seems obvious that this acceptance in principle of American proposals and budget vote caused the Soviet revisions of MBFR strategy: on the one hand, their weapons' modernization was accelerated and on the other the Russians attempted to force their WPT allies to increase their military budgets likewise. This pressure, however, failed in the case of Poland, which because of its economic crisis froze military expenditure at the existing levels. As for Rumania it rejected the Soviet proposals out of hand and thus revealed the most serious crisis in the WPT alliance since its inception in 1955. These then appeared to be the reasons behind the sudden Soviet flexibility and constructive proposals in Vienna. If the economic situation in the Eastern European countries, "near worthless and economically burdensome allies," deteriorated still further, the USSR might be forced to employ more effective means of compulsion with all the obvious consequences for the WPT and world peace.

By February 1981, after seven years of talking, NATO and WPT negotiators had reached no agreement of any permanent value. During the 26th Congress of the Soviet Communist Party, President Brezhnev made certain proposals on both strategic and conventional agreements with the West, which if backed by concessions, could have injected new dynamism into SALT II and MBFR talks, but nothing concrete followed the congress speech.

Left:
A Pershing 2 missile of the type to replace existing medium-range delivery systems in Europe.

XXVI
ЛЕНИНСКИМ КУРСОМ –
К ПОБЕДЕ КОММУНИЗМА!
ПЛАНЫ ПАРТИИ –
ПЛАНЫ НАРОДА!
РЕШЕНИЯ XXVI СЪЕЗДА КПСС – ВЫПОЛНИМ!

CHAPTER TWO

DETENTE AND INTERNATIONAL INSTABILITY

Russian self-propelled gun during a May Day march. Traditionally the May Day march provides the Soviets with a propaganda exercise to show their military might.

It is perhaps not so surprising that since the signature of SALT I in 1972, which established the "peaceful process" called detente and replaced the Cold War, the world has become even more unstable, chiefly because of the differences in interpreting detente. From the very beginning the Soviets stressed that detente did not mean the end of their ideological competition with the United States. This "dynamic" aspect of the detente process was perhaps overstressed, for the Americans came to believe that while ideological competition would continue, a political moratorium on "territorial" expansion by both sides would be in force. However, almost immediately after the Helsinki conference in 1975, the Soviet Union made clear the difference in interpreting detente. Thus during the conference Soviet Foreign Minister, Andrey Gromyko, told the amazed Americans that their Middle East policy was contrary to detente: they were leaving the Soviet Union out of the area and this seemed to him inadmissible. As if to drive the point home, the Soviets began to act unilaterally as well.

In Africa, the Portuguese empire had collapsed as a result of a revolution in Portugal itself. The revolutionary government declared that it would grant independence to all its colonies, particularly Angola and Mozambique. By 1975 Angola was independent, but a civil war was raging in the country between the left- and right-wing nationalist factions. When the left government appealed to Soviet Russia for military aid the Russians granted it immediately: but apart from sending war materiel the Soviets ordered 15,000 Cuban troops to redress the balance in favor of the left. This was the first unilateral intervention in international politics by the Soviet Union since 1973, when

Below:
North Vietnam tanks enter the Presidential palace in Saigon after the collapse of the South Vietnamese Army on May 1, 1975. US pride took another humiliating blow as its former ally fell to communism.

the Soviet-American agreement on the prevention of nuclear war was solemnly signed. It was on this agreed document that the rules of detente was laid down in print: (1) institutionalizing and facilitating international crisis management; (2) instituting self-restraint and encouraging others to be prudent. It was precisely because of this agreement that the Americans ceased to use force in Cambodia on August 15, 1973 and refused to get involved in the civil war in Angola. The Soviet Union failed to interpret the agreement in the same way. Subsequently, in July 1974, it signed a Treaty of Friendship with the Somali Republic which as a result received massive military aid and in return permitted the Russians to build up a tactical and strategic base at Berbera. In Africa the Soviet Union began to discurse military aid

on a large scale; apart from Somalia and Angola, Guinea, Guinea-Bissau, Mali, Mozambique, Nigeria, and Uganda began to benefit. The Soviets proceeded cautiously, step by step, always ready to adjust their political and military penetration, if circumstances changed, or the Americans protested too vehemently, but nonetheless clearly acting against the spirit of Helsinki and detente.

After the Soviets started acting unilaterally in Angola and Somalia, the American administration which had political obligations in South Vietnam began to act unilaterally also to support the regime there. When however, American public opinion and Congress turned against the US government's involvement in that area and refused further assistance to the South Vietnamese, the latter promptly col-

lapsed; the leaders fled abroad while the North Vietnamese armored divisions raced south to take Saigon. It was evident that the Soviets did not even try to restrain their North Vietnamese allies and the USA became dissatisfied with detente. In December 1975 the Chinese leader, Mao Tse-tung, told President Ford to stand firm against the Soviets in Europe, Africa, and Southeast Asia, or they would expand their hegemony, detente or no detente. To the Americans Communist Mao seemed right. At that time Dr. Kissinger visited Moscow to continue SALT II negotiations; he tried to link further progress with Soviet withdrawal from Angola. However, the Russians would have none of it. They could see that the Ford administration was not likely to survive its term of office and since they disliked the idea of disengagement in Angola, there

simply was no progress in SALT II negotiations; so world-wide destabilization continued.

The Russians then took advantage of the inexperience of the new Carter administration to expand their influence even more vigorously, while SALT II negotiations continued to drag on inconclusively until the summer of 1979. With ex-President Nixon and Dr. Kissinger progress in strategic negotiations had been invariably linked with some political or military concessions on the Soviet side. Even the Helsinki conference itself, so much opposed by Britain, had brought two concessions from the USSR: the West Berlin settlement and MBFR talks between NATO and the WPT. Admittedly these concessions proved to be only "preliminary," and in both cases the Russians were in a position to reverse them, if the final agreement proved unworkable or otherwise unsatisfactory. Thus the Western concessions at Helsinki, namely legitimizing internationally the postwar arrangements in Eastern Europe, was not matched by an equivalent Soviet concession. The renunciation of force as a means in international politics by the USSR was never conceded and the continued use of force would shortly lead to increased tensions, and finally to the same Cold War confrontation as in the 1950s.

In 1977, after three years of Soviet military aid, the Somali President, Siad Barre, felt himself strong enough to invade the neighboring Ethiopia whose province Ogaden he claimed for his country. Ethiopia had recently been weakened by an internal upheaval, in which the ruling emperor Haile Selassie was ousted and power taken over by revolutionary army officers. Previously Ethiopia had a security agreement with the USA, now it renounced it and turned to the USSR for military aid, as it continued its old war in another province, Eritrea, which had demanded independence for itself. Initially the Somalis proved successful and occupied almost the whole of Ogaden. Then Ethiopia appealed to the Soviets for additional help. At first the Soviets tried to mediate between their two allies, but when this proved in vain, they made a choice; 20,000 Cuban troops were diverted to Ethiopia with some 3,000 Soviet technicians and advisers. Over $2,000,000,000,000,000 of arms and equipment were airlifted and by 1978 President Barre was forced to abandon Ogaden. The Soviet base at Berbera was exchanged for another base at Masawa. To the Americans this was the final illustration of the Soviet interpretation of the renunciation of force in international politics.

In Africa Soviet active involvement continued unabated, by proxy, with Cuban troops,

Fidel Castro in Miscow. Cuba still enjoys a special relationship with the Soviet Union. Cuba has intervened in Angola and Ethiopia on behalf of the Sovet Union.

in spite of competition from China, which had agreements with Cameroon, Equatorial Guinea, Guinea, Mali, and Tanzania. In 1978 after a *coup d'etat* in South Yemen, East German advisers and technicians were sent there to stabilize the new revolutionary regime. In the same year, the Russians, taking advantage of the civil war in Rhodesia, came to an agreement with Mozambique by which the Zimbabwe guerillas were trained by East German military instructors. However, in 1978 the Russians overreached themselves for the first time in Africa. Zaire, a giant of a territory with feet of clay, was suddenly invaded from Angola. The invasion force consisted of the former Katangese autonomous army which had retreated to Angola after its defeat in Zaire, living there forgotten near the border. The ruling Angolan revolutionaries suspected Zaire of encouraging and supporting their own guerillas and were now in a sense turning the tables on them. The Katangese forces advanced easily, defeating the Zaire forces on their way, but Zaire appealed for aid to France. France responded immediately and airlifted paratroopers to the invaded province of Zaire, so the Katangese forces were soon stopped and beaten back to Angola. Thus it was France, in no way involved in strategic and political agreements with the Super Powers, which had intervened in far away Africa and for a time put a stop to further Soviet expansion.

Thus the whole of 1978 seemed to have accentuated the alarming expansion of the USSR, as the Americans interpreted it. Shortly after the Zaire crisis, the Soviet ally Vietnam invaded Campuchia, where a particularly murderous regime had installed itself after the fall of Prince Sihanuk. It was significant that the Pol Pot regime maintained close ties with China. At the same time the Vietnamese began to expel ethnic Chinese, especially from former South Vietnam. The massive exodus of the so-called boat people started and the Americans naturally

Left:
A Somarli soldier displays Russian arms, captured from the Ethiopians.

A Nike Hercules surface-to-air missile supplied by the US to Taiwan forces. Since 1978 the USA has "normalized" trade relations with the Republic of China, which is now importing US military hardware. Since the death of Chairman Mao the new Chinese leadership has become anxious to import Western technology.

blamed the Russians for this. By then Western reactions made it clear to the USSR that countermeasures were contemplated and would follow. In April 1978 NATO accepted in principle the new neutron bombs which the USA offered the alliance; the three percent increase in military budgets was also voted. Dr. Brzezinski, on a visit to China, appealed to the Chinese leaders to join the West against the USSR: as if in response, the Sino-Japanese Peace Treaty, which was signed at this time, contained a hegemony clause, obviously directed against Soviet pretensions in Southeast Asia. Chairman Hua Kuofeng's highly provocative visit to Rumania, Yugoslavia, and Iran was meant as a warning to the Russians to keep their hands off these countries. Later in 1978 US-Chinese relations were "normalized" and China was able to purchase defensive weapons from the USA. Throughout this year the Americans sent advanced weapons to Israel, Iran, Turkey, while warning Ethiopia not to go too far in Ogaden and taking this opportunity to denounce the Cuban "mercenaries" fighting the war. In the United States more and more influential people were voicing their doubts about the SALT II agreements still being negotiated. The growing

tension between China and Vietnam preceding the Vietnamese invasion of Campuchia, inspired the USSR and Vietnam to conclude a treaty of friendship and cooperation and only then risk the invasion. From both Super Powers' point of view a state of crisis had been reached and the USSR revised its international strategy.

This Soviet revision of strategy was more a restatement of priorities rather than principles which remained the same. The most important principle now became the irreversibility of the socialist revolution. This in fact meant that the USSR was prepared to go to war in order to uphold the communist regimes of Poland, Czechoslovakia, East Germany, Bulgaria, Rumania, and Hungary. A less clear undertaking was made on behalf of Yugoslavia, Cuba, Mongolia, and North Korea. Laos, Vietnam, and Campuchia were also included in this group of privileged nations, but the Soviet obligations were even less clear than with the previous group. (Though this restatement of the vital interests of the USSR was largely intended for internal hegemonial purposes, it would soon have external consequences as far as Poland was concerned. The Soviet Union like the Americans in Asia, became concerned with the

domino theory in their sphere of influence: if one satellite was allowed to break away, all would want to follow.) A second principle was that the Soviet defense umbrella would be extended to the new self-proclaimed Marxist states such as Angola, the Congo, Ethiopia, Mozambique, Syria, Afghanistan, and South Yemen. They would be entitled to all sorts of aid and even military assistance (intervention) if threatened internally or externally. A third principle was that friendly countries, such as Libya and Iraq would continue to receive weapons and technical aid, and a fourth principle was that the favored trade partners would be West Germany, France, Italy, and Japan. It now seemed obvious that this was a reappraisal of priorities in the face of an approaching crisis. However, instead of helping the USSR to cope with the crisis more effectively, it in fact made Soviet position more inflexible and increased the possibility of a conflict between the Super Powers, which it was supposed to prevent.

In January 1979 Vice-Premier Deng Xiaoping visited the United States and his visit was a great success. As soon as he returned to China, the Chinese army invaded the north of Vietnam in order to "administer that country a punishment for the invasion of Campuchia." The Soviets already saw American hands behind this war, especially since they themselves had just concluded a defense treaty with Vietnam, which was supposed to protect the latter against such possibility. However, the Chinese armies, after "punishing" the Vietnamese, pulled out of the country and the conflict did not escalate. Nonetheless international tensions rose visibly and the USSR was publicly humiliated.

Also in January 1979 the Shah of Iran fled from his country and a revolution swept through it, a faithful and favored ally of the United States. In turn the other Super Power was publicly humiliated and this in fact led to a temporary rapprochement between them. After seven years of abortive negotiations the Super Powers suddenly made mutual concessions and the SALT II treaty was ready for signature in June 1979. President Brezhnev and Carter flew to Vienna and solemnly signed the treaty, which had to be ratified by the American and Soviet legislative bodies.

There were misgivings in the United States about the treaty during the negotiating stages; now after its precipitate signature and subsequent humiliations in Iran the treaty was seen by American public opinion as a confirmation of an American decline in international affairs and it became increasingly evident that it would not be ratified by the US Senate. If the Americans

still hesitated, the Soviets became quite convinced that SALT II was dead and with it detente. As a result of the cumulative effects of failing detente the USSR was ready to make some remarkable decisions which would threaten world peace. In December 1979 NATO voted to accept in principle 600 updated IMBMs which the Americans offered the alliance. At the same time Iranian students seized the US embassy in Teheran and there was visible disarray in Washington. Still the Russians expected the Americans to intervene in Iran and in turn they had their own intervention ready. In 1978 they had concluded a treaty of alliance with revolutionary Afghanistan, where the political situation then degenerated as the minute communist factions struggled for power among themselves. During Christmas 1979 the Soviet army finally invaded the country bringing thus "massive aid to the Afghan revolution."

President Carter, although busy with the Iranian crisis, reacted with surprising firmness. He was advised that the Soviet invasion signified a new phase in Soviet expansion, in a particularly volatile region. The US military claimed that Iran and Pakistan had been outflanked, that the Russians were aiming at a warm-water port in the Indian ocean, and that oil supplies to the West as a whole were threatened. Carter therefore advised the Senate to suspend the consideration of the SALT II treaty and cut supplies of grain to the USSR, which had been negotiated in the early 1970s. Thus the USSR had to pay dearly for this "offensive" decision. In addition the USA was joined by Western Europe, Third World countries, and certain WPT countries as well, in their public and less public condemnation of Soviet intervention in Afghanistan. World tensions rose and a cold war confrontation became a real possibility. In the early 1980s three countries, Iran, Yugoslavia, and Poland became the flashpoints of a possible conflict between the Super Powers.

IRAN

The unexpected collapse of the pro-Western regime in Iran made of this country a potentially serious cause of a world conflict, for Iran, together with other, largely Arab, states in this area of the world, control the strategic commodity for the West, oil. The American Joint

Chiefs of Staff foresaw this danger when in 1980 they stated that ". . . in a situation of increasing competition for scarce resources, the potential for conflict looms large in the 1980s. . . ."

When in 1953 the American Central Intelligence Agency carried out one of its most successful operations, namely ousting Premier Mossadegh from power, and substituting him with Reza Pahlavi, nothing seemed more improbable than that the Shah's regime should collapse. The Shah was young, full of good intentions, liberally minded; apparently he would lead the country from centuries of decline to a new renaissance, solidly based on Western science, industry, and political system.

However, despite his good intentions, the Shah proved unable to cope with his country's political and economic problems. In politics he wanted to base himself on the 1906 Islamic Constitution and act as a constitutional monarch. Instead he and his family tried to dominate everything, take credit for all the progress that the nation made, and derive advantage from the oil wealth which continued to accrue regardless of the political regime. In fact according to the liberal opposition (in a declaration signed in 1977 by the Shah's last Premier, Dr. Bakhtiar) the Shah disregarded the constitution and acted as an ancient Persian despot with no individual human rights respected, much less guaranteed. He was apparently wasting the oil wealth, the country's only asset, creating devastating inflation, causing food shortages and housing deficiencies. This open letter addressed to the Shah in June 1977 summed up the grievances of the rising middle class which was supposed and in fact did share in the economic boom that was set into motion by the accrued oil revenues. These Iranian "liberals" however, were not the only ones to complain about the Shah's mismanagement.

Since 1945, when the Russian armies had occupied Northern Iran, a left-wing political opposition had struggled against the Shah's regime. In the crises in 1946 and again in 1953, the Tudeh party was defeated politically quite easily and it turned to clandestine struggle. In the 1970s there existed four groups of political guerillas; the (Moslem) Mojahidins and (Marxist) Fedayeens were particularly active in large cities, causing the Shah's regime a great deal of trouble, and were the excuse for maintaining the security police, SAVAK, and employing inhuman methods to combat these opposition forces. The Fedayeens were hunted down by the SAVAK mercilessly and suffered heavy casualties. On the whole the SAVAK, by savage methods, brought these guerilla groups under control, until 1978, when the channels for arms entering Iran were suddenly unlocked and the battered guerillas could reorganize and reequip themselves with modern arms.

Paradoxically it was the three most fundamental reforms which the Shah launched as part of the modernization of Iran, namely land reform, emancipation of women, and industrial development which provoked and gave rise to the real opposition to the existing regime and ultimately caused its downfall. The new economic system, which was to bring about the industrialization of the country, provoked the traditionalist economy of the bazaar to revolt against the Shah. The bazaar, which was the basis of the Iranian economic system, controlling two-thirds of wholesale trade and much of foreign trade (except oil), proved itself to be a great political mobilizer. In 1906 it was thanks to this institution that the constitution had been approved. The Shah's return from exile in 1953 was also largely due to the bazaar's influence. However, by the 1970s the bazaaris felt sufficiently threatened by the Shah's economic policies to be converted by the Moslem clergy to opposition to the Shah. The Merchant Association then threw its weight behind the masses of unemployed, also taking financial care of the strikers and victims of the Shah's repression. They were aided and abetted in their demolition work by students and emancipated women, who for reasons of their own, also hated the Shah's regime. However, the most decisive force behind the movement against the Shah was the Moslem clergy.

Though some of the clergy approved the 1906 constitution, many fundamentalist clergymen remained in opposition to it. Since the 1930s, the most consistent opposition leader had been Ayatollah Khomeini. In 1941 he published a book in which he attacked the Pahlavis as corrupters of his brand of the Moslem religion, the shiism. Khomeini and subsequently the whole shiite clergy (the mullahs, hafezez, and hojjats) rigorously opposed the Shah: his land reform, because it threatened land owned by the mosques; the emancipation of women, because it was against their tradition; the Shah's regime in general, because it spread moral corruption. From their point of view, the so-called islamic regime of the Shah was unreliable as a source of financial support and it also failed to combat heretical movements such as Bahaiism. Above all it was the "corruption of the faith and its practice" that made the clergy rebellious. The clergy could rely for support on the conservative, agricultural masses, largely left out of the economic boom, but with dissatisfaction spreading elsewhere, the clergy proved capable of uniting all the disparate elements against the Shah. Still, in 1963 when Ayatollah Khomeini criticized him publicly, the Shah had him arrested and subsequently deported to Iraq. Khomeini's arrest then provoked mass demonstrations, which the Shah ordered to be suppressed by the army, a task which was achieved at the time.

It became clear that the Shah could maintain himself in power only thanks to the SAVAK and the army, both of which he personally controlled. However, when the opposition forces succeeded in mobilizing the urban and agricultural masses, it became clear even to the Americans, who supported him unflinchingly, that the Shah would have to relinquish power. The Shah chose to remain blind: he continued to underestimate the strength of the opposition and increasingly depended on military and political hardliners. As he desired all the credit for his modernization drive, he could not now distance himself from the errors and misdeeds of his government which had conducted modernization in his name. Because of his political and economic dependence on the United States he also offended Iranian nationalist feelings and his concessions, when they came, were either inadequate or too late.

Finally in the summer of 1978 a wave of strikes, riots, and demonstrations hit Iran. As previously the Shah ordered repression: in Tabriz there were 100 dead; in Isphahan also 100, but in September in Teheran the Black Friday riot left 600 dead among the demonstrators. Encouraged by Khomeini, who had moved from Iraq to France, demonstrators and strikers hardened their resistance. The Shah's military government, apart from killing people *en masse*, totally failed to control the strikes which paralyzed the economy, and demonstrations which stopped life itself in its tracks. On December 9, 1978, over a million demonstrators flooded Teheran, and with junior officers and conscripts demoralized, apparently on American advice, the Shah decided to leave his country before the revolutionary wave engulfed him. On December 30, 1978 he appointed Dr. Bakhtiar as his Premier and soon afterward flew out to Egypt, never to return.

The hapless Bakhtiar dissolved the SAVAK and promised the Iranian people all the reforms that he had demanded from the Shah. However, even his colleagues from the National Front deserted him, preferring to join the Khomeini camp. On February 9, 1979 after the Air Force cadets, who were pro-Khomeini, mutinied and successfully resisted the assaults on their bar-

racks made by the Imperial Guard units, the Iranian armed forces dissolved in chaos, and Dr. Bakhtiar was left without any power to influence the situation in Iran. He could not prevent Khomeini returning from France, and had to run for his life after the Ayatollah's guardians of the revolution began to purge the whole of Iran. Khomeini appointed Dr. Bazargan as his Premier and gradually a takeover was accomplished, though political stability was not restored. A wave of executions also failed to stem the prevailing chaos, and when the Shah was permitted to visit the USA, revolutionary students stormed the American embassy and took almost all diplomats and staff as hostages.

Previously the Iranian revolution had turned against alleged Western corruption; now this ideological contention was turned into action. American installations against the USSR had been dismantled; Western military programs were unilaterally terminated; technicians were expelled; businessmen arrested and otherwise harassed. The former fortress of the West against the USSR and communism seemed ripe to fall victim to the Iranian left, especially the Tudeh (Communist) Party, which remained the only organized body politic in the revolutionary chaos. Miraculously Khomeini succeeded in keeping a check on both the various non-

Reza Pahlavi, the Shah of Iran, was brought to power with C.I.A. help but the Americans did nothing to bolster up his shaky regime in 1979. Once ousted from power he sought exile in Egypt and died shortly afterward.

Persian minorities and the left by means of revolutionary purges and executions. Once the US hostage crisis had been resolved, internal stability did not return and instead Iraq invaded the south of Iran. President Bani Sadr was dismissed in 1981 and had to run for his life back to France. Although the Americans sent their naval and air units to the Persian Gulf, to prop up the morale of neighboring Arab oil states, Iran remained, with its internal power vacuum, a temptation for its neighbor, the USSR, to try its hand at solving local problems or "fish in troubled waters." The Americans, after the Soviet invasion of Afghanistan, declared the Persian Gulf area as of vital importance to the USA and the West in an effort to keep the Soviets at bay, and in 1980 rapidly created the Long Range Joint Task Force to dissuade the Soviets still further. However, the Iranian puzzling problem remains as does the possibility of political change in that country in favor of the USSR which would lead to an East-West confrontation, probably resulting in a strategic conflict.

YUGOSLAVIA

Once before this area was responsible for a world conflict. In 1914 the assassination of Archduke Francis Ferdinand at Sarajevo by Serbian nationalists was the direct cause of World War I. Long before and also after this conflict the language of international politics retained the word "balkanization" meaning an explosive situation in the region, in which the Super Powers had been involved without actually having a decisive control over their minor allies: this lack of control and the resulting anarchy in world affairs ultimately led to world-wide conflicts. In 1918 Balkan nationalistic conflicts were ostensibly solved by the creation of independent national states in Rumania, Bulgaria, and above all Yugoslavia. In fact the nationalist unrest continued; even though the Super Powers, Turkey and Austria-Hungary, either no longer counted or existed. However this did not prevent the succession states having nationalist tensions in the region and conflicts within themselves; this was particularly true of Yugoslavia which seemed to have inherited all the minorities of the defunct Super Powers: Yugoslavia's

ruling Serbian dynasty had to cope with rebellious Croats, culturally superior Slovenes, restless Macedonians, revanchist Hungarians, with Greeks and Albanians thrown in. At first the king Alexander wanted to be a constitutional monarch, but when the dominant nationalities, the Serbs and Croats, began to sort out their quarrels in parliament by shooting each other during parliamentary discussions, he became a dictator, only to be assassinated during his visit to France with the French foreign minister, Barthou. Even World War II, which devastated Yugoslavia, failed to calm internal, nationalistic passions. Internecine bloodshed conducted mainly by the Croat Ustashi continued and a new force, the partisans, led by a communist called Josef Broz, who subsequently was known as Marshal Tito, further complicated the political situation.

After struggling against the Germans and his Yugoslav rivals, Marshal Tito moved with his partisan armies into Belgrade and installed himself in the royal palace there. However, for the moment, after the bloodshed of the war, nationalist passions were exhausted and Tito skillfully consolidated his power to become an undisputed communist ruler in a country which scarcely had an industrial proletariat, but on the contrary, whose dominant nationality, the Serbs, were politically and economically underdeveloped. Tito himself was a Croat, but his political machinations proved too much for his internal rivals, so that he and his minute communist elite succeeded in performing a major miracle by pacifying and ruling this Balkan country.

From 1945 Yugoslavia was an enthusiastic member of the Communist bloc and in the three succeeding years Tito even fancied himself as successor to Stalin, the recognized leader of this bloc. Marshal Stalin was not amused by Tito's aspirations and sponsored a conspiracy against him in Yugoslavia. Tito comfortably anticipated the machinations of his fellow Communist and when he defeated the Soviet conspiracy at home, Stalin had him and Yugoslavia publicly expelled from the Communist· bloc (or better its ideological front organization, termed Cominform). In 1948 Tito had to invoke Yugoslav nationalism to impress on the Soviets not to invade the country, and once again he proved successful. The Yugoslav communist elite was backed by the nations and nationalities so that Stalin was dissuaded from ordering his armies to march and conquer the turbulent communist, erstwhile ally, and bring it back into the orthodox fold under his domination. Thus until 1955 Tito and the Yugoslav

Communists came to practice a different type of communism from that of the Soviet brand. The communist elite still ran the country, but contrary to the Soviet Party, it left out of its running the economy, instituting what is nowadays termed the self-management economic system. When in 1955 Yugoslavia became reconciled with the USSR and the other communist countries, the Yugoslav system was recognized as a communist system; the Yugoslavs also insisted that part of the reconciliation process was the recognition by the Soviets and other communists of their political and military non-alignment. After this "official" reconciliation Tito developed normal relations with the USSR and the bloc, soon to be called the Warsaw Pact. While Tito was alive (he died in May 1980) he was skillful enough to make use of these renewed relations to the benefit of himself and his country, balancing communist influence and economic aid with Western influence and aid. Politically Tito also kept in balance the orthodox and liberal tendencies within the Communist Party. Thus he did not hesitate to purge Djilas and Serbian liberal Communists, when they became too vociferous and extreme; neither did he hesitate to put on trial conservative communists, when it suited him.

Thus Soviet-Yugoslav reconciliation was never complete, for the leaders distrusted each other: periodically a worsening of relations was followed by temporary improvement. In 1972 economic agreements were found to damage the Yugoslav economy and when currency difficulty arose, the agreement was practically nullified. Tito most vehemently condemned Soviet intervention in Czechoslovakia in 1968 and kept his ill-equipped army on alert to dissuade the Soviet army doing the same to Yugoslavia. After all, as in Czechoslovakia, the Soviets could find in Yugoslavia a few communists who would have invited them to intervene on their behalf. In fact a Czech deserter, General Sejna, divulged the existence of a contingency plan to invade Yugoslavia by the Warsaw Pact armies, if this communist country suddenly or gradually lapsed into anarchy. Above all the periodic ups and downs in Soviet-Yugoslav relations went to show that Tito was only able to keep his country independent, because there existed a state of tension between the USSR and the USA. In case of relaxation, that is detente, Tito and his successors would find it increasingly difficult to balance the Super Powers against each other to their benefit.

Furthermore the Soviet Union was quick to use the points of friction within Yugoslavia to its advantage: it was fully aware that some

Marshal Tito was President of Yugoslavia from 1946 until his death in 1980. He followed an independent foreign policy and helped to start the movement of non-aligned countries.

700,000 Serbs lived in Croatia causing nationalist frictions. The same situation pertained to Kossovo, where the Albanians were restless. Above all Macedonia was subject to claims by Bulgaria, the most orthodox of the Soviet allies. It is true that the exploitation of these frictions proved unsuccessful while Marshal Tito was alive. However, after his death, the situation would undoubtedly be more favorable to the Soviets, for there would be a whole series of successors to one Tito, (the so-called collective presidency), and the minority problem would remain as acute as before.

In December 1979, some six months before Tito's death, the USSR proved to the Yugoslavs beyond any doubt how much their fears had been justified. In 1973, after a *coup d'etat* in Afghanistan, the Afghan monarchy, which had ruled the country since 1923 and kept it independent, was overthrown and General Daud became President of the Afghan Republic. The People's Democratic Party (the name used by

Right:
Kiev; pride of the Soviet Fleet.

Far right:
MiG-23 Flogger.

Below:
Soviet Global Power Projection.

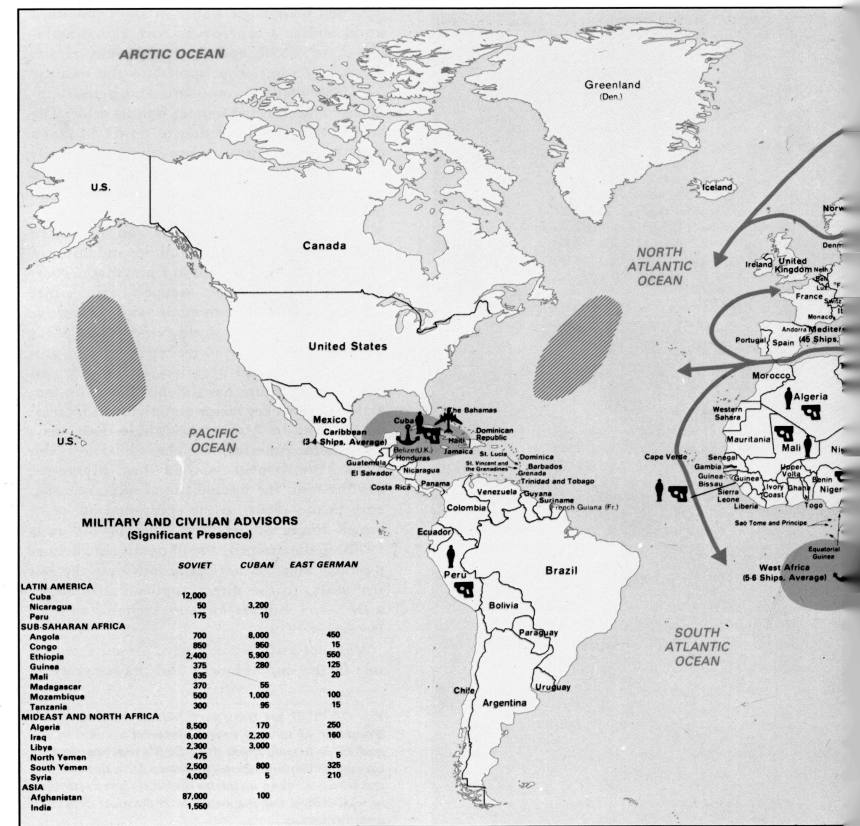

ARCTIC OCEAN

Greenland
(Den.)

U.S.

Canada

Iceland

NORTH
ATLANTIC
OCEAN

Norw

Ireland United
Kingdom

Denm

Neth
Bel
Lux

France
Switz

It

Monaco

Andorra Mediter
(45 Ships,

Portugal Spain

Morocco

United States

PACIFIC
OCEAN

U.S.

Mexico

Caribbean
(3-4 Ships, Average)

Cuba

The Bahamas

Haiti

Dominican
Republic

Belize(U.K.)

Jamaica

St. Lucia

Guatemala

Honduras

St. Vincent and
the Grenadines

Dominica

Barbados

El Salvador

Nicaragua

Grenada

Trinidad and Tobago

Costa Rica

Panama

Venezuela

Guyana

Colombia

Suriname

French Guiana (Fr.)

Cape Verde

Western
Sahara

Algeria

Mauritania

Mali

Senegal

Ni

Gambia

Guinea-
Bissau

Guinea

Upper
Volta

Benin

Sierra
Leone

Ivory
Coast

Ghana

Niger

Liberia

Togo

Sao Tome and Principe

Equatorial
Guinea

West Africa
(5-6 Ships, Average)

Ecuador

Peru

Brazil

Bolivia

Paraguay

SOUTH
ATLANTIC
OCEAN

Chile

Uruguay

Argentina

MILITARY AND CIVILIAN ADVISORS
(Significant Presence)

	SOVIET	CUBAN	EAST GERMAN
LATIN AMERICA			
Cuba	12,000		
Nicaragua	50	3,200	
Peru	175	10	
SUB-SAHARAN AFRICA			
Angola	700	8,000	450
Congo	850	950	15
Ethiopia	2,400	5,900	550
Guinea	375	280	125
Mali	635		20
Madagascar	370	55	
Mozambique	500	1,000	100
Tanzania	300	95	15
MIDEAST AND NORTH AFRICA			
Algeria	8,500	170	250
Iraq	8,000	2,200	160
Libya	2,300	3,000	
North Yemen	475		5
South Yemen	2,500	800	325
Syria	4,000	5	210
ASIA			
Afghanistan	87,000	100	
India	1,550		

68

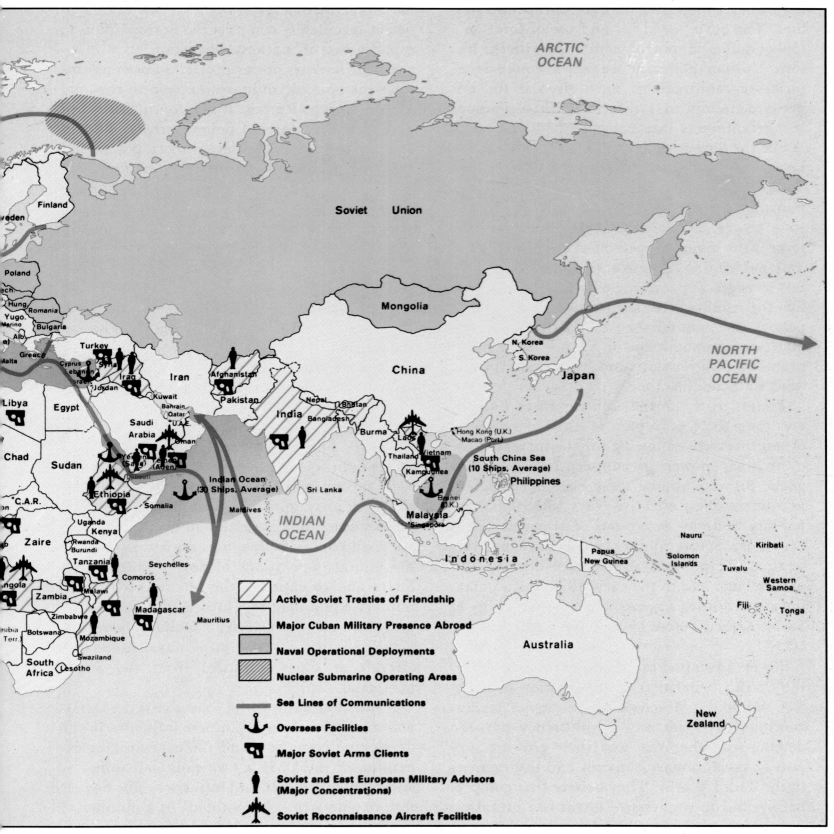

ARCTIC OCEAN

Soviet Union

NORTH PACIFIC OCEAN

Mongolia

China

Finland

Poland

Romania

Bulgaria

Turkey

Greece

Cyprus

Syria

Iraq

Iran

Afghanistan

Pakistan

Nepal

Bhutan

India

Bangladesh

Burma

N. Korea

S. Korea

Japan

Kuwait
Bahrain
Qatar
U.A.E.
Oman

Saudi Arabia

Libya

Egypt

Chad

Sudan

Yemen (San'a)

Ethiopia

Somalia

C.A.R.

Zaire

Uganda
Rwanda
Burundi
Kenya

Tanzania

Angola

Zambia
Malawi

Zimbabwe

Botswana

South Africa

Swaziland
Lesotho

Madagascar

Mauritius

Comoros

Seychelles

Indian Ocean
(30 Ships, Average)

INDIAN OCEAN

Maldives

Sri Lanka

Mozambique

Laos
Thailand
Vietnam
Kampuchea

Hong Kong (U.K.)
Macao (Port.)

South China Sea
(10 Ships, Average)

Philippines

Malaysia
Singapore

Brunei (U.K.)

Indonesia

Australia

Papua New Guinea

Solomon Islands

Nauru

Kiribati

Tuvalu

Western Samoa

Fiji

Tonga

New Zealand

| | Active Soviet Treaties of Friendship |
| Major Cuban Military Presence Abroad |
| Naval Operational Deployments |
| Nuclear Submarine Operating Areas |
| Sea Lines of Communications |
| Overseas Facilities |
| Major Soviet Arms Clients |
| Soviet and East European Military Advisors (Major Concentrations) |
| Soviet Reconnaissance Aircraft Facilities |

the Communist Party), founded clandestinely in 1965, began to plot against Daud and on April 27, 1978 seized power in another *coup d'etat*. Daud was executed and succeeded by the Secretary General of the Communist Party, Nur Mohammad Taraki. At the same time Afghanistan became a people's democratic republic. However, Taraki only had time to conclude a treaty of friendship and cooperation with the Soviet Union. In September 1979, after he had returned from abroad, he was toppled from power (and executed) by Hafizullah Amin, fellow leader of the Khalk communist faction. Security rapidly deteriorated in Afghanistan, while various Afghan communist factions struggled for power. In December 1979 events came to a head: Amin and his group, including all his family, women and children, were massacred, after the Russians had thrown their weight behind the Parcham faction. But General I. Paputin, Soviet Deputy Minister of the Interior, who had been sent to Kabul with a team of security experts, was also killed during a *coup de main*. The new leader, Babrak Karmal, immediately appealed to the USSR to "save the communist revolution by sending troops in its support." The Red Army responded magnanimously and despite winter conditions it occupied the capital and gradually the whole country. Thus the USSR demonstrated to the world in general and to Yugoslavia in particular that it was prepared to act with decisive power and invade and occupy any communist country in which the struggling factions made an appeal to it. The Yugoslavs became extremely worried and for a good reason.

In Yugoslavia, following Tito's death, the transition seemed peaceful enough. However, as the Yugoslavs always expected political trouble to come either from the Serbs or the Croats, and the latter were known to maintain clandestine party relations with the USSR, events there became even more complicated and dangerous. In March/April 1981, quite unexpectedly, violent disorders broke out in the Kossovo province, inhabited largely by Albanians: the Yugoslav army mercilessly put down the nationalist insurrection, the Albanians claiming that some 2,000 young men were killed. In this case the Yugoslav Albanians could only appeal to the badly armed Albanians in the neighboring homeland, and in any case the combined forces would have been no match for the Yugoslav army. Thus this trouble was not a real test. None of the big powers was involved in this conflict, for as well as the USSR earlier, China had broken relations with the Albanian communists. However, given the ease with which this insurrection was started, it is a serious warning to the West: it seems only a question of time before the Yugoslav communists will have on hand a political and possibly military insurrection in Croatia, and in that case, both the winning and the losing parties will probably appeal to the Soviet Union to resolve this latent domestic issue, whatever consequences for the world at large, as demonstrated in Afghanistan.

POLAND

In the 1980s Poland seems to be the most likely cause of a super power conflict. Not only was it the immediate cause of World War II, but because of its traditional (historical) antagonism toward the Russian Empire and then the Soviet Communist Empire, it seems most likely that the "chain reaction," historically always responsible for major conflicts, will be set in motion there. It is now almost 40 years since Poland experienced the last mass insurrection in Warsaw which ended so sadly and which ensured Poland's incorporation into the Soviet hegemony.

In 1947, after a manipulated election, which was won overwhelmingly by the communist dominated electoral bloc, Poland formally submitted to Stalin's designs: he then launched a long-term campaign aimed at the destruction of the peasantry and the Catholic Church in Poland. In the same year an important official of the US State Department, George Kennan, reflected on American impotence *vis a vis* Stalin's treatment of Poland and sounded, all the same, a hopeful note: ". . . however demoralized and overwhelmed the Poles may seem now, in the future they will prove such an embarrassment to the Russians that they will be made to reflect on the folly of wanting to dominate Poland. . . ." While Stalin was alive and while the tiny communist ruling group was able to use terror, Poland appeared subdued, and there was no rioting or bloodshed, even after Cardinal Wyshinsky, Primate of the Polish Church, was put in custody. However, as soon as Stalin was dead (and with him the local tyrant, Bierut), the Poles rose in revolt. In June 1956 at Poznan, while foreigners attended the international industrial fair, workers rose against bad living conditions and went on strike. But the Communist Government refused them just wages

and better conditions, although a communist faction, led by Wladyslaw Gomulka, successfully exploited this revolt to install itself in power. In turn Gomulka was dismissed from power in 1970, after mishandling another revolt: while Polish workers demanded better conditions and higher wages, he ordered increases in the price of basic foods. Although the Polish army with tanks sorted out this particular social problem of the communist regime, Poland henceforth appeared to be the powder keg of the Soviet hegemony, ready to blow up as soon as social conditions appeared to deteriorate.

Gomulka's successor, Edward Gierek, tried for ten years to improve Polish living standards, thus staving off a similar showdown with the Poles. Between 1971–75 Poland went through an industrial boom, unprecedented even in Communist Eastern Europe. This boom was partially financed by Western loans and was the result of a more liberal policy toward private agriculture. However, by 1976 it became clear that the communist authorities could not even manage this economic boom: since that year the Polish GNP failed to reach its planned level. In 1979 it even dropped 2 percent compared to 1978, another unprecedented phenomenon in the Soviet bloc. While in 1976 the industrial growth was 9.3 percent, in 1979 it was 2.8 percent and in agricultural production there was a drop 1 percent. Throughout these years wage demands on the contrary continued to grow until an economic crisis was reached which disorganized the whole of the Polish economy.

By 1980 the GNP had plunged by 4 percent, industrial production decreased by 3 percent and drought reduced agricultural production by 15 percent. In Warsaw house building was fulfilled by only 35.8 percent of the planned targets. Foreign debts also increased: from 4.1 thousand million export zlotys in 1979 to 57 thousand million. Debts to capitalist countries amounted to $23,000,000,000,000. By the end of 1980 exports decreased by 6.5 percent, while the prices of imports, especially of grain and fodder, increased by 26 percent. Gross agricultural production was 9.6 percent smaller than in 1979 and grain harvest was 3.2 million tons short. In contrast nominal monthly wages rose by 12.8 percent and in the last quarter of 1980 by 20 percent; overall price rises were in the order of 10 percent, but for the basic foodstuffs they were more than 14 percent. By July 1980, when the distribution system all but collapsed, the Poles became vitally interested in solving a catastrophic economic situation, which the public (communist) authorities failed to control, by whatever means, even by strikes. In a series of spontaneous strikes, started in the Lenin dockyards at Gdansk, and followed by the occupation of their places of work, the Polish workers established independent trade unions, which in turn demanded public agreements with the Communist Government as a preliminary for calling off the strikes.

Already in 1976 Poland had had a wave of strikes against the lowering of living standards, but the authorities had succeeded in isolating the strikers, dividing and arresting the strike leaders. This time the workers seemed to have learned from that experience: ad hoc strike committees were elected in all the enterprises on strike and they took contact with each other to coordinate their demands to the government.

Below:
Soviet sailors on a May Day parade.
The strength of Soviet adventurism
comes from the knowledge that it
is the largest military might in
the world.

Far left:
The Polish government at a
Communist Party meeting during
the Solidarity crisis. Fear of popular
unrest paralyzed the Praesidium
during the initial stages of the crisis.

recognition: they were the workers' trade unions (and subsequently of the peasants), calling themselves Solidarity. Walesa, backed by the united strike movement, and the regional Communist Party Secretary, Fiszbach, made the government agree to the workers' demands and demonstrated once again that communism was no real power in Poland, and that it depended entirely on Soviet bayonets which established it in that country in 1945 and sustained it throughout. However, as soon as the Communist Government and the Polish Party capitulated and agreed to satisfy Walesa's economic and political demands, the Soviet Union began to put pressure on its communist ally, though the crisis was her own fault.

While in the past the Soviet Union could not sufficiently help Poland economically, it certainly gave the Communist Poles a free hand in the economy: provided the West granted them credits, the Poles were the freest satellite of the Soviet hegemony. But as soon as this policy began to have domestic repercussions, the USSR dogmatically recalled "the international communist obligations of fraternal Poland." In practice it meant that the Communist Party of Poland had no right to grant economic, and above all political concessions, to its working class. However, the economic and moral bankruptcy of the Polish Communists was so complete as to leave them no option, and they made it plain to their principal ally, the USSR, and to minor allies, the German Democratic Republic and Czechoslovakia, the most disturbed by the Polish development. In fact the Soviet response to events in Poland became almost monotonous: as soon as the free trade unions, Solidarity, advanced demands, however justified, the USSR and the two Warsaw Pact allies, arranged military exercises along the Polish border, sometimes involving Poland, sometimes not. The situation was very similar to that in July 1968 in Czechoslovakia, where further liberalization was slowed down with a show of power by the Soviets and Warsaw Pact.

Nonetheless, with the West having economic interests in Poland, and above all, with the USA far from indifferent to the possible occupation of Poland by the Warsaw Pact armies, the situation is not really comparable to that of Czechoslovakia in 1968. In the end the internal situation in Poland deteriorated to such an extent that the Soviets even tried to postpone the fraternal Communist Party Congress. By 1981 Gierek's men who had taken over from Gomulka's, were mercilessly purged; some were expelled from the party; many committed suicide. In July 1981 the rest were ousted from power at the Communist

At Gdansk, the dismissed worker, Lech Walesa, was elected chairman of the strike committee and he soon extended his influence all over the country. In August 1980 the government began to negotiate with these unofficial strike committees which immediately demanded legal

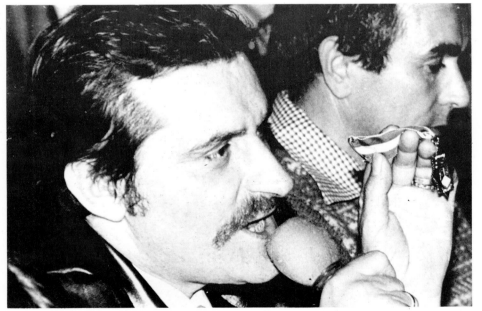

Party Congress about which the Soviets had entertained such doubts. Still the Congress changed nothing of the reality of Poland and the party itself appears as superfluous as before. On the other hand, the newly freed forces, especially the Solidarity union, are clamoring for a real expression of their newly acquired power. Once again the USSR notified the world that it would hold land, air, and sea exercises in September 1981; as if by accident these would take place along the Eastern border of Poland and in the Baltic sea. Despite the imposition of martial law by General Jaruzelski and the detention of Solidarity leaders the power problem in Poland is unresolved; Poland's place in the Soviet hegemony is unclear. This is an intolerable situation for the Soviet Super Power which cannot be allowed to go on for long. In time, perhaps, in the not-too-distant future, when the Soviets initiate a military action against Poland, the consequences of it can only be fatal for the peace of the whole world.

From this analysis it is clear that international tensions are likely to increase in the 1980s. Albeit the Super Powers seem deterred from a direct confrontation which could easily escalate into a strategic conflict, they both appear less and less capable of managing crises within their hegemonies, as Iran and Afghanistan have shown. The most acute danger to world peace in the 1980s appears to be the possibility that because of ideological inflexibility the Super Powers may be dragged by their allies or clients into a theater conflict. Such an occurrence would be devastating for the whole world because of the accumulated strategic armament on both sides.

Above:
Lech Walesa was chairman of the Gdansk dockyard strike committee in 1980. This position propelled him to national fame and he was elected leader of the workers' free trade union, Solidarity.

Top:
Walesa and a member of the Polish government during the negotiations about Solidarity's status.

CHAPTER THREE

SOVIET MILITARY POWER

The United States and the Soviet Union, which emerged from World War II not only as victors, but also as decisive world powers, the Super Powers, have mistrusted each other ever since the end of that conflict. As early as October 1945 President Truman ordered General Dwight D. Eisenhower, then his military supremo, to prepare a contingency plan, *Totality*, for war against Soviet Russia in Europe, if the Red Army continued to expand westward, as it had done in Eastern Europe. *Totality* was the first emergency war plan by one erstwhile ally against the other. It is remembered as such only because it became publicly known, (we as yet know practically nothing about Soviet contingency planning) and militarily it had no value whatsoever. The Americans demobilized so rapidly as to give *Totality* no teeth: the plan was only worth the paper it was written on. Still it marked the emergence of the Soviet military threat.

However since the Americans, and with them the West Europeans, were interested in postwar international stability and security, they began to develop and rely increasingly on the new atomic power, tested so devastatingly on Japan in August 1945, as a counter to this largely theoretical Russian threat. With the monopoly of the atomic bomb, the United States developed a completely novel strategy, totally different from the *Totality* plan. In October 1945 the US Air Force produced a strategic proposal, *Strategic Vulnerability of Russia to a Limited Air Attack*, which visualized a limited air intervention with atomic bombs on 20 Russian cities, whose objective would be to destroy the Soviet capacity to wage war by wiping out Soviet industrial and political centers. These proposals were a marked departure in concept from the American contingency plans before and after World War II.

The same perception of the Russian military threat forced the United States, and its ally, Great Britain, to prepare for an all-out global war. The American Chiefs of Staff authorized this first emergency war plan over Berlin in 1948. The British government ordered war alert all round in June 1948, as if the outbreak of World War III were imminent. War panic in the West was general and all the non-communist governments were taking emergency measures: the French government, for example, prepared for its evacuation to Algeria. This general panic curiously enough was not the result of an increased Soviet military threat, as the US interpreted the Russian blockade of Berlin, (the Americans had a strategic plan, *Broiler*, and were prepared to use atomic bombs over Berlin in June 1948). With hindsight we know that Stalin was only probing the West

politically. In the military sense the Soviet "threat" was unimpressive. In 1945 Stalin had 11,365,000 Red Army men under his command. By 1948, when he put pressure on the Americans over Berlin, he only had some 2,874,000 troops, mainly garrison soldiers, with whom no grandiose expansion was possible. Stalin needed demobilization for obvious domestic economic requirements: reconstruction and further industrialization. Nonetheless the ratio of combat divisions, 175:10, which caused panic in the West, exposed Western weakness rather than Russian strength. All the same Stalin's political probings always gave the impression of being backed by Soviet military power. But in June 1948 Stalin knew full well, from his intelligence sources, of the American determination to hold on to the city and he did not allow the Berlin crisis to escalate. In fact it was solved quite peacefully a year later. Curiously enough, it was an ideological conflict, which at this stage, brought the Super Powers face to face to the very edge of war. The Russians felt this threat in 1947, when the United States offered Western Europe economic aid in the form of the Marshall Plan. They interpreted this move by "imperialist capitalism" as an attempt to create large standing armies (West Germany included), which, with the backing of US Navy and atomic-equipped Strategic Air Command, would threaten Soviet Russia. This bellicose Western policy was countered by the equally bellicose establishment of the Cominform in September 1947. In this "ideological" encounter, the Russians seem to have been more successful. Certainly Greece and Turkey had been saved from communism; by contrast the whole of Eastern Europe had finally succumbed to it. The United States and the West passively witnessed political takeovers by the Russians in Hungary, Poland, Rumania, throughout 1947; in Czechoslovakia in February 1948, and in June 1948 in Finland, though that country kept her bruised sovereignty. Curiously enough, this series of power takeovers obliged the USA to draw up an ideological response. The plan, *Charioteer*, emphasized the Russian political threat to world peace, making the communist ideology responsible for international tensions at this stage: "the class struggle of the proletariat against the bourgeoisie in order to dominate the world." Therefore the objective of this new plan was twofold, military and political: the Soviet war capacity was to be destroyed *manu militaris*; the Soviet Union would then be compelled to withdraw within its 1939 borders; it would have to abandon its ideology and with it the idea of world domination, and a new Soviet government would have to be created which would be peace-loving. All this would be brought about by US strategic air operations from bases in Britain and West Europe, in which some 133 atomic bombs would be dropped on 70 Soviet cities, within 30 days of the outbreak of war. If the USSR failed to surrender after this first strike, the second strike, spread over 24 months, would follow, in which 200 further atomic bombs would be dropped on Soviet Russia: some 40 percent of its industry would be destroyed and six to seven million workers would perish. However, Soviet advance in Europe would "definitely be halted." This then was the most serious Western response to Soviet military threats and political expansion and since it became known to Soviet leaders, Stalin's reaction was conciliatory, at least in the political sense. He compromised in Finland; while the Berlin crisis also ended in a compromise. But he urgently needed to acquire the first atomic device, which he tested probably in August 1949. The acquisition of the bomb by Russia finally knocked the atomic teeth out of the American contingency plans. Henceforth the balance of power, or as Churchill used to call it, the balance of terror, operated, and old-fashioned conventional wars had to be fought once again to bring about any territorial gain or "victory" for either Super Power.

On June 1, 1949 in a top secret annex to a contingency plan to counter a Soviet invasion of the Western world, the United States Chiefs of Staff considered the current estimates of the Soviet Army consisting of 175 divisions as correct. The largest proportion, some 125, were deployed west of the Ural Mountains. Most significantly 105 of these combat divisions were located along the western and south western

frontiers and in occupied Eastern Europe (only some 20 divisions were stationed in the internal military districts of the USSR). Even to a layman this seemed to be an aggressive deployment of Soviet military capacity. (Only 36 divisions were deployed in areas adjacent to Iran, Afghanistan, and China, and 14 divisions in the Far Eastern seaboard.) The aggressiveness of the deployment transformed itself into a real military "threat" when satellite armies were added to the Soviet ones.

	Troops	Divisions
Albania	50,000	3
Bulgaria	80,000	10
Czechoslovakia	130,000	10
Finland	23,000	3
Hungary	65,000	4
Poland	138,000	16
Rumania	150,000	18
Yugoslavia	240,000	33
	876,000	97

(In 1949 the US considered both Finland and Yugoslavia to be satellites of the USSR).

Although the satellite armies magnified the Soviet threat "an analysis of the dispositions of satellite units disclosed no significant strategic pattern." Thus the US Chiefs of Staff rightly considered the satellite armies and their deployment non-aggressive. However, they failed to take into consideration the Asian "satellites," China and North Korea, who a year later provoked and became involved in a "hot" war.

With 2.7 million under arms the Soviet Union has the largest army in the world.

Soviet naval forces have developed enormously in the last 20 years.

great strides in biological, chemical, and missiles warfare, but according to them, these developments did not constitute a significant enough threat to the West. They also estimated, quite wrongly, that the earliest date by which the Soviets might have exploded their first atomic bomb would be mid-1953. Because of this mistake Soviet weaknesses as perceived by the US Chiefs of Staff now seem unrealistic:

(1) Lack of atomic weapons as opposed to potential enemies who possess them;
(2) The Soviet Surface Navy is comparatively weak, lacks strategic mobility and could support only limited amphibious operations;
(3) The long-range air force lacks experience under combat conditions;
(4) The aviation gasoline supply position is tight;
(5) Shortage of trained technical personnel;
(6) Certain Soviet industries are highly concentrated in relatively few areas;
(7) There are dissatisfied and dissident groups within the Soviet Union susceptible to exploitation by aggressive clandestine and psychological warfare.

It was therefore concluded that "the Soviets have the combat power to overrun key areas in Europe and Asia." "Following the seizure of certain key areas in Europe and in Asia, the capabilities of the Soviet Union to occupy, hold and exploit these areas would, to a great extent, depend upon the ability of opposing forces to exploit successfully those weaknesses enumerated above."

It was anticipated that the Soviet armed forces would invade Western and Southern Europe simultaneously with invasions in the Balkans, Near and Far East, (the six Soviet divisions in the Far East would occupy the Korean peninsula within 18 days.) The main thrust by some 45 divisions would be through Germany, to neutralize initially France and Britain. France was to be occupied within 50 days and the whole of the Iberian peninsula within 243. All these targets were within Soviet military capabilities and it was therefore no surprise that the Western allies formed a defensive alliance, NATO, and launched rearmament programs. However the anticipated conflict, a direct clash between the Super Powers and their allies, did not take place in the late 1940s nor in the 1950s, though there was a "hot" conflict in Korea in 1950.

While Stalin was alive the threat of a military conflict between the Super Powers was less than under his successors. With hindsight we can see that Stalin was essentially a politician interested in manipulating international affairs, and a classical military strategist. He agreed to fix a 3:1 ratio of troops in his favor, because he

American calculations and analyses of the Soviet threat also included Soviet mobilization potential, combat efficiency, development of new weapons, Soviet weakness and concluded with an overall balance sheet. Thus it was thought that the Soviet Union could mobilize an additional 170 divisions within one month of a conflict: within six months 470 divisions and within a year, 520 divisions. Significantly the US military leaders thought "the postwar reorganization of the Soviet army along modern mobile mechanized lines, plus a year-round intensive training schedule, and generally successful efforts to reconstitute sagging morale, have imparted to the Soviet Army as a whole a combat efficiency initially in excess of that of any existing army in the world today (1949)." Therefore, at least in the initial stage of a conflict, which the US anticipated, the Soviet armies would be very successful.

In the assessment of development of new weapons, the American Chiefs of Staff were right in thinking that the Soviets had made

calculated that such a ratio would balance the American advantage of having atomic weapons, but otherwise he simply refused to acknowledge any change in strategy, above all that atomic weapons might have brought into world politics. In 1946 Stalin declared that atomic bombs were not as serious as the "imperialists" made out: they were there mainly to intimidate but they did not themselves decide a war. Stalin stuck to his wartime theory of "constant factors":
(1) the stability of the home front; (2) the morale of firmed forces; (3) the quantity and quality of divisions; (4) the armament of the armed forces and (5) the ability of commanders (largely himself). These "factors" would decide the outcome of any conflict between East and West. On the other hand he was most conscious of his weaknesses and knew them better than the American military leaders, his presumed opponents. He compromised over Berlin, never launched his armies against Finland or Yugoslavia, though he seriously considered an intervention in those two countries. Above all, he did nothing to upset the balance of power in Central Europe and Germany, which undoubtedly would have provoked a military conflict. Instead, in order to defuse the tensions in Europe, he agreed to the North Koreans fighting a war by proxy in the Far East. In Europe he continued his political

moves to prevent the reestablishment of Western Germany and its rearmament. Even though the Soviet atomic bomb was developed while Stalin was alive, no one dared to raise the nuclear issue and its implications for warfare. Therefore only conventional conflicts could be envisaged, but Stalin was politically determined to avoid them. Only after Stalin's death, in March 1953, did Soviet generals begin in secret to talk about atomic bombs, while Prime Minister Georgy Malenkov announced to the world that the Soviets had tested a hydrogen bomb. In 1955, when the debate became public, Marshals Pavel Rotmistrov, Ivan Bagramyan and Sergei Biryuzov seemed to be more concerned with pre-emptive nuclear strikes than with the military, political and economic implications of nuclear warfare. In the development of a strategic doctrine the Soviets proceeded erratically, albeit it was obvious that a new era in warfare was ushered in. In the end Marshal Georgy Zhukov, then Minister of Defense, carried the day and forced his views even on the politicians; the Malenkov faction which opposed him was ousted and the Khrushchev faction, which favored him, gave him a free hand. The problem was no longer mutual deterrence or how to prevent a nuclear war, but how to wage one. Finally a completely new military doctrine was developed.

NATO map drawn in 1957 indicating Soviet centers of control and mining targets.

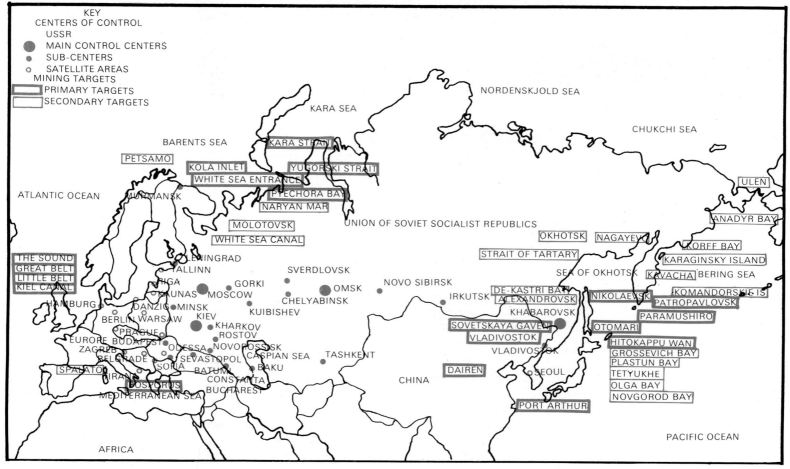

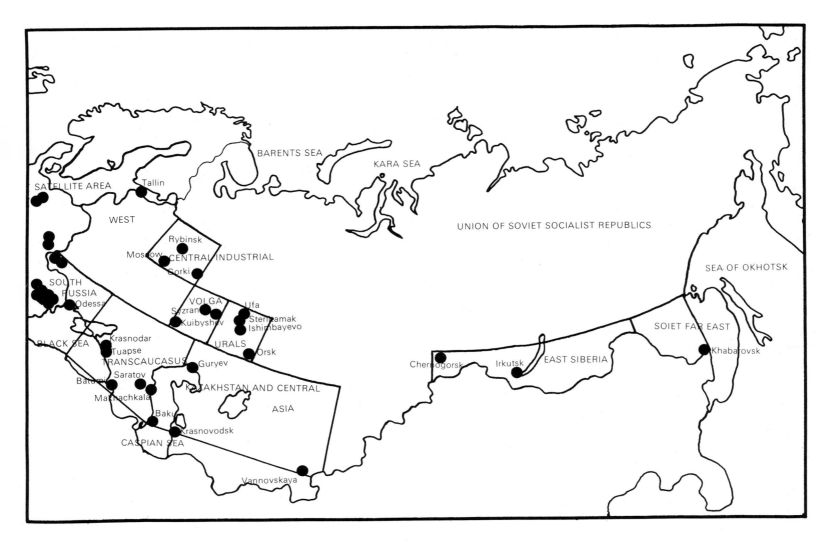

Map labels:
BARENTS SEA
KARA SEA
SATELLITE AREA   Tallin
WEST
Rybinsk
Moscow CENTRAL INDUSTRIAL
Gorki
SOUTH RUSSIA
Odessa
VOLGA   Ufa
Syzran   Sterlitamak
Kuibyshev   Ishimbayevo
Krasnodar
Tuapse   URALS   Orsk
TRANSCAUCASUS   Guryev
Saratov
Batumi   KAZAKHSTAN AND CENTRAL
BLACK SEA
Makhachkala   ASIA
Baku
Krasnovodsk
CASPIAN SEA
Vannovskaya
UNION OF SOVIET SOCIALIST REPUBLICS
SEA OF OKHOTSK
SOIET FAR EAST
Chernogorsk   Irkutsk   EAST SIBERIA   Khabarovsk

Soviet Petroleum targets in 1957.

Although as usual in the USSR the political leader Khrushchev was credited with the development of the strategic doctrine and formulation of policy, the real theorists were Marshals Vasily Sokolovsky and Rodion Malinovsky: the latter became Minister of Defense after Marshal Zhukov's dismissal in 1957. Colonel Oleg Penkovsky's "defection" gave the West a clear picture of Soviet military thinking as well as strategic capabilities under Prime Minister Khrushchev. Since 1953, with growing economic strains the Soviet emphasis on conventional forces was superseded by a nuclear posture, coupled with a belief in the "old" doctrine of mutual deterrence. Krushchev embraced this new policy with vigor, even verging on nuclear-mania, in the words of his future critics. Thus between 1957–64 Soviet conventional forces were reduced from 140 division to 75. However in order to avoid "irresponsible assumptions of risks" Khrushchev granted Soviet military leaders increases in general purpose forces and above all carried out a vigorous build-up in mixed offensive and defensive strategic systems. In turn military leaders convinced Soviet politicians of the concept of nuclear sufficiency, which made winning a nuclear conflict *possible*, and which meant that a large quantity of nuclear devices and delivery vehicles were made available to them.

It is clear that the new policy had several weaknesses. It was definitely a great advance on Stalin's strategic thinking, but the Soviet theory of short limited nuclear war gave Soviet leaders virtually no options: nonetheless the immediate results of this new policy were encouraging. The vigorous concentration on delivery vehicles, intermediate and intercontinental missiles, brought instant success: in 1957 the USSR launched its first earth satellite, Sputnik. A "missile gap" was perceived in the United States which now definitely diverted the Americans from conventional rearmament to strategic armament, including delivery vehicles. However, the Soviet Union instantly used the missiles politically and the phase of "missile diplomacy" was inaugurated by the impatient Khrushchev. The first manifestation came in the turbulent year of 1956, when the threat of missiles was used against France and Britain during the Suez operation. The Americans brushed it aside and only understood its real meaning in 1957, after the Soviet earth satellite had been launched. In the Far East the Soviets used their supposed missile superiority in the conflict over the offshore islands between the Chinese communists and nationalists. Rather incautiously Khrushchev also attempted to use his missile superiority in solving the "old" Berlin problem, but by then a new vigorous president, Kennedy, had been elected in the United States and he quickly put Soviet missile diplomacy to the test.

In the late 1950s Fidel Castro seized power in Cuba and eventually adopted communist policies and turned to the Soviet Union as an ally, for military as well as economic support. Then late in 1962, the American U-2 planes discovered in Cuba silos for firing Soviet IMBMs. The Soviet Union constantly claimed that Cuba was supplied with purely defensive weapons in order to protect itself against external invasions. But in 1962 the Americans suddenly discovered nine missile sites: six with four launchers, and three with four IRBMs, the range of which was 2,200 miles and which were clearly offensive as they could reach several American cities. The latter silos were still under construction, but the USSR had already based in Cuba some 42 IL-28 strategic medium bombers and 42 MRBMs with a range of some 1,000 miles. It is even now unclear why Khrushchev permitted this missile

build-up in Cuba, but in October 1962 the Americans were determined to test Soviet intentions. President Kennedy placed his 157 ICBMs on alert (it is estimated that the USSR had some 125 ICBMs at this stage); American B-47s and B-52s were dispersed and remained airborne throughout the crisis. The Americans also assembled conventional forces in their southern states in sufficient numbers, ready to invade Cuba if their demands for the dismantling of offensive weapons were not met. Premier Khrushchev's bluff had been called and "reprehensible capitulation" was forced on him, which 18 months later cost him his position as Soviet leader.

The shock of this first nuclear confrontation was felt world-wide, above all by the Super Powers. At first both reacted in a positive way: never again must a point of mutual extermination be reached. There followed talks on nuclear and conventional disarmament, or at least disarmament by stages during a process of reduced international tension and Super Power cooperation, called detente. However much was achieved politically after 1962, militarily the world remained unchanged: disarmament did not come about, instead, strategic inferiority was turned by the Soviets into strategic superiority, at least as far as ICBMs and megaton yields of warheads were concerned, and this gave them confidence to face even the possibility of a nuclear conflict.

	Soviet ICBMs	US ICBMs	Soviet SLBMs	US SLBMs
1959	some	none	none	none
1960	35	18	none	32
1961	50	63	some	56
1962	75	294	some	144
1963	100	424	100	244
1964	200	834	120	416
1965	270	854	120	496
1966	300	904	125	592
1967	460	1054	130	656
1968	800	1054	130	656
1969	1050–1350	1054	160–200	656
1970	1300–1440	1054	280–350	656
1971	up to 1500	1054	up to 400	656
1972	1550	1054	580	656
1972 SALT	1618	1054	650	656

Right:
Cuban missiles reach Mariel Port
prior to installation.

Below:
Cuban missile sites.

Far right:
An A-4 Skyhawk attack aircraft is
prepared for launching during the
Cuban crisis.

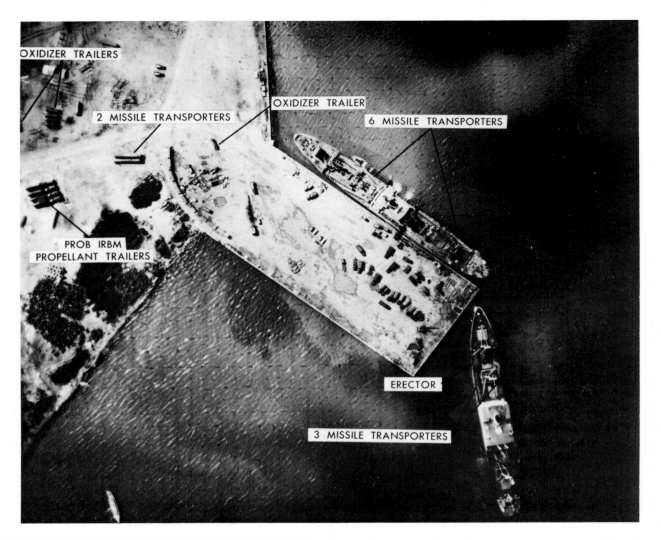

OXIDIZER TRAILERS

2 MISSILE TRANSPORTERS

OXIDIZER TRAILER

6 MISSILE TRANSPORTERS

PROB IRBM
PROPELLANT TRAILERS

ERECTOR

3 MISSILE TRANSPORTERS

MISSILE ERECTOR

THEODOLITE STATION

5 TRUCKS UNDER
CAMOUFLAGE NETTING

CABLE

5 TRUCKS UNDER
CAMOUFLAGE NETTING

MISSILE SHELTER TENTS

Right:
The SS-11 ICBM has a 500-kiloton yield.

Since 1965, when Secretary of Defense McNammara, imposed an unilateral nuclear restraint on the United States, the Soviet Union has made an immense strategic effort: between 1965 and 1970 the numbers of ICBMs jumped from 340 to over 1,200, among which were some 220 older missiles, but 270 of them were the super missiles SS-9 and 825 the latest SS-11 and SS-13. This was the result of a conscious policy of the post-Khrushchev leadership, whose other priorities (after the strategic one) included an increased airlift capacity (as demonstrated in 1967 in the Middle East, in 1968 in Czechoslovakia and in 1979 in Afghanistan); and an incredibly enlarged naval capacity making the Soviet Union a really global power with interests in East and West Africa, the Persian Gulf, the Middle East and the Indian Ocean, all served by this new Soviet Navy. In addition the Soviets have reestablished and slightly increased their ground forces in Eastern Europe and the Far East in response to internal hegemonial crises (Czechoslovakia 1968; China 1969; Poland 1980). Thus between 1967–77, Soviet increases in troops were 700,000 (300,000 for China), (140,000 — five divisions — in Czechoslovakia after 1968) and a 60 percent increase in aircraft intended mainly for the Far Eastern War theater. All these Soviet developments have seriously eroded the US strategic deterrent. The Soviets have also increased their civil defense (for example by dispersing industrial capacities); their super missiles made US ICBM sites vulnerable and their rigid commitment to first-strike capacity, made the USA nervous and war-jumpy. Thus in the most contemporary phase of world politics, in the 1980s, the Soviet military "threat" to the stability of world peace assumed new dimensions but continued to rest on the old Soviet commit-

The SS-9 Scarp ICBM with 20 megaton yield is part of the Soviet rocket armory developed in the late 1950s.

Inset:
APDS at a May Day parade.

Below:
The SCUD, battle-support weapon system, can carry a nuclear warhead and has a range of 280km (174 miles).

Soviet *Stenka* class torpedo boats in the Baltic.

ment to military power, their military doctrine, weapons and the deployment of military power, as under Stalin.

In 1980, according to the estimates of the US Joint Chiefs of Staff, the current Soviet military posture is alarming. In the absence of a SALT II, or a similar agreement, the United States has to respond to the anticipated military development with another arms race, comparable to the one preceding the Cuban missile crisis in 1962. What makes this Soviet challenge even more mystifying than the previous one is the Soviet refusal to permit the verification of strategic and conventional disarmament agreements negotiated with the USA or NATO.

Since the refusal to ratify the SALT II agreement by the USA, the Soviet Union has continued to deploy its latest ICBMs at an alarming pace: in 1980 it deployed 1,398 ICBMs (SS-13, SS-17, SS-18 and SS-19). It converted 300 outmoded SS-9s into SS-18s; 150 SS-11s were

likewise converted into SS-17s; all these systems were deployed in silos separate from those of the SS-19s, whose 360 silos have been specially strengthened. In 1980 the Soviet Union deployed some 950 SLBMs, mainly on Delta III class submarines which are equipped with SS-N-18 (the only MIRVed) missiles. What is even more alarming is the development of the Typhoon class submarine which would have 20 tubes to carry the SS-N-18s. It appears that in long-range aviation the USA is also lagging behind Soviet development: of the 800 LRA aircraft, 600 of them can carry ASMs, of these some 70 Backfires are the most dangerous, for they have the capacity to strike against the USA itself. Apart from 150 Bisons and Bears and 320 Badgers, the Soviets also deployed some 140 Blinders, similar to the American aircraft, B-1, which is still in the development stage. Some 10,000 SAMs and 2,600 interceptors were added to the Soviet strategic might; the

Above:
An SA-2 Guideline antiaircraft medium/high altitude missile.

Top:
TU-122 Backfire swing-wing supersonic aircraft has a combat radius of 3,570 miles at Mach 2 which brings it in range of America. It is used as a nuclear strategic bomber.

Left:
The modern Soviet Navy practicing anti-nuclear drill.

Right:
The TR can carry 16 troops and is seen here carrying the AT-3 Sagger and antitank missile.

Above:
BMP – armøred personnel carrier – carries six men. It is lightweight and easily transported by air giving the Soviets an edge in terms of mobility and speed.

Above:
SA-B Gechko amphibious antiaircraft weapon comparable to the
European Roland system. It has
two radar which allows two
missiles to be launched separately.

Left:
SA-2 Guideline antiaircraft missiles.

most sophisticated SAM is the SA-X-10 being currently deployed. This strategic posture is complemented by the ABM-1b system, the so-called Galoshe, whose protective complexes are deployed round Moscow; by Henhouse, the early warning radars; by Dog and Cat House, battle management radars and Try Add engagement radars.

The Soviets have always rejected the concept of the balance of terror, or as others have put it, the Mutually Assured Destruction (MAD) factor in case of a strategic conflict. They have always argued that: (1) strategic system superiority and (2) political system superiority would combine and bring them victory. Though voices were raised, even in the USSR, against these strategic concepts, the Russians have not modified them. Their strategic doctrine emphasizes surprise and preemption, but is made subordinate to political decisions and objectives; in other words the Communist Party and its leadership reserve to themselves final military options and therefore also the modifications of doctrine, if and when they become necessary. Because of this differing concept of deterrence, targetting dif-ferences arise between the Super Powers. Soviet priorities are as follows:

(1) Destruction of the means of nuclear attack by heavy and accurate ICBMs;
(2) Destruction of troop-basing systems by high-yield weapons;
(3) Destruction of war support industries by ICBMs and SLBMs;
(4) Destruction of the centers of administration by accurate high-yield weapons;
(5) Destruction of the rear and transport system by numerous warheads.

Moreover targetting differences automatically mean requirement differences which, coupled with doctrinal ones, make strategic disarmament practically impossible, and instead, increase mutual competitions and suspicions. Since 1972 when the SALT I agreement fixed the Soviet numbers of ICBMs at 1,618, the Soviets have developed four new ICBM systems, compared to the one new American system. In the USSR only 159 old SS-7 and SS-8 were left in service, while the heavy SS-9s have been reduced from 288 to 252. However, the latest SS-18 "super" missile was deployed in 1975, and it is ap-

MiG-19 all-weather fighters.

parently 16 to 40 times more powerful than the American equivalent, Minuteman III, (it also has between 8 to 10 MIRVs). The Russians have deployed 60 SS-13, 100 SS-19, and 900 of the light SS-11 with an unknown number of the mobile missiles SS-20. In addition there are two medium range systems deployed by the Russians: SS-14, mobile Scamp and SS-X-Z, mobile Scrooge. Because of the extreme Soviet secrecy and "aggressive" doctrine the Americans seem convinced that all this Soviet missile might has been created to destroy them in one preemptive attack: they argue that the Russians want to achieve a decisive superiority over them and then, politics permitting, they will strike them down. However, many non-American experts are less pessimistic and argue that Soviet strategic might is essentially defensive and that (according to Professor John Erickson), even the huge SS-9 missile was developed not as a first-strike capacity, but to counter the American defensive systems. So far strategic experiences from the past indicate that a strategic conflict between the Super Powers is unlikely, and whether the Soviets acknowledge it or not, in practice, the balance of terror, or mutual deterrence, is operative. Thus on the one hand the Soviets have begun the expensive process of hardening their missile sites; on the other hand, they have never put their strategic bombers on a general alert; only 11–15 percent of their nuclear submarines are at sea, while only 50

AMD amphibious personnel carrier.

percent of their ICBMs are fire-launch ready at any time, as compared to 98 percent of the US; their air defenses are always in a low state of readiness and even their mobile SS-20 missiles, their latest offensive development, are not really mobile, but are based in garrisons. Thus, while the danger of a bilateral strategic conflict is always there, it is more likely that if a nuclear conflict should break out it would not be as a result of a first-strike attack, but rather an escalation of a theater war conflict. Despite powerful arguments on both sides, it appears that, in the strategic domain, the Super Powers have reached a stalemate: consequently Soviet superiority in theater warfare is the more likely cause of war in the 1980s.

It has already been stated that after Premier Khrushchev's fall in 1964, the Soviet ground forces were "reestablished" both in Europe and the Far East, particularly against China; since 1968 doctrinal changes justified this military conventional build-up. Doctrinally then the Soviets seek "a margin of advantage" within the combined arms concept of the theater warfare. The doctrine presupposes dual, nuclear and non-nuclear, forces which do not represent "an escalation of the conflict" but are independent of each other. The Soviet forces involved in theater warfare are of four types: (1) Nuclear — disposing of FROG-7, SCUD Cruise and SS-12 missiles; (2) conventional, with tactics of assault and encirclement; (3) chemical troops equipped

with VX and GB nerve gas as well as mustard gas, and finally (4) irregular forces, the highly specialized *vysotniki* and *reidoniki* combined with five East German paratroop battalions and the 6th Polish Paratroop division.

The latest survey of Soviet theater forces sounds most impressive as well as alarming. In 1980, according to the US Joint Chiefs of Staff, Soviet theater nuclear forces deployed some 450 MRBMs (mainly SS-4 and SS-5), single MIRVed missiles, and 180 SS-20 (3 MIRVed) mobile missiles, which so alarmed the Western European allies in NATO. Altogether some 300 SS-20s are targetted on Western Europe, the Middle East, China and Japan. Tactical rockets, FROG-3s and 5s were being

replaced by FROG-7s and above all SS-21s. However, the latest SCUD A and B were considered as nuclear delivery vehicles equivalent to the SS-X-23 system. Beyond FROG and SCUD ranges the Soviets deployed the Scaleboard missiles, SS-12s. In tactical aviation the Fencer, Flogger and Fitter aircraft appear as formidable weapons, enhancing the capability of Soviet theater forces. As the main battle tank, the Soviet forces in Germany deploy the T-64s and the Western Military District, the pivot of Soviet defensive and offensive intentions *vis a vis* Western Europe, deployed the formidable T-72s; ground forces were equipped with self-propelled 122mm and 152mm guns, and with surface-to-surface missiles, SS-21s and SS-22s. Thus ground

Above:
An ASU-85 self-propelled gun.

Top:
The MiG-23 Flogger is a single-seat tactical attack and all-weather interceptor. It has an armament of a 23mm Gatling gun with five barrels and carries up to 4,000 lb of missiles or bombs. It has a maximum speed of Mach 2.3.

Left:
BTR on parade.

Far right:
A FROG missile tactical rocket has a range of 20km and is capable of carrying a nuclear warhead.

Below:
The T-72 is the most advanced Russian battle tank. It has 122mm cannon and is being put into service throughout Warsaw Pact armies.

Above:
A Mi-24 Hind D Helicopter
gunship. It is a ground support
helicopter capable of carrying
12/14 troops and has machine
gun and rock pod mountings on the
prominent stub-wings at the side.

Right:
A mobile patrol boat of the Soviet
Navy shows the modernization
which has taken place at a
remarkable pace.

Far right:
A Kynda Class cruiser which has
multiple rocket missile launchers
and is comparable in sophistication
to any Western ship of its kind.

forces deployment is seemingly offensive, with some 170 Soviet and 50 non-Soviet divisions, which are organized in 16 military districts, four groups of forces in Eastern Europe, the Army of Afghanistan and forces in Mongolia. The best forces (class 1 and 2) are deployed against NATO, while some 42 divisions are deployed against China. Most of the Soviet military districts contain strategic reserves, while the latest deployment of some 26 divisions is directed against Turkey and the Middle East. (Some 85,000 troops are deployed in Afghanistan). Some 4,800 fighter aircraft, (1,200 against China) are deployed in the four war theaters together with 5,200 helicopters (Hind D currently being replaced by Hind E). The Soviet worldwide military posture is emphasized by the deployment of 271 surface warships, 120 patrol boats, 285 submarines, and 86 amphibious crafts, all of which give the Soviet Union's posture historically quite unprecedented capacity.

From past experiences, such as, for example, the Dniepr maneuvers, it is clear that Soviet contingency planning concentrates on a conflict in Europe, the initial phase of which, at least, would be conventional in character. The Soviets envisage a short conflict in which the first echelon divisions (mainly Soviet) would suffer heavy losses from frontal attacks, which they would deliver on the enemy. Therefore Soviet ground forces amount to some 1,825,000 men, organized in 170 divisions, of which 105

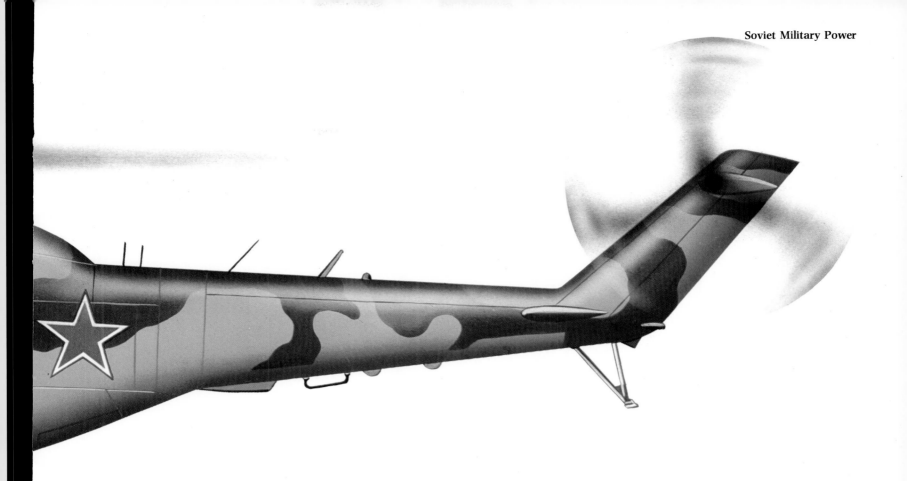

are first- or second-class ones. They are equipped with some 45,000 tanks, 55,000 armored personnel carriers; 19,000 pieces of artillery and with 720 multiple rocket launcher tubes per division; they are supported by 4,600 combat aircraft. Military consumables are prepositioned and the forward deployment of large equipment is widely practiced. Soviet élite troops are also prepositioned in East Germany: 20th Guard Army has its HQ at Eberswald; 3rd Shock Army is deployed in the Magdeburg-Stendal area and 8th Guard Army is stationed around Weimar. The 3rd Shock Army, for example, has 55,000 troops in its ranks with 1,200 tanks, 1,100 personnel carriers and 400 pieces of artillery. Thus a vigorous Soviet offensive in the Central

European area would only require "topping up" of the Soviet ground forces — mass mobilization would deprive the Soviets of the element of surprise. In 1979 the Druzhba maneuvers rehearsed all the aspects of theater warfare: they were preceded by thorough exercises in preparation of theater nuclear weapons; military division of labor was demonstrated: amphibious operations were carried out in the Baltic sea; winter warfare was practiced in the Carpathian mountains; and mobile operations enacted on the plains of Hungary. Territorially the USSR relies on its buffer zone in Eastern Europe: additional military power is derived from the Warsaw Pact which organizes the East European buffer to buttress the Soviet military power.

An SS-15 Scrooge ICBM.

Soviet Military Infrastructure

SS Praesidium L. I. Brezhnev	Council of Ministers N. A. Tikhonov	C.P. Politburo L. I. Brezhnev	Central Committee
Supreme Soviet	Ministry of Defense	Minister of Defense D. F. Ustinov	

Main Military Council

Warsaw Pact Marshal Kulikov	Chief of Staff Marshal Ogarkov	1st Vice-Minister Marshal Sokolov	GLAV PUR A General Yepishev
Strategic Rockets A General Tolubko	Ground Forces A General Petrov	P.V.O. Air Marshal Koldunov	Navy Admiral Gorshkov
Air Force Air Marshal Kutakhov	Airborne Forces A General Margelov	Inspectorate Marshal Moskalenko	Civil Defense A General Altunin
Construction C General Shestolapov	Rear Services A General Kurkotkin	Armament Production C General Shabanov	Transport, Supply & Medical Services

Soviet National Air Defense P.V.O. in 1982

joint

Warsaw Pact C in C Air Marshal Koldunov	National C in C Air Marshal Koldunov		
Chief of Staff General Sozinov	1st Deputy General Okunev		Political Administration General Khalipov
Deputy General Podgorny	Department of Armament General Grennikov	Deputy General Baydukov	Deputy General Votintsev
Dep Rear General Shevchuk	Dep Combat Tr General Ghishkov	Dep Fighter A General Borovykh	
Assistant C in C School General Bryukhanov	Dep Radio Technology General Beregovoy	Dep Zenith Rock General Gurinov	

The T-62 battle tank alongside an older T-55, which is still in service.

It was only in May 1955 that the countries of the Soviet hegemony signed a formal alliance treaty in Warsaw. Up till then the Soviet armed forces were exclusively responsible for the security of both the USSR and Eastern Europe. They had arrived in Central Europe and particularly in Germany in pursuance of war. After World War II Stalin decided to fill in the power vacuum in Eastern Europe left by the defeat of Germany, and as a consequence Eastern European states were subjugated to become part of the Soviet security zone. Stalin intended to neutralize Germany so that it would never again, either itself or in conjunction with the West, invade the USSR. However, by subjugating Eastern Europe and by satellising the area, Stalin aroused such fears in Western Europe and elsewhere as to force the Western Europeans and the USA into a defensive alliance, NATO. Stalin could not reply to this "aggressive" response in like manner: the Red Army's domination of the area was total, although Eastern Europe had only recently been "satellised." Thus Stalin could not trust individual countries, to ensure the security of his buffer to any extent.

Curiously for historical reasons, this military solution was preferred in Eastern Europe by Stalin and his successors. In the past invasions of Imperial Russia and the Soviet Union, came from the Poles, Swedes, French and Germans, and a defensive zone of buffer states seemed necessary for the security of the Soviet Union. However, after World War II, when this policy was put into practice, it was extended not only to Eastern Europe, but also to the Middle East (Iran, Turkey) and the Far East (Afghanistan, Sinkiang and Mongolia). The military occupation of the buffer zone was imposed on Stalin and his successors, paradoxically again, by history: because of the traditional hostility of the occupied nations toward Russia. However, this military solution suited Stalin politically very well: the military occupation of such an extensive area enabled Stalin to keep large armies in existence and therefore maintain the status of the Super Power for which the Russians and their Soviet successors had a peculiar craving. The military occupation enabled Stalin to maintain the *status quo* of his newly established hegemony and further "satellise" these once proudly independent nations so as to "convert" them into communist states friendly toward the communist motherland, the USSR. Thus from the beginning the buffer zone seemed essentially

ADPs at a May Day parade. As well as acting as a propaganda morale-boosting exercise, the May Day parades are a show piece for potential customers.

FROG missile at a May Day parade. Soviet missiles are sold to the Eastern European satellites and deployed in those countries as part of the Warsaw Pact posture.

ideological in purpose, enforcing communist parties' domination in the national states, but also defensive, providing the USSR with space in which to deploy its forces and maneuver them in the available space in case of an invasion. After "satellisation" the buffer zone assumed also political importance, for the satellised states, Poland, Hungary, Rumania, Czechoslovakia, Bulgaria and East Germany exhibited the same Soviet patterns of behavior and ways of administration. In the security field the Soviet KGB could freely operate throughout the buffer, while earlier, immediately after the war, there were also certain economic and technological advantages to be gained from the buffer by the USSR.

However, after Stalin's death in 1953 political and military conditions in the Soviet hegemony had changed: the presence of Soviet troops in Eastern Europe (except in Czechoslovakia where there were none) had to be justified internationally and a greater financial contribution toward the maintenance of security was also expected from the members of the hegemony. Moreover, in 1955 the Soviet occupation forces left Austria, after a peace treaty had been signed. Thus the legal basis for keeping Soviet troops stationed in Hungary vanished and it was felt something had to be done to replace this legal fiction by another. At the same time West

Germany had just become a member of NATO: nine days later it was announced that the Warsaw Pact had been signed by the USSR, Poland, East Germany, Czechoslovakia, Rumania, Hungary, Bulgaria, and Albania. (Subsequently Albania denounced the pact in 1961). Formally the new communist organization was the Eastern equivalent of NATO. But the chief difference between NATO and WPT (also termed Warsaw Treaty Organization and abbreviated WTO) was that the latter served to make the USSR even more predominant in military affairs: in fact the WPT perpetuated the Soviet military control of the hegemony.

As before, since its inception in 1955 the joint high command of the WPT was invariably in Soviet hands: Marshals Ivan Koniev, Andrey Grechko, Ivan Yakubovsky were followed by the present incumbent, Marshal Victor Kulikov. For some 15 years the Commander in Chief of the WPT, supported by the Joint Armed Forces Staff, all situated in Moscow, was paramount: but after the upheaval that followed the invasion of Czechoslovakia in 1968, the pact organization was improved and several more effective political and military bodies were added.

From 1955 onward the WPT had the Political Consultative Committee (PCC), whose secretary general has been Nikolai Firyubin, since 1966 (all along Deputy Minister of Foreign

Affairs) which met regularly twice a year, discussed foreign and military policies and made its recommendations to the C in C of the WPT. In practice the C in C took no notice of this committee, as in any case, it acted as a transmission belt of the Soviet State apparatus, and the C in C of the WPT received his policy directives directly from the Soviet politburo via the Ministry of Defense whose directorate it had been until the reorganization. In 1969 the PCC, senior

body of the WPT, was strengthened and among other things it became the chief organ for the formulation of policy initiatives between the two blocs, NATO-WPT. It should also be pointed out that despite its strengthening the PCC remains an artificial body cut off from the power base: it has never formulated any worthwhile policy leading to its declared aim, the dissolution of the blocs. And even if by some miracle this aim was achieved, the Soviet Union

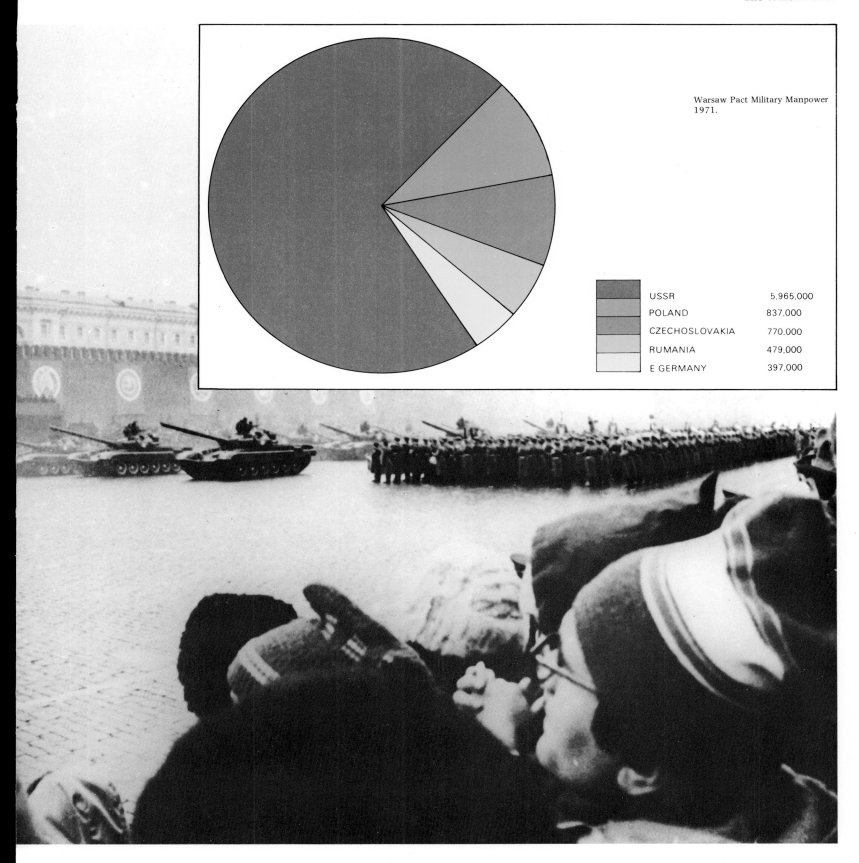

Warsaw Pact Military Manpower 1971.

USSR	5,965,000
POLAND	837,000
CZECHOSLOVAKIA	770,000
RUMANIA	479,000
E GERMANY	397,000

has enough bilateral arrangements within the WPT to preserve the *status quo* of the alliance. On the other hand the PCC has never succeeded in imposing on the country of the alliance any policy that was really against their national interests. Rumania is the most striking example of this weakness of the WPT: since the 1950s it has not pursued identical foreign policies with the other members of the pact. In addition it successfully opposed the stationing of the WPT troops on its territory and did not take part in various WPT exercises (and the occupation of Czechoslovakia in 1968) on other states' territories. In 1978 it went as far as to veto military budget increases which the other countries accepted without demur (Poland's budget was frozen, because of its desperate economic position).

Thus it is clear that the 1969 reforms failed to strengthen the WPT, since they did not succeed

Impressive display of Soviet military power for both NATO and Warsaw Pact allies to think about.

109

in bringing about smoother working together and increased participation of the minor allies; nonetheless much has been achieved. Although the WPT HQ is still in Moscow, it has ceased to be a directorate of the Soviet Ministry of Defense; instead it is a multinational staff attached to the Ministry. Marshal Kulikov, C in C of the Joint Forces, is now obliged to take note of the political initiatives of the strengthened PCC. In addition he has a committee of defense ministers to help him in formulating military policies of the pact. Another body politic was added to the WPT structures in 1969: it is the Military Council which emphasizes the communist parties' domination of the alliance. The Combined Staff was also transformed: Soviet Army General Gribkov is the Joint Chief of Staff; however, each member of the alliance is now represented by a deputy chief of staff. But the inspectorate of the Pact remains under overwhelming Soviet domination (General Pastushenko); so does the new Military Technical Committee of the Pact (General Fabrikov). As if to emphasize the

Russian troops, the human materiel of the Russian war machine.

military futility of the WPT the Joint HQ has no operational capacity in peacetime: it has no logistics capacity, no transport system and no supply services at its disposal. In addition, the air defense responsibilities for the WPT area belong to the Soviet Homeland Command (ADC). Consequently it seems that the WPT's role is purely ideological-political, that it serves as a watchdog and controller of the more or less unwilling allies. Recent estimates indicate that at least three allies (Poland, Hungary, and Rumania) exhibit more than questionable loyalty to the alliance; on the other hand Czechoslovakia, Bulgaria, and the German Democratic Republic show much greater loyalty; though in case of a conflict this professed loyalty would certainly be put to a terrible test. In any case all the NSWPT allies want more political independence from the Soviet Union and in this pursuit they are likely to cause the WPT more problems than benefits.

Since the Russians use the WPT chiefly to control their allies, the usefulness of the pact appears militarily questionable. Despite this three additional points demonstrate the utility of the WPT to the USSR: (1) the WPT has always fitted extremely tidily into the overall strategy of the USSR; (2) from the political point of view the pact has also offered certain advantages to the USSR; and (3) in the military-industrial effort (this point is the most neglected by Western analysts), the Pact is the most useful. While the USSR has been trying, in both the strategic and conventional fields, to preserve and increase the margin of advantage over the West, which it had achieved after an enormous effort in the 1970s, the WPT has greatly aided the USSR in this effort. Even if the Soviet aim remains strategic defense, the USSR nevertheless plans a further expansion of power projections means (air and naval resources) as well as battle techniques and general purposes forces. The WPT is not only a useful testing ground, but also an industrial producer of the new weapon systems.

Since 1955 the Soviet contribution to the Pact's military posture was 25–26 divisions, which after 1968 rose to 31–32 divisions. The Pact's armies are formed into four groups: (1) East Germany (5 Army HQs – 19 Soviet divisions supported by 6 German divisions under the overall command of Army General M. M. Zaitsev). (2) Northern Group in Poland (with 2 or 3 Soviet divisions – some 30,000 troops and 2 air divisions supported by 15 Polish divisions with 3,800 tanks and 750 combat aircraft – under the command of Lieutenant General Y. F. Zarudin.) (3) Central Group in Czechoslovakia

(5 or 6 Soviet divisions, some 60–70,000 troops and 2 air divisions supported by 5 Czechoslovak divisions with 5,000 combat aircraft under the command of Colonel General M. G. Grigorev) and (4) Southern Group in Hungary (4 divisions and 1 or 2 air divisions commanded by Colonel General F. F. Krivda). Thus the nominal order of battle of the WPT is impressive: 31 Soviet and 54 (or 56–58) non-Soviet divisions representing some 935,000 troops with 16,000 tanks, 3,680 combat aircraft and 3,500 tactical nuclear weapons. All this military might represents in fact the Soviet forward deployment in Europe and additional forces can be drawn from the total of 5.2 million Soviet troops (including internal security troops) organized in 16 military districts backed by four fleets based in the Baltic, Black Sea and Northern and Pacific Oceans. By any criterion this is the greatest military force ever gathered in peacetime in Europe.

The WPT's declared objective is collective security to discourage aggression: member states are obligated to render each other military assistance, but the alliance also legitimizes interventions on allied territory. The WPT's military strength is obvious; but its fatal weakness lies in its last objective: if any of the allied countries, for whatever reason, decided to leave the alliance, the Pact can reverse this decision. Thus in 1953 the Soviet armed forces put an end to the East German revolt: in 1956 they intervened in Poland and then with real force in Hungary: always either because of internal breakdown or because of the threat of leaving the alliance. As late as 1968 Soviet armies marched into Czechoslovakia to restore "hegemonial security." The strategic objectives of the USSR and WPT appear incompatible: to ensure the USSR's and the WPT's security can be contradictory. This contradiction unresolved, the WPT remains a political threat to the USSR, and has to be kept in check with the naked exhibition of military power.

In the 1980s the Soviet domination of the WPT, both in theory and practice, appears unabated: the USSR spends between five to 10 times more on weapons than the non-Soviet members of the pact and Soviet forces constitute four-fifths of the pact forces. Because of economic difficulties among the non-Soviet pact members, Soviet military expenditure is likely to increase still further, all this extra effort going into the maintenance and increase of the margin of advantage over NATO. Though this may sound defensive in doctrine, an aggressive development is clearly discernible. For the 1980s Soviet military specialists devised a new concept of combined arms which means that the Soviet Army will develop the capability to wage theater wars at all levels: nuclear, conventional, as well as chemical. Since the defection of China from the communist bloc, the Soviet military specialists have also developed the concept of independent theater option, a two-front war configuration, applicable to both the European and Far Eastern war theaters. The build-up in chemical warfare will undoubtedly provoke an American reaction, and all these weapons and armament increases are bound to make a Soviet-American arms race most likely.

T-34s in East Germany at the end of World War II. In 1953 Russian T-34 tanks were used to put down a revolt in East Germany.

111

Far right:
The T-62 battle tank.

Below:
T-55s are still in service.

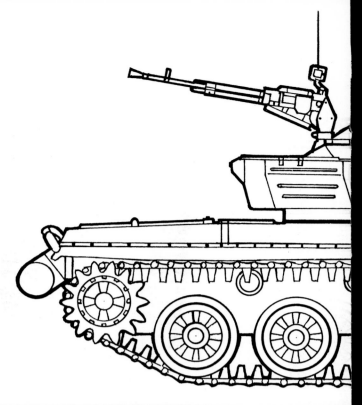

However, it must be pointed out that often Soviet military initiatives stem from their reactions to American developments and improvements. In the 1980s the Soviet armed forces will introduce and deploy tactical (field) ABMs as a response to American and NATO improvements of theater nuclear forces, in particular the production of the neutron bombs. In response to the envisaged deployment of NATO'S Pershing 2 and Cruise missiles, the Soviet PVO (Strategic Air Defense) will be equipped with vastly improved surface to air missiles. During the current decade the Soviet armed forces will produce great improvements in their C3 system (command, control, communication), in which they have lagged far behind the United States. Likewise, in reaction to

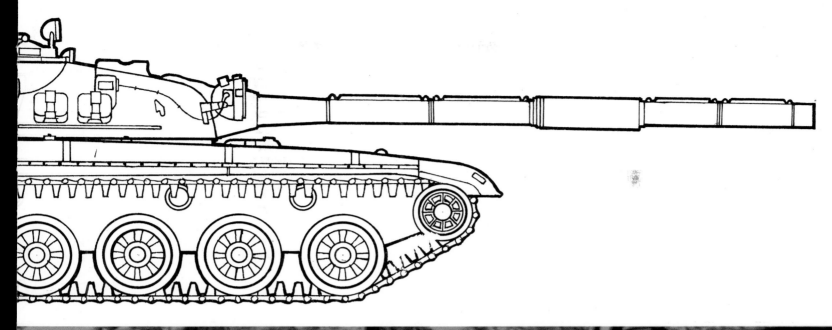

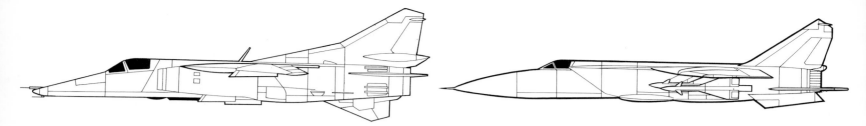

American advances, Soviet electronic warfare capacity will be greatly improved. However, many other improvements are not in response to anything in the West and must be interpreted as aggressive moves, straight and simple: tremendous efforts are put into improvements of munitions, combat engineering support and above all MBT T-80 which is being currently tested.

If the modernization of Soviet armed forces within the WPT and the doctrine on which the deployment is based give these forces an aggressive character, the nominal order of battle of Marshal Kulikov's SWPT 32 divisions strengthens this view still further: although these divisions are class 1 or 2, Kulikov apparently commands only elements of these divisions, and in case of a conflict would be unlikely to field them in such strength. In all events the deployment of Soviet forces in Germany is most impressive for both NATO and the WPT countries: five Army HQs (2nd Guard Tank Army, 20th Guards Army, 8th Guards Army, 1st Guards Tank Army, 3rd Shock Army) altogether 19 divisions, one artillery division, the 16th Air Army (with 848 aircraft — its wartime strength is 1,700 aircraft) with the bulk of Soviet tanks stationed there (T-64/T-72, some 4,020 — only the GSFG deploys the T-64 as MBT, T-62s some 2,030 and T-54/T-55 2,040). This show of overwhelming strength makes the East German Volksarmee pale into insignificance: its 3rd and 5th Army HQ consist of two tank and four motor rifle divisions with 340 aircraft (including MiG-23), some 50 T-72s; 2,500 T-54/T55s and 330 guns.

In the Northern Group Soviet deployment is less impressive, though capable of checking any restlessness of the Polish Army: with Army HQ at Legnica there are the 20th Tank and 38th Tank divisions stationed there (these divisions could be augmented to 3–4 divisions at short notice). The Polish National Army makes up the strength of the NGSF; organized in three Army HQs (Warsaw, Pomorze, and Silesia), it contains 5 tank and 8 motor-rifle divisions. With the 6th Airborne and 1st Sea-landing Divisions, stiffened by 675 aircraft, some 50 T-72s and 3,430 T-54/T-55s as well as 1,250 guns (including the 122mm SP guns) the Polish army is a formidable force, and would indeed take some checking.

Since 1968 a new group of forces was added to the WPT deployment: some 6 divisions (10th, 13th, and 51st tank and 16th, 55th and 66th Motor-Rifle divisions) with 100–150 air-

craft and an unknown number of T-72s, 1,150 T-62s, and 180 T-54/T-55s. Again the Czechoslovak People's Army supplements this Soviet force to make it impressive: organized in two Army HQs (Western-Prague and Eastern-Trenčín) it consists of 5 tanks and 5 motor-rifle divisions with the 7th and 10th Air Army (some 460 aircraft including MiG-23) over 100 T-72s and 3,600 T-54/T-55s and 950 guns (including 122mm SP guns).

Compared to the northern tier, the Southern group appears ramshackle. The Soviets deploy some 4 to 5 divisions with 275 aircraft and the bulk of T-62s (1,140) with only some T-72 deployed. Soviet forces are stationed in Hungary but there are no Soviet forces in Bulgaria or Rumania. The Hungarian People's Army is the smallest in size (1 tank and 5 motor-rifle divisions with 150 aircraft) and the Rumanian Army, while more impressive in numbers (2 tank and 8 motor-rifle divisions with 300 aircraft) is badly equipped and trained. In the southern tier it seems that the Soviets rely on the Bulgarian Army organized in three Army HQs (Sofia, Plovdiv and Plevna) and containing 2 tank and 8 motor-rifle divisions with 165 aircraft; over 100 T-62s, 200 T-54s and 700 guns supplement this pivotal force of the WPT's southern tier.

Given the doubtful reliability of the non-Soviet WPT forces, the aggressiveness of the WPT deployment is therefore somewhat blunted. It would nevertheless enable the Soviet forces to launch a powerful ground thrust coupled with preemptive air strikes. The aggressive design of the WPT forces is further blunted (as has been pointed out) by their lack of mobilization mechanism, logistic support, PVO anti-air defense. However, this overwhelming dependence of the WPT on the Soviet defense system gives the impression that the Soviets, unable to trust their allies, rely largely on their military machinery. This impression is further confirmed by the fact that Soviet forces most recently appear to be organized in three TVD (teatr voyyennykh deystvyi-theater war groups) which include Soviet military districts facing NATO, hence the direction from which historically the invasions of the Russian territory came from. The Northern TVD, which consists of the Leningrad MD and elements of the Baltic MD has as its operational commander General Postnikov. The Western TVD is centered on the SGFG, includes the Volksarmee and its operational commander is General Zaitsev. The 3rd TVD is centered on the Kiev MD with elements from Odessa MD,

Carpathian MD, and Central GSF. General Gerasimov, C in C of the Kiev MD, is the operational commander. This alternative organization therefore appears as the real military set up of the Soviet Union; it is equipped with all the service branches necessary to conduct an aggressive or defensive war. The WPT military organization thus presents the world and NATO with a dilemma: with non-operational strength, Soviet defensive arrangements have the appearance of a defensive set up; with the doctrine which stresses "in-place, unreinforced Soviet offensive, requiring the topping up of select attack formations with specialists and tank crews in prepositioned places" it certainly appears to be an aggressive set up. The real explanation of the utility of the WPT organization is probably non-military, political. It is a historical fact that

the Russians have been able to maintain their hegemony in Eastern Europe by military force only: with so many puzzling aspects, the WPT seems to point to this historical explanation. After all the WPT has also a political objective, namely to keep Western Europe in political check; its secondary purpose is undoubtedly to keep the Communist hegemony intact. And this objective seems to be the WPT's most serious weakness: it is possible to "keep the margin of advantage" over NATO almost *ad infinitum* considering the slow progress of the MBRF talks; however, after 1980 and the events in Poland, it is practically impossible to imagine that Soviet military forces could keep the Soviet hegemony intact. This fact then represents the gravest danger to world peace in the 1980s.

Warsaw Pact Organization in 1982

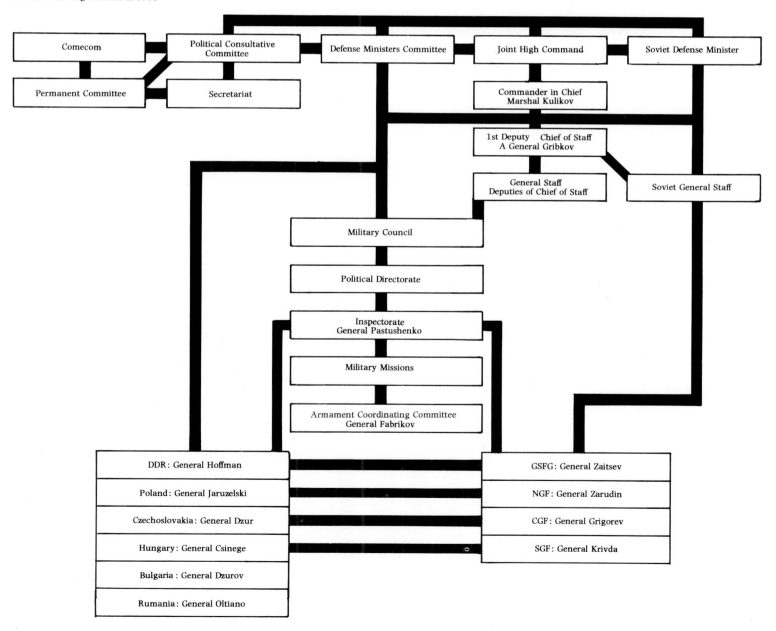

The Multiple Rocket Launcher is the most advanced piece of rocket technology in the US armory. It can fire all 12 missiles in less than one minute and automatically reaims the remaining rockets between individual launches.

CHAPTER FIVE

AMERICAN MILITARY POWER

U S ARMY

After World War II the Americans hoped to demobilize and send home their armies within two years of the cessation of hostilities. That is what President Roosevelt told Premier Stalin would happen at Yalta in February 1945, though he omitted to mention it to the other ally, the British Prime Minister. However Roosevelt died two months later and it seemed with him his promise to return to relative isolationism. Immediately after World War II the United States began to demobilize its armed forces then amounting to some 11,000,000 men. This demobilization was accelerated after the unconditional surrender of Japan in August 1945. The United States rightly considered itself quite secure in a world which had so recently witnessed a demonstration of their atomic power. In addition the instrument for the maintenance of international peace, the United Nations, created by the victors at Yalta, had begun to function, however gropingly. After the last war leaders' summit conference in Germany at Potsdam it was widely believed that all the problems of peace would be solved by means of international conferences.

However, while the American Secretaries of State, James Byrnes and George Marshall, grappled with the problems of drawing up peace treaties which would formalize the new international balance of power, American power was diminishing all the time: while in 1945 the Americans had 11,600,000 men and women under arms the numbers had fallen to 2,500,000 in August 1946. Furthermore the President was forced by inflationary pressures to cut $1,650,000,000,000 from the defense budget, which meant that US armed forces fell below the 2,000,000 mark. Nonetheless the United States still felt confident of its power because of its monopoly of atomic weapons and a GNP of $300 billion which in the devastated world of 1945 made them the only Super Power all round. It was only after the political setbacks in 1947 that the United States realized the correlation between political power and military and economic power. By 1947 when Poland, Rumania, Hungary, and Bulgaria had finally gone communist, with Greece and Turkey under threat of a communist takeover from the inside and under Soviet external pressure, President Truman, after consultations with Congress, announced on March 12, 1947 his doctrine: the United States must support all free nations against being subverted by internal minorities or external pressures. To avoid such a fate the president asked the Congress to permit him to send to threatened countries American civilian and military advisers and grant them aid to the

tune of $400 millions.

Two months earlier, on January 6, 1947, this same Republican-dominated Congress, had trimmed both foreign aid and defense budgets. Already Truman had had to reduce military spending by $1.65 billion, so that in 1947 his military expenditure totaled $3.4 billion, which was lower than in 1946. US demobilization continued at an accelerated rate and it was widely thought that American troops would pull out of Europe altogether in 1947, as President Roosevelt had pledged to Prime Minister Stalin. It was therefore a great surprise for the world at large, when American Congress not only granted Greece and Turkey $400 million in aid, but also agreed to a $100 million loan. It seems clear that the difficulties the Americans were experiencing with the USSR on the terms of the peace settlement, had finally made an impact on the US politicians if not on the general public; in 1946 according to a poll only 23 percent of Americans considered foreign affairs important. On March 15, 1947 the Prime Ministers of Turkey and Greece welcomed this generous American offer; three days later US warships paid a formal visit to Pireus and Istanbul and the Truman doctrine became a reality.

Although all the Soviet and many of the American analysts claimed that this American action launched the Cold War, the claim is contradicted by facts. In 1947 the Joint Chiefs of Staff failed to perceive any military threat from the USSR and continued to run down their forces until in 1948 they were left with some 10 divisions and 1.4 million troops in all services. It was clear that the frictions in international politics were the result of political decisions and that as long as the USSR avoided threatening the US militarily, American demobilization and reduced spending on defense would continue.

The show of strength over Greece and Turkey was backed by the Marshall Aid program which the United States launched in the summer of 1947. Observing that the weakness of the Greek and Turkish governments was partly caused by their weak economies, the Secretary of State, General Marshall, lent his name to an international reconstruction project, with the USSR and those Eastern European states dominated by the communists, invited to participate. On the face of it this American economic aid program appeared to be one of the most generous offers made and Western Europe availed itself of it with enthusiasm. Premier Stalin, however, reacted quite unpredictably: he ordered his foreign minister, Molotov, to reject the offer of aid and walk out of the Paris preparatory talks. Furthermore Stalin ordered his "allies,"

Josef Stalin was able to manipulate international relations in a masterly way at the end of World War II. Pro-Soviet governments were installed in Eastern Europe without any US or Western European response.

Poland and Czechoslovakia, who had already accepted the American invitation, to turn it down and promised them Soviet economic aid. Stalin reasoned that the Marshall Plan was a political maneuver by which American "imperialism" intended to enslave Western and Eastern European nations, the USSR included. Stalin was probably wrong in his political analysis. His rejection of aid brought relief all round in the USA. However it clearly indicated that the former allies were no longer on speaking terms and would soon become adversaries, if they had not reached that stage already. Stalin's reaction was to reestablish the communist international movement, which he called Cominform. East and West European communist parties sent delegates to Eastern Poland, where the foundation meeting took place in September 1947. The Soviet delegates, Georgy Malenkov and Andrey Zhdanov, reiterated the Soviet analysis of international affairs, namely that the world was divided into two camps, an imperialist and a democratic camp (the latter apparently being the Soviet) and that hostility was inevitable: the Cold War was launched.

Not even after this double rebuff did the Americans move against the Soviets, either in Europe or elsewhere. They permitted Korea to be divided into the Northern Communist-dominated and the Southern part. The *coup d'état* in Czechoslovakia ran its course without even a token gesture by the USA, while Finland saved its independence despite the USA. However, the situation in Germany and particularly in Berlin, was becoming critical, especially when in December 1947, Molotov insisted that the other allies accept his solution of the German problem: a unified Germany which would pay heavy reparations to the USSR. The Council of Foreign Ministers adjourned *sine die* and the Western Allies prepared for unilateral measures in Germany. Since the European economies could not be reconstructed without Germany, it was decided to send Marshall aid to Western Germany and the first step was a currency reform both in the Western zones and Berlin. The Soviets could

The Yalta Conference took place in February 1945 at the end of World War II. Roosevelt and Stalin came to a gentlemen's agreement over world domination. Roosevelt's death two months later put an end to this agreement.

119

Allied planes break the blockade of Berlin in July 1948.

do nothing about the Western zones of Germany without a war, but they could cause plenty of trouble for the Western Allies in Berlin, which was isolated within the Soviet zone of occupation.

On March 5, 1948 US General Clay cabled Washington from Berlin that he had a feeling that a sudden war was possible in the city. He could not back this feeling with Soviet military moves, but the atmosphere in Europe and particularly in Berlin was heavy with expectation. Whether they wanted it or not the Super Powers had finally drawn the dividing line in Europe and the divided capital of the Third Reich remained the last issue. Two weeks after General Clay's alarm American military planners reviewed contingency war plans, while President Truman began to exploit the crisis in Europe politically. He finally got through Congress the Marshall Aid Plan, but failed to get universal military training enacted. Congress only agreed to a restoration of selective military service. By April 1948 the Four-Power Control Council fell apart over the currency reform and the four victorious powers began to abuse one another publicly. On June 18, 1948 after the currency reform had been enforced in the Western zones the Soviets announced that they included the whole of Berlin in their zone. When the US introduced the new German Marks in Western Berlin the Soviet armies sealed the capital off from the West.

The blockade of Berlin began on June 24, 1948. Surprisingly it was not a land challenge to the West as General Clay had anticipated. The Soviets chose to challenge Western power in the air. The 2,000,000 Germans living in the western parts of the old capital had enough food for 36 days and coal for 45. To break the Soviet blockade the Americans had three choices: (1) either start a general war, or (2) break the blockade in a land armed thrust, or (3) break it in the air.

Not surprisingly war alarm spread all over the world. The British government issued its instructions to diplomatic representatives in case of war. The US military leaders reviewed their options. They rejected the first because the Soviets were known to have heavy superiority in armed forces while the 12 American nuclear devices, which were available at this time, were not thought capable of redressing this conventional imbalance. The second option was equally inoperable; Soviet amor and troops were again superior to anything that the US and the West could muster in Europe. Thus the Americans were left with the third option and took it up with typical enthusiasm and thoroughness. On July 22, 1948 the first aircraft involved in the Berlin airlift took off from bases in West Germany.

Although the airlift beat the Soviet blockade the consequences of the Berlin crisis were manifold. Firstly, it forced the US Air Force to expand its air frame production colossally: by 1949 the production was increased threefold. Next, the USA formed its first advanced forces base in Britain by establishing there the 1st Strategic Air Command on July 15, 1948. Thirdly, the Americans were finally able to establish intelligence networks *vis a vis* the Soviet hegemony, and finally, it forced the Soviets to resolve the Berlin crisis by negotiation. In May 1949 Stalin agreed to lift the blockade, but by then President Truman and the American public were convinced that there existed a Russian threat to world peace, that it had to be faced and logical conclusions had to be drawn: the military budget could no longer be kept down; research work had to start on a new, Hydrogen super bomb, and on new strategic delivery vehicles. However, the most important political consequence of the blockade was that Germany was finally divided; so was Europe.

In the United States selective military service was resumed and the military asked for $3,000,000,000,000 supplemental appropriation. The 70-Group Air Force was established and defense appropriations for FY1950 jumped to $12,000,000,000,000 (the JCS asked for $14,400,000,000,000), though in 1949 the US defense spending totaled $13,500,000,000,000, because of European emergencies. In addition because of NATO the USA launched the rearmament of its allies in the military assistance program which amounted to $4,800,000,000,000 by 1949. Thus in 1949 the United States spent $18,700,000,000,000 on defense, raised the manpower of its armed forces to 2,000,000 men and formed a defense alliance, NATO, the first such alliance in peacetime to which the USA belonged.

Albeit NATO was the result of a European initiative, the US would not have joined it but for the Soviet military threat, particularly in Berlin. The first step had been taken by Britain in 1947, when it had become clear that the war-time alliance would not reestablish a lasting peace. As a safeguard against a future Germany, France and Britain signed the treaty of Dunkirk, which was a purely political alliance to re-assure Western Europe psychologically; the Benelux countries would join it for the same reason. On March 17, 1948 the enlarged treaty was signed in Brussels with the enemy unnamed, designated simply as "all and any aggressor." In response to the Berlin crisis the Americans initiated Western European defense talks, which would bring about American association in the defense of Europe before "the actual outbreak of war." The aim of this eventual alliance was to give the West Europeans the political and psychological reassurance, they so badly needed.

To the Americans the future alliance had an even greater significance than to the Europeans: they thought that once the European powers had recovered their economic and military strength they could contain the Soviet "threat" on their own. However, this American aim was then and has remained wishful thinking, for although the Europeans in time recovered both military and economic strength they never regained political will.

Only during the crisis year of 1948 was there a political will to conclude a defensive alliance between the Western powers. Britain was reluctantly willing to join the United States in reestablishing the balance of power in Europe: this was the British concept of protection against the Soviet "threat." The French changed their minds after the communist *coup d'état* in Czechoslovakia: Foreign Minister Bidault informed US Secretary of State that "France was ready for political and military cooperation with

The life-line to Berlin. Allied aircraft bring vital food supplies to Berlin. Here American personnel unload from a USAF Dakota.

Above:
The North Atlantic Treaty
Organization meet for the first time.

Far right:
French military pride suffered a
severe blow at Dien Bien Phu.

Below:
A column of Vietminh infantry
marching out of Dien Bien Phu
after the battle in which French
troops suffered a crippling defeat.

the USA." The minor West Europeans allies, Belgium, Holland, and Luxemburg, were willing to follow the two Great Powers. Washington talks started on July 6, 1948 and within two months they proved a diplomatic success. By September 1948 the proposed alliance represented a collective response of the Brussels Treaty countries, joined by the United States and Canada, to an armed threat coming from the Soviet bloc. All the other European countries outside Soviet hegemony were invited to join the proposed alliance. Denmark, Iceland, Italy, Norway, and Portugal immediately availed themselves of this invitation, while Ireland and Sweden declined it. The latter promised to reconsider the refusal to join, in case the Soviets renewed their "threat" to Finland, either by an internal takeover or occupation. The treaty, setting up the alliance, was formally signed on April 4, 1949. Soviet Foreign Minister Molotov

described it as an aggressive alliance violating the Potsdam agreement and Franco-Soviet and Anglo-Soviet friendship treaties.

After signing the North Atlantic Treaty Western Europeans began to feel politically more secure and as is usual with sovereign allies immediately disputes broke out within the alliance. On September 22, 1949 Truman asked Congress for $13,000,000,000,000 to put military teeth into the political alliance, called the North Atlantic Treaty Organization, and immediately abbreviated as NATO. In Dean Acheson's words (he became the new Secretary of State) "NATO required sufficient strength to make it impossible for an aggressor to achieve a quick and easy victory." However, as soon as the funds for rearmament were allocated (Europe received $4,800,000,000,000) disputes broke out again about the allocation, the American Joint Chiefs of Staff wanting more for themselves. On September 17, 1949 the NATO council met for the first time to resolve financial disputes and immediately ran into political difficulties. Although the European allies agreed to the American demand to set up the German Federal Republic, France consistently opposed its rearmament, and above all the creation of a new German army. Neither were the NATO allies keen to set up the military organization. It took two years before General Eisenhower, appointed the Supreme Allied Commander of the new organization, could establish his HQ outside Paris. It would have taken even longer had the Korean war not broken out in June 1950.

Until the outbreak of the Korean war the military aspects of the NATO alliance were almost exclusively an American problem. On the

whole the Europeans, up to 1950, considered German rearmament more of a threat to world peace than Soviet expansion. They were confirmed in their analysis of international politics in May 1949, when the Berlin blockade was resolved peacefully. After the war scares in 1948 the international balance of power seemed to have been stabilized and Soviet responses were political rather than military. When the West established West Germany the Soviets set up East Germany. The Soviets answered NATO's financial allocations and Western rearmament by launching rather bizarre peace movements and world peace congresses. Until the Korean war the USSR felt militarily secure and did not respond with rearmament, particularly after it had succeeded in testing its own atomic device in September 1949. Thus paradoxically, at this point in 1949, when an absolute balance of power had been established in the world, the two Super Powers refused to acknowledge it and instead searched worldwide to destabilize it.

The causes of destabilization were manifold. With a sudden shock the Americans realized that the Cold War was not just a European confrontation: Britain was coping with a communist insurrection in Malaya and France in Indochina. After the collapse of nationalist China and communist seizure of power in that country the Americans suddenly realized (probably quite mistakenly) that the Soviet-communist challenge was worldwide and they would have to face it on this basis. Internally the United States was seized by political hysteria, MacCarthyism, which ascribed all internal and external troubles to a world-wide communist conspiracy. Senator Joseph MacCarthy con-

Above:
US troops fighting in Korea under the auspices of the UN.

ing. The other thesis, namely that the conflict in Korea was part of General Douglas MacArthur's crusade to roll back communism, also lacks conviction. It now appears that the Korean conflict was one of those chance clashes of the Super Powers in the explosive climate of the Cold War. In itself it was less important than its consequences. The Americans finally realized that they were the only Western power with world-wide interests and capabilities. The world was at last divided between the Super Powers, and the Third World would appear later.

After the defeat of Japan in August 1945 Korea had been occupied by the Soviet and US armies, who after establishing two different systems of government both left. In March 1949 Russia concluded an economic agreement with North Korea which enabled the North to maintain a 100,000-strong army. In the South the Americans were so concerned with establishing a democratic political system that they neglected the Korean economy and security. No standing army was raised or trained, and only a small gendarmerie force was left behind. Also in 1949, the United States concluded an agreement with Dr. Syngman Rhee, the South Korean President, but US economic and military aid only began to arrive slowly. Dr. Rhee was not popular in the United States because of his record on human rights. To make him more acceptable the Americans forced Dr. Rhee to hold another election on May 30, 1950 and his opponents won handsomely by getting 120 seats in the 210-seat legislative assembly. Before political consequences could be drawn from the electoral defeat of Rhee, the South was invaded. This gave rise to the legend that Dr. Rhee provoked the invasion from the North in order to remain in power.

On June 25, 1950 four North Korean divisions supported by 70 Russian-built tanks launched the invasion of the South from four different points. The Americans were utterly bewildered and had no forces to spare to help the South Koreans. On the one hand General MacArthur forced Washington to order the 7th Fleet in the Pacific to sail into the straits of Formosa to protect General Chiang Kai-shek from Chinese communist invasion. On the other hand the general ordered the US Air Force to attack North Korean targets in the South, as the Southern forces had been routed and soon controlled only the southern-most tip of the Korean peninsula, the Pusan perimeter.

Politically the Americans reacted much more effectively. The Soviet Union was boycotting the United Nations so President Truman appealed

ducted public witch hunts to "root out communism in the United States." All these factors served to divert American attention from Europe, and in 1950 particularly, to Asia.

It would be an oversimplification to state that once the USSR had been contained in Europe, it turned to Asia. The origin of the Korean conflict is even nowadays shrouded in mystery. All that is known is the fact that Stalin gave permission to Kim Il Sun, the North Korean communist leader, to invade the South without consulting his Chinese communist allies. The Soviet explanation that the North Koreans were lured into war by the United States and the South Korean leader, Syngman Rhee, so that President Truman could get through Congress his rearmament program, sounds unconvinc-

to the Security Council to stop the North Korean invasion. On June 27, 1950 the Security Council, in the absence of a Soviet veto, condemned North Korea as an aggressor and asked member states to aid the South. On June 30, 1950 President Truman responded to the Security Council resolution by committing American ground and air forces "to restore South Korean borders." General MacArthur was then appointed the United Nations Commander in Chief and his (future) forces were given the task to "repel armed attack and restore international peace." But MacArthur had very few troops to counter the North Koreans and for a time limited himself to aerial bombing of targets both in the South and North. Throughout August 1950 the American Air Force hammered the North disrupting supply lines and harassing Northern troops in positions round Pusan. Finally after the arrival of reinforcements, MacArthur ordered an outflanking operation on

the river Inchon, some 25 miles from Seoul, the South Korean capital. Two US divisions, after a shaky start, cut the North Korean forces to ribbons; they had to retreat from Pusan not to be cut off. On September 27, 1950 MacArthur ordered the invasion of North Korea.

The United Nations approved the invasion on the grounds that the two Koreas would be reunited, which was the original North Korean aim. At the same time MacArthur was bent on "punishing the invader" and took the conflict highly personally: he was fighting the North and the North should surrender to him personally. When in October 1950 MacArthur had under his command a formidable United Nations force which was fast approaching the Yalu river, the border between Korea and China, the conflict was far from being his personal affair. Both President Truman and General Bradley, chairman of JCS, had warned the general of the danger of Chinese intervention, but instead of

Above:
General Douglas MacArthur, Commander in Chief of UN troops in Korea, was sacked by President Truman for insubordination during the Korean war.

Below:
UN troops make an amphibious landing at Inchon during the Korean war. This daring operation took the North Koreans by surprise and within a month UN troops had routed communist troops in South Korea.

heeding their warning he announced his "last offensive before going back home" on November 24, 1950. It was known that the communist Chinese had amassed 2,000,000 troops along the Yalu border. By the fall of 1950 Premier Chou En-lai had persuaded Stalin to send these armies the latest modern weapons which in the words of General Peng Tu-huai would enable the Chinese to obliterate the United Nations in Korea. Two days after MacArthur's announcement of the "last offensive" the Chinese armies struck on a broad front, split, trapped and destroyed large contingents of United Nations' troops. Within three weeks the United Nations' forces had been driven out of the North and Seoul was again in Chinese hands. Panic-stricken MacArthur considered the evacuation of the whole peninsula. Though the Chinese spoke of the reunification of the Koreas, they appealed for an armistice, which

was a clear indication of their intention not to proceed any farther and repeat the errors of the North Korean invasion. By March 1951 General Matthew Ridgway, who had taken over operations on the spot, had driven the Chinese out of Seoul and back to the 38th parallel, the old dividing line. Henceforth there was no large-scale fighting in Korea, but an armistice was only agreed in 1953. Chinese intervention in Korea and the anti-communist crusade of Senator MacCarthy forced Truman into proclaiming a state of national emergency, despite his Chiefs of Staff incessantly proclaiming that the war in Korea was in the wrong place, against the wrong enemy and at the wrong time. US military budget for FY1951 jumped to the massive $50,000,000,000,000 and in Europe the integration of NATO forces was forced through by the United States; in addition a firm decision was made on the rearmament of West Germany.

The United States were reacting to communist probes rather than anticipating them, dragging its NATO allies along with them. Although most military leaders opposed such a massive involvement in South Asia General MacArthur's policy of "fighting communism in Asia rather than Europe" was never quite abandoned. Some 720,000 troops, largely American, continued to be tied down in Korea until 1953, even after Truman had dismissed MacArthur for insubordination. American involvement in Asia suited Premier Stalin who continued to plan Korea-style operations against Finland and Yugoslavia. Still Stalin learned a lesson in Korea, since the "probing by proxy" had produced such an US overreaction: his probes into Finland and Yugoslavia had to remain in the planning stage for fear of a similar US overreaction in Europe. He concentrated exclusively on the blocking of West German rearmament. Initially the shock of Korea had a galvanizing effect on NATO in Europe. While the Europeans thought that the USSR would employ similar tactics in Europe to those in Asia they continued to back the United States both politically in the United Nations, and militarily by sending token forces to fight in Korea. However, when it became clear that US military efforts would be concentrated in Asia for some considerable time and after Truman had not taken NATO decisions seriously enough in December 1950, political cracks began to appear in the alliance. Perhaps it was symbolic that General Eisenhower, NATO's C in C, installed his headquarters in France with very few NATO forces under his command.

Henceforth the Europeans and particularly the French became reluctant allies. They reasoned that since the United States felt comparatively safe in their 'continental fortress," and sent huge armies to Asia, where there were no direct European interests, Western Europe had to bear the brunt of the military burden. France, which considered itself particularly burdened with three divisions deployed in Germany, 16 divisions in France and 10 in Indochina, resented the American C in C, unified military command and German rearmament to boot.

Then it was realized that the Korea-type action was unique and would not be repeated in Europe, or Germany. That was at least the conclusion reached by a special US study committee (members C. Bohlen, G. Kennan, G. Hilger), and which also recommended that large-scale retaliation against the USSR over the Korean conflict was unnecessary. This made the European allies even more reluctant, while the Americans became, if anything, more forceful. Greece and Turkey were admitted to NATO in 1952 and, despite French maneuvering, West Germany was rearmed and in 1955 also became member of NATO. The United States quadrupled its rearmament program, Britain raised its national service to two years and military expenditure to 12 percent of its GNP, while France increased its military expenditure by 30 percent. It is true that the Americans

The B-52 Stratofortress was first flown in April 1952. It has a range of 12,500 miles and can carry numerous missile systems including the Cruise missile. It forms the bulk of the US bomber force.

Above:
The B-47 was the first strategic bomber to be powered solely by jet engines.

Right:
B-52 strategic heavy bomber was the standard US bomber for over 20 years.

increased their military commitment in Europe and particularly in Germany, but this was largely in response to the new military doctrine "forward strategy" rather than European political or military appeals.

In February 1952 under the pretext of a possible Korean-type attack in Europe the Americans forced through the NATO political council the greatest and hollowest decision: by the end of 1952 NATO would field 50 divisions, 4,000 aircraft, and 704 major combat vessels. For 1953 the aim was even more incredible: 75 divisions and 4,000 aircraft. With the receding danger of war the Europeans simply ignored these military targets; besides rearmament was already imposing an intolerable burden on European economies. In any case the stress on conventional rearmament began to appear exaggerated. By the end of 1948 the Strategic Air Command with its B-50 and B-36 aircraft and advanced bases in Britain and the Far East was able to pose a substantial strategic-nuclear threat to the USSR. With the modernization of aircraft, B-47 jets were brought in and the all-jet heavy bomber B-52 was test flown in April 1952. They were capable of delivering the new Hydrogen bombs (tested on November 1, 1952) and inflicting immense damage on the USSR. The argument for increased conventional rearmament was evaporating. By October 1952 Britain had also tested its nuclear device, and the Soviets followed suit by testing their H-bomb in August 1953. Cracks within the NATO alliance became cleavages and for all practical purposes the United States left its European allies to fend for themselves, safeguarding their own interests and security from some 450 military bases in 36 countries.

Whether it was admitted or not a conventional balance of power existed between the Super Powers and their allies; the same now applied to the balance of terror as strategic-nuclear balance was then termed. The United States thereafter developed a strategic doctrine which upheld the existing balance of terror by making the purpose of strategic systems the prevention of strategic conflict rather than

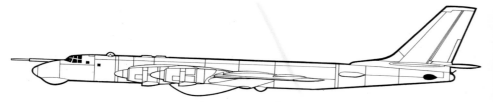

winning it. The new Eisenhower administration (General Eisenhower was elected President in November 1952) expressed the strategic doctrine in more political terms: conventional wars were to be limited to border skirmishes; however, conflicts of the Korean type were to be treated as strategic. The administration therefore decided to depend primarily on the great capacity "to retaliate, instantly, by means and at places of our choosing." Europe was obviously excluded from this policy and the Soviets made it clear that this was the way they understood and interpreted this new US policy. In 1955 the Soviets began to speak about Soviet "rockets" and launched their own nuclear diplomacy. Both Super Powers, each for its own purposes, had reached a stage of bilateral antagonism which hardly took into account their respective allies.

As previously the Soviets took advantage of mutual deterrence first, and the US continued with its traditional overreaction. During the Suez crisis, when the US allies, France and Britain, joined Israel and attacked Egypt, the Soviets threatened obliquely with 'rocket' retaliation. The United States had to make it publicly clear that even though it did not approve the actions of its allies in Egypt, it still considered them under its nuclear "umbrella" and any aggressive act against them by the Soviets would provoke "massive retaliation." However the Soviets continued to use strategic threats regardless: in 1958 during the Quemay-Matsu Islands crisis and over Berlin. In 1960 the Soviets threatened to obliterate the European bases for US U-2 aircraft. Politically American prestige was constantly being eroded and the NATO allies became seriously disquieted: with the "growing" Soviet nuclear ascendance it was thought that the USA would either leave NATO defenseless or drag the alliance into a suicidal war. At the root of the Eisenhower administration's insecure overreactions lay the

Above, right and below:
The Tupolev Bear long-range reconnaissance aircraft can carry the Kangaroo missile but has now been superseded by the Backfire bomber.

belief that there existed a disparity in delivery vehicles between the Super Powers, the so-called first missile gap. This explained why a US administration, elected on the claim to "roll back communism," did nothing, when Eastern Europe was convulsed by a series of revolts in 1953, and in 1956 by a revolution in Hungary. Nothing was done either about Soviet armed intervention in the latter country, or the threats of an intervention in Poland at almost the same time.

Late in 1954 the Soviets displayed a jet bomber, Bear, which had intercontinental capacity. Furthermore, during the May Day celebrations in the following year they exhibited a number of Bison aircraft which were of the same class as B-52s and completely deceived the American leadership. The US leaders believed in this "bomber gap" and subsequently also in the "missile gap" and permitted the Soviets to make political capital out of them. The Americans then began feverishly to close this supposed gap. B-52 bases in Spain and Morocco became operational in 1957 and the Polaris program was launched in 1956 to be operational in 1960. Still the US seemed to have no luck with counter-development: in October 1957 the Soviets launched their first Sputnik, artificial earth satellite, while US Atlas rockets were being tested. However, without being aware of it, the US quickly reversed this situation of uncertainty by improving its strategic posture, by having one-third of its strategic bombers on constant 24-hour alert. The final resolution of this American dilemma occurred only in October 1962, after the Cuban missile crisis.

Soon after seizing power in Cuba in 1959, Fidel Castro turned to the USSR to seek economic and military aid. In April 1961 the US-sponsored invasion of Cuba was defeated and on September 2, 1962 Cuba and the Soviet Union signed a security pact. The pact was to ensure Cuba's defense against an external aggressor and Soviet missiles were to be installed on the island, as well as Soviet medium-range bombers, IL-28s. The Americans became aware of these Cuban developments in August 1962, when a U-2 spy plane identified SAM-2 sites. President Kennedy warned the Soviets that offensive Soviet missiles in Cuba would not be tolerated and Premier Khrushchev denied that there were any offensive missiles there. Foreign Minister Gromyko reiterated these denials, but on October 14, 1962 the Americans obtained aerial photographs of missile ramps at Cristobal, and the Cuban missile crisis as a bilateral, Super Power nuclear confrontation broke out on an unsuspecting world.

In fact the Soviet missile deployment in Cuba was gigantic especially if compared to the American missile deployment in Turkey, where there were 15 Thor-Jupiter missiles. The Soviets already had 42 IL-28 aircraft on the island and 42 MRBMs (range 1,000 miles) brought in by Soviet ships. The Americans identified nine missile sites; six of these sites, consisting of four launchers, were for the MRBMs already assembled on the island. Three sites were destined for IRBMs (range 2,200 miles) which were still en route on Soviet ships. It was estimated that these missiles were capable of inflicting 80,000,000 casualties if fired on the United States. Since all this military might was not in Cuba to assure the defense of that island, the Americans took it on themselves unilaterally to clear it of these offensive weapons.

President Kennedy started secret meetings with his security advisers on October 16. They discussed all the options that presented themselves: either they ignored the developments in Cuba or invaded the island to seize the offensive arsenal. A surprise attack on the missile sites was also a possibility, but in the end Kennedy decided on a whole series of counter-measures. On October 22 the President publicly announced his intentions: the Soviets had to withdraw the offensive weapon system from Cuba and until this was done the island would be placed under a naval quarantine. At the same time the President placed all ICBMs (103 Atlas and 54 Titan missiles) on alert as well as the 105 MRBMs

135

(Thor-Jupiter missiles) and 144 Polaris missile. All the B-47s and B-52s were dispersed and remained airborne throughout the crisis; 37 aircraft carriers ensured the blockade of Cuba as well as sea deterrence. Faced with this display of military power and show of resolution by the young US President, the Soviet leader accepted all the American demands on October 28, 1962. Subsequently it transpired that the supposed missile and bomber gaps had never existed: the US had deployed 406 ICBMs as compared to 125 Soviet ones. In long-range aviation the proportion was 1,600 US to 190 Soviet. Apart from the military triumph the US damaged the Soviet international reputation and even caused an internal upheaval in the USSR. In 1964 the Soviet leader Khrushchev, was dismissed, largely because of his blundering over Cuba.

The Cuban confrontation demonstrated the bilateral nature of international politics. Only the Super Powers could afford the heavy expenditure involved in the production of nuclear warheads and delivery vehicles. US defense expenditure rose between 1954 and 1964 from $42.7 billion to $51.2 billion. Between 1966 and 1970 the US spent $400 billion on defense, the annual peak was reached in 1969, when $81 billion were spent. The

various arms control agreements and political detente kept US defense spending under the annual $80 billion. However, in the dangerous 1980s it has jumped up again, stimulated by an arms race with the USSR and inflation to $180 billion. Throughout the 1970s Soviet military expenditure was 30 percent higher than the US and with renewed international insecurity, especially after the Soviets had invaded Afghanistan in 1979, the United States attempted to catch up with their antagonist. CIA estimates of Soviet expenditure were being revised: thus apparently in 1979 the Soviets spent $222 billion on defense which was 50 percent higher than the US. In 1981 the CIA estimate of $185 billion of Soviet defense spending was again higher than the US, but in view of the latest research findings it still has to be revised upward. Nonetheless for the average 9 percent of GNP spent by the US annually since 1950, the US Super Power can boast a formidable defense establishment.

When the US triad of (1) land-based missiles, (2) strategic bombers and (3) strategic submarines is compared to the Soviet one, it is clear that the Soviets must have spent a much greater proportion of their GNP on defense. They invariably produced twice as many weapons systems as the Americans:

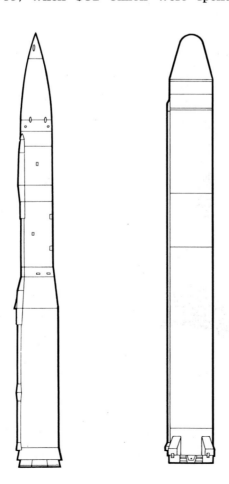

USSR	USA
Since 1960 ICBMs	
SS-11	Titan II
SS-13	Minuteman II
SS-17	
SS-18	Minuteman III
SS-19	

	SLBMs	
SS-N-4		Polaris A-3
SS-N-5		Poseidon
SS-N-6		
SS-N-8		
SS-N-18		

	Bombers	
Badger		B-52
Bear		FB-111
Bison		
Blinder		
Backfire		

In absolute terms the US deploys 1,052 land-based ICBMs: 52 aging Titan II; 450 Minuteman II and 550 Minuteman III. Since President Reagan's election in 1980 the US has decided to develop and produce MX missiles to enhance survivability and increase deterrence. The characteristics of the US ICBMs are their high alert rate, redundant and secure communications, modest annual operation costs, as well as modest maintenance. The ICBMs are highly responsive, have great accuracy and reliability and rapid retargetting capability coupled with assured penetration. However, increasingly in the 1980s their silos are vulnerable to a Soviet strategic strike.

Because of high survivability, the deterrence value of US SLBMs is even higher than the land-based ICBMs. Since 1959 the US has deployed 41 nuclear submarines of the Polaris type. In the 1970s 31 Polaris SSBMs were converted into an updated Poseidon system (two Polaris were deactivated and eight were converted into submarine-hunting vessels). In the 1980s the US deploys 19 Poseidons with C-3 missiles and 11 Poseidons with C-4 missiles which have a range of 7,400km. One Poseidon will be back-fitted with the Trident I in 1982. Each Trident I has independently targetted RVs and its range not only increases its operational area but also preserves its survivability against possible future Soviet anti-submarine capabilities. Trident SSBNs, which will go into production in 1982, will have higher speed and will make less noise than the Poseidon and Polaris SSBNs. Each Trident will have in addition 24 missiles (Trident I) and improvements are planned in command, control, and communications all of which will enhance the new submarines' survivability and connectivity with strategic force C-3 elements and complement force endurance.

While the US ICBMs provide rapidly retargettable weapons capable of destroying any land-based missiles and the SSBNs are comparatively invulnerable when at sea, the manned-strategic bombers add to the triad a basic dimension of flexibility. They can be launched prior to the decision to launch the ICBMs, which are computer-programed and therefore cannot be manipulated in the same way as the bombers. The bombers are also of political utility: they can be launched to indicate national resolve and then recalled, if the situation changes. They are the only force which can engage unanticipated or mobile targets, are easily reusable and can deliver strategic and conventional payloads accurately on diverse targets. The bulk of this force is formed by the B-52 long-range bombers, some 316 of them. In addition there are 60

The USS *Benjamin Franklin* is a Trident missile submarine.

Right:
A Trident missile emerges after a
sea launch trial.

Far left:
The USS *Ohio* during sea trials off
Groton, Connecticut.

Below:
The USS *Ohio* is an Ohio Class A
Trident missile submarine seen
here during sea trials.

141

Right:
A T-111 all-weather attack
bomber which has a maximum
speed of Mach 2 and a range of
3,165 miles. With a maximum
bomb capacity of 31,500, the
F-111 is certainly a formidable
weapon.

Below:
Another F-111 but modified to the
requirements of a strategic bomber.

F-111 bombers which are designed for low-altitude and high-speed penetration. While the existing strategic bombers will have to be used until the next century, (as there are no planned replacements) their survivability will be improved in 1982: in December of that year the air-launched Cruise missiles will be carried by B-52s thus reducing their exposure to present air-defense systems. However the unpredictability of Soviet development in defensive and offensive air weapons systems makes it imperative for the US to provide a new multi-role strategic aircraft and the decision made by President Reagan to build 100 B-1 aircraft may fill this gap.

The back-up systems for the strategic bombing force are the aerial refueling and reconnaissance forces. The refueling tanker force was originally acquired to extend the range of the strategic bombers but is currently committed to the single integrated operational plan (SIOP). The SIOP means that strategic bombers can fly non-stop to remote targets, penetrate deep strike areas and return home or to overseas bases. The US Air Force has 615 KC-135 tankers including 128 reserve aircraft. In addition these refueling aircraft extend the range and capability of strategic airlifts, command and control, and reconnaissance; they are also usable for the rapid global deployment and employment of tactical air forces. The increasing importance of the refueling forces led to the procurement of 12 KC-10 aircraft: in the 1980s many more will have to be procured to ensure the rapid deployment of the RDJTF to potential crisis areas, such as Southeast Asia or the Middle East.

The reconnaissance forces are indispensable for the SAC as they provide the surveillance, reconnaissance and target acquisition missions.

Below:
A Boeing B-52 Stratofortress unloads its bombs during a mission over Vietnam.

Above:
The Galosh (ABM-1) antiballistic missile is a three-stage missile with an estimated range of 188 miles (300km). It has a nuclear warhead with a megaton range.

Above center:
Land-based radar provides detailed information about enemy missile and aircraft movements.

Above right:
Radar from the Safeguard ABM system. Its development was scrapped in 1976 due to prohibitive costs.

Below right:
AWACS airborne warning and control system aircraft in flight.

They are subdivided into two general types: the strategic and tactical standoff, and penetration systems. The reconnaissance forces come under the appellation of strategic air-breathing systems and consist of eight U-2B, nine SR-71 and 14 RC-135 aircraft. In addition they include 12 RF-4C aircraft with side-looking airborne radar; five RF-4Cs with tactical electronic reconnaissance sensors; 90 OV-1D Mohawk aircraft with SLAR. Though no electronic improvements are planned, the force itself will be operational until the next century and will be adequate for tactical reconnaissance.

In the early 1970s the United States was contemplating building its own strategic defensive systems. The equivalent of the Soviet Galosh ABM, deployed round Moscow, was to be the Safeguard ABM. The development of this ABM system proved prohibitive, $50 billion, and it was therefore canceled, after the Soviets and the US signed the SALT I agreement in 1972, under whose terms both sides froze the development of ABM systems. In any case the ABM systems are only a part, and often not the most essential, of strategic defense systems. The more essential parts of the SDS are those which provide timely, unambiguous, and reliable warning as well as assessment of aerospace attack. They are integral to any retaliatory strategic response, they defend US conduct of operations in space, limit damage to strategic retaliatory forces and C^3. There are three ballistic missile early warning systems, one perimeter acquisition radar attack characterization system radar, one FPS-85, one FSS-7 SLBM detection radar and two PAVE PAWS SLBM detection and warning radars devoted to these tasks. Atmospheric surveillance of North American airspace is performed by the distant early warning line of 31 radars, but these radars are antiquated and they will soon be reduced to 13. There are

The interior of an AWACS airplane.

also 46 radars of the joint, civilian and military, surveillance supports guarding the North American airspace. However both these defensive lines will soon be replaced by airborne warning and control system aircraft, the AWACSs.

As part of the strategic deterrent the United States maintains theater nuclear forces, whose bulk represents American participation in NATO. They can be used in Europe either in response to a conventional, chemical, or limited nuclear attack, or as an indication of levels of nuclear conflict, whether it threatens to escalate to a general nuclear conflict. Currently American forces are equipped with a mixture of nuclear delivery systems many of which can be used with conventional munition. Thus, for example, both 8-inch and 155mm howitzers, which are conventional guns, can fire atomic projectiles. For shorter ranges American forces deploy the Lance missile; for longer the Pershing 1A missiles. As part of NATO modernization the latter will be replaced by 108 Pershing 2 missiles and 464 ground-launched Cruise missiles. In addition, the United States maintains theater aviation, chemical retaliatory forces, electronic warfare forces, and other highly sophisticated arms.

Compared to this strategic and theater weapons panoply the size of the American armed forces appears quite modest. The US Army

deploys 16 active divisions, eight reserve divisions, 25 reserve brigades, and four armored cavalry regiments. Of these 11 active divisions are stationed in the United States (one in Hawaii). Four active divisions, three reserve brigades, and two armored cavalry regiments are deployed in Europe; one active division is in Korea while Berlin, Alaska, and Panama each retain one theater defense brigade. To these units the rapid deployment joint task force should be added, which only recently held its first exercise in the Middle East and Africa.

As there exists a Soviet superiority in conventional arms in the European war theater US MBTs, antitank weapons, and tactical aviation deployed there, are of great importance. Currently the US Army deploys 884 older M-60A1 tanks which are being converted into the more advanced M-60A3s which in 1981 will amount to 2,480. The latest tank development, XM-1, was tested operationally in 1980: 7,058 have been ordered and they will start coming off the production line in 1981 at 30 every month and 60 every month after 1983. The replacement of the infantry and cavalry fighting vehicles, the M-113 carriers, began in 1980. The new IFV affords greater firepower, mobility and protection; the IFVs mount an automatic 25mm cannon, a 7.62mm co-axial gun and a

Above and above left:
The M-112 Armored Personnel
Carrier is used extensively by the
US Army and NATO allies. It is
also being replaced gradually by
the newer 1FV.

Left and below:
The M-60 is the main battle tank
for the US Army. The latest tank
development is the XM-1 which
will supersdede the M-60.

1,260 such vehicles.

With Soviet armor improvements the US Army is improving its primary antitank guided missile systems too. At the moment there are some 100,000 unimproved 5-inch TOW missiles and by 1986 12,000 improved missiles (5-inch and 6-inch configurational) will be procured every year. The M-72A2 light antitank weapon will be replaced by the VIPER (light-weight, shoulder fired short-range missile), 93,000 of which will be deployed in 1982. In 1980 the US Army procured 2,100 of the 155mm laser-guided projectiles (Copperhead) which will vastly improve the antitank capability of existing artillery weapons. By 1990 the army hopes to have 276 multiple launch selfpropelled launchers with 360,000 missiles. Scatterable mines (FASCAM), ground emplaced mines (GEMSS) and 155mm artillery-delivered mines complete the defensive arrangements of the US Army *vis a vis* Soviet armor superiority in Europe.

Tactical air force appears also inferior to the Soviets at least in numbers: currently the US Air Force deploys 26 active wings and 11 reserve

tube-launched, optically tracked, wire-guided antitank weapon system. Some 464 IFVs will be in service in 1982 and by 1986 the US Army will dispose of 3,048 such vehicles. In 1982 the M-9 armored combat earthmover will be produced (87 vehicles); these are rapid diggers of fighting positions for tank and infantry weapons and antitank ditches. In view of the Soviet armored superiority this is an important weapon; the US Army hopes ultimately to dispose of some

Left:
The F-4 all-weather multi-role fighter aircraft first flown in May 1958 and entered into service in February 1960. It has a maximum speed of Mach 2.27 and a maximum range of 2,300 miles. It can carry a wide range and quantity of weapons and is one of the most versatile of the American fighter aircraft.

Below:
The Chaparral, the mobile surface-to-air guided missile, in various stages of operational readiness.

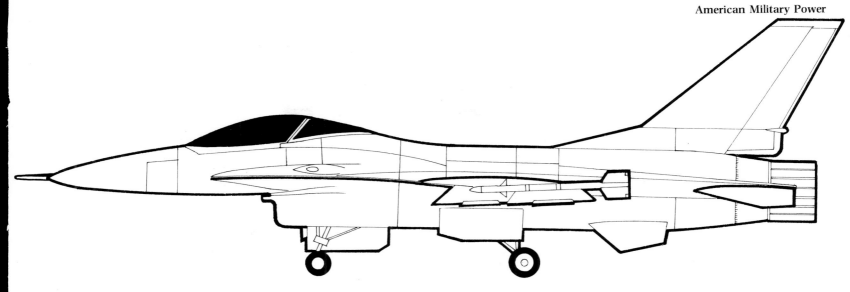

wings. Each three squadron wing fields 72 aircraft; thus there are only 1,692 active fighters and 822 reserve fighters. Both active and reserve wings deploy 354 F-15s, 312 A-7s, 372 A-10s and 252 F-111s for specialized operations along with 162 F-16s and 954 F-4s which are multi-role aircraft. They are supported by 84 F-4Gs and 24 F-105Gs (electromagnetic aircraft) 215 RF-4C (reconnaissance aircraft) 22 E-3As (airborne warning and control aircraft) and 252 OV-10s, OA-37s, and O-2s (tactical aircontrol aircraft). Soviet air superiority will be offset by the replacement of the aging F-4s by the A-10s, F-15s and F-16 which are currently in production and are to be delivered to reequip 40 wings by 1986.

Above:
The F-15 is an air superiority fighter developed to bridge the gap in air superiority thought to have been gained by the Soviet MiG-23 and 25. It was first flown in July 1972 and has a top flight speed of Mach 2.5 and a maximum range of 3.450 miles.

Center left and top:
The F-16 fighter-bomber was developed as a high-speed fighter.

Far left:
The F-16 fighter-bomber launches a medium-range air-to-air missile at a speed of Mach 0.85 at an altitude of 20,000 ft. The top picture shows "Mach diamonds" in the exhaust plume as its velocity reaches supersonic speed.

Left:
OV-10 tactical support aircraft gives close support to ground forces.

CHAPTER SIX

THE NORTH ATLANTIC TREATY ORGANIZATION

The French aircraft carrier *Foch* with two Super Etendards on its flight deck. These aircraft can carry Exocet missiles, which have proved so effective in the Falklands crisis.

Although France felt uneasy about NATO from the very beginning, when in the 1950s it became clear that the USSR would not attack Western Europe, most of the other members of the alliance also became restless. From the start the European allies found it difficult to reconcile social and economic progress with security which required of them heavy financial expenditure. At first the United States joined France in opposing a central military command, but would not allow any other all the privilege of supreme control over its national forces even in Germany. Weapons' procurement was another stumbling block: standardization was impossible and national specialization was difficult to control. In the 1950s when France and Britain became absorbed in colonial wars and upholding their own national interests (Suez 1956), as a military tool the alliance simply went into abeyance. The real turning point for the alliance came in 1958 when the new President of France, General Charles de Gaulle suggested a nuclear directorate for NATO, which would have comprised the USA, France, and Britain only. After President Eisenhower had rejected this French proposal the alliance showed signs of strain.

In 1954, when US rockets and missiles arrived in Germany they were intended for US forces only and Marshal Philippe Juin, then commander of NATO ground forces in Europe, was not allowed to know the nature and number of tactical nuclear weapons under his command. This coupled with President de Gaulle's nuclear disappointment led to the withdrawal of France from the military structures of NATO in 1966. In 1974 France was followed by Greece which saw no sense in belonging to an alliance unable to protect her against a fellow ally, Turkey, which had invaded and occupied part of Cyprus. Moreover the rest of the European allies lost confidence in the US nuclear umbrella, especially in the 1970s, when American-Soviet detente agreements indicated that the erstwhile antagonistic Super Powers were in reality aiming at a world condominium.

In mitigation the Americans have periodically attempted to right certain imbalances within the alliance. President Kennedy's idea of the multilateral force for NATO as a remedial measure came to nothing; Admiral Radford's recommendations which would have placed reliance

for the defense of Europe primarily on tactical as well as strategic weapons was abruptly reversed by the Kennedy administration, and if anything further confused the alliance; even the distribution of tactical nuclear weapons among NATO armies failed to resolve the fundamental problem, namely that the alliance was useless for Europe. The Americans made this abundantly clear, when in 1962 they acted unilaterally in Cuba and then became involved, again unilaterally, in Vietnam. In the meantime France unilaterally developed its nuclear *force de frappe*, which after 1957 provided Europe with a really independent nuclear deterrent.

Currently NATO has its supreme head-quarters in Brussels (since 1966 when France left the military organization) from which it plans and commands the European area (less Britain, France, Iceland, and Portugal). The supreme commander has at his disposal over 3,000 delivery vehicles for 6,000 tactical nuclear warheads. Although the tactical nuclear weapons are spread all over Europe (excepting Luxemburg, Norway and Denmark) they are

Nike Hercules is a surface-to-air missile which has both a conventifnal and nuclear capability. It can also be fitted with an antitank warhead consisting of several sub-munitions with automatic guidance systems. Although the Nike missile is considered outdated it still has a very important role to play in a limited war.

US ARMY

US ARMY

in American custody and therefore cannot be used by the other NATO allies (except France which has independent tactical weapons and some British tactical weapons). The supreme commander has some 66 divisions earmarked for his command in peacetime with 3,400 tactical aircraft spread over Europe's 200 air-fields with a back-up system of storage depots, fuel pipelines and signal communications. Since 1978 there exists an integrated NATO early warning system which includes US AWACS aircraft.

NATO command in Europe is subdivided into the Northern, Central and Southern sectors. Northern command HQ is at Kolsaas in Norway and is responsible for the defense of Denmark, Norway, Northern Germany and the Baltic approaches. Most of the Danish and Norvegian armed forces are earmarked for this command, while Germany has assigned to it one division, two air wings and its Baltic fleet. NATO's southern command is situated in Naples, Italy and its task is the defense of Greece, Italy, and Turkey. Land forces assigned to it include 22 Turkish divisions, eight Italian, and 13 Greek (Greece rejoined NATO in 1980 but will probably leave it again). These countries' tactical air forces also come under the southern command, which

because of its Mediterranean and Black Sea duties comprises the bulk of Allied naval forces.

The Central Europe command has always been considered the most important. Its HQ is at Brunssum in Holland and commands the bulk of NATO land forces as well as tactical aviation. Its northern army group is centered on Munchen-Gladbach; its central group is at Seckenheim, while its air force HQ at Ramstein. These forces

Right:
Two F-4 multi-role fighter aircraft fly over northern Italy.

Bottom left:
Lockheed F-104 Starfighter all-weather interceptor, called the "missile with a man in it." Gradually being replaced by the F-15, it provides the mainstay of the less developed countries in NATO. It has a maximum speed of Mach 2.2 and a range of 1,380 miles. It carries up to 4,000 lb. equipped with small missiles and a 20mm M61 Vulcan multi-barrel cannon.

Below:
The Panavia Tornado is a joint British, German, and Italian project. The Tornado multi-role swing-wing fighter-bomber can carry an impressive load of weapons at 1.5 Mach.

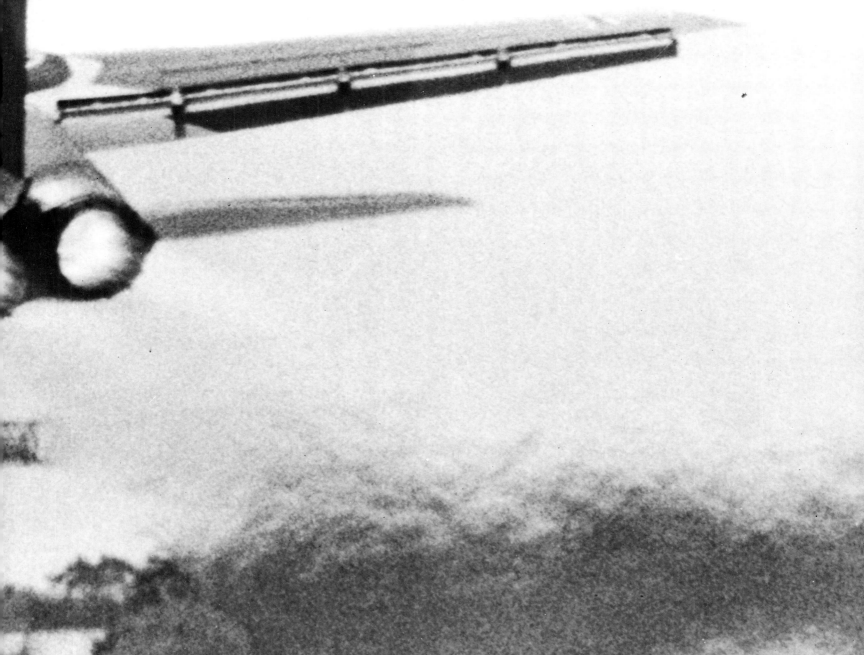

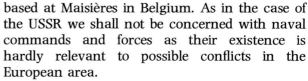

amount to 26 divisions and 2,200 tactical aircraft. In the northern sector which runs along the Liège-Göttingen line there are Belgian, Dutch, British, four Germans divisions, and one US brigade. The 2nd Tactical Air Force supports these ground forces. The southern sector contains the bulk of US armed forces in Europe, seven German divisions and a Canadian brigade group supported by the 4th Tactical Air Force. In addition NATO forces in Europe comprise a mobile force (AMF) based in Seckenheim air forces based in the United Kingdom (HQ at High Wycombe) and the early warning command

based at Maisières in Belgium. As in the case of the USSR we shall not be concerned with naval commands and forces as their existence is hardly relevant to possible conflicts in the European area.

Contrary to the Warsaw Pact arrangements the United States, while permanently controling the supreme allied command, is not the largest manpower contributor to the allied forces. The US Army maintains in Europe 219,729 men; the bulk of whom are stationed in Germany: 208,000 of them comprising two army corps, two armored and two mechanized divisions with one armored and two mechanized brigades and two armored cavalry regiments. These ground forces are backed up by four air-defense squadrons and 3,000 NBTs. In West Berlin there is an infantry brigade (4,000 men), in Greece 569 men, in Italy 3,760, in Holland 1,000, and Turkey 1,200 men. The US Air Force deploys on the European continent 54,000 men and in Britain 20,500 men. Thus in Britain the air force consists of four wings: four squadrons with 84 A-10s, two squadrons with 36 RF-4Cs; one squadron with F-55Es and 16 C-130s, also 29 KC-135 tankers and four there are certain strategic units and one tactical wing consisting of three squadrons of F-4s, A-10s and F-15s. Five combat wings are based in Germany: three squadrons with 66 EC-135s. In Spain, Italy, Greece, and Turkey F-111s, two squadrons with 42 A-10s, eight squadrons with 144 F-4s and three squadrons with 54 F-15s. One squadron of F-15s is deployed in the Netherlands; one air defense

Below:
Leopard II battle tanks. They are deployed by Germany, France, Italy, Canada, and several other countries.

Left:
The Socprion tank was designed for use in conditions demanding high power to weight ratio, low ground pressure and positive traction over bog, swamp, and snow. It is the first fighting vehicle built amost entirely of aluminium and carries a 76mm gun mounted on a 360 degree transverse turret.

Right:
Italian M-60 tanks. The Italian Army has some 300 M-60 A1s.

163

squadron in Iceland and a total of 29 fighter squadrons elsewhere.

European NATO allies provide the bulk of the land forces as well as tactical aviation. Belgian armed forces amount to 65,000 men; air force 20,100. Belgium fields 25,000 men (one army corps, one division, one armored and one mechanized brigades and one HAWK battalion) in Germany, but in case of a conflict all her armed forces automatically come under NATO command. They include one battalion equipped with four Lance missiles; two battalions for air defense equipped with 36 HAWK; five engineering battalions and four aviation squadrons. The Belgian Army is equipped with 334 Leopard (German) tanks; 55 M-47 (US) tanks and 133 Scorpion (British) tanks; it has 153 AFVs; 1,123 APCs and a large number of up-to-date howitzers and guns. Its air force consists of 144

Above:
A Leopard II tank gives support to British troops during NATO exercises.

Far left top:
The Scorpion light reconnaissance tank built entirely of aluminium and used by many NATO countries. countries.

Left:
A Scorpion tank, a Fox armored car and a Chieftain main battle tank are the main armored elements of the British Army.

Top:
Leopard II tanks.

combat aircraft: three squadrons with 54 Mirage 5BA/Ds; two squadrons with 36 F/TF-104Gs; 18 F-16A/Bs; 18 Mirages 5BR and a variety of other aircraft. It also has 72 Nike Hercules SAM missiles. This demonstration of a minor ally's contribution to NATO is comparable to that of Canada: (one mechanized brigade

of 3,000 men, 59 Leopard MBTs, 375 APCs; three fighter squadrons consisting of 42 CF-104 aircraft and helicopters); to Denmark's: armed forces 19,300 men and air force 7,600; Greece: ground forces 150,000 organized in three military regions and an air force of 24,500 men; it also deploys 36 Nike Hercules SAM missiles and 36 Nike Ajax missiles. Luxemburg's army consists of 690 men and they are all under NATO command. The Netherlands' army comprises 67,000 men organized in two armored and four mechanized brigades with one battalion with Lance missiles. The air force consists of 19,000 men in five fighter squadrons equipped with 54 NF-5As and 36 F-104Gs. Norway's army consists of 18,000 men organized in two brigades; the air force has 115 combat aircraft manned by 10,000 men. Portugal's army has 47,000 men organized in six regional commands. Its air force maintains 85 combat aircraft manned by 10,500 men. Finally Turkey's army amounts to 470,000 men and air force to 53,000. The army is organized into four army HQs, while the air force has 325 combat aircraft.

Turkey also has 96 Nike Hercules SAMs.

It is obvious that the armed forces of Britain, Italy and Germany make the most substantial contribution to NATO and they far exceed the forces of the minor allies. The British army of the Rhine amounts to 55,000 troops organized in a corps HQ consisting of four armored divisions, one artillery division and the 5th Field Force. There is also one infantry brigade stationed in West Berlin (3,100 men). The Royal Air Force fields 10,800 men who form two squadrons of Phantom FGR-2s, two squadrons of Buccaneer aircraft, five squadrons of Jaguars; two squadrons of Rapiers SAMs. In Germany there is also one squadron of RAF regiment, Wessex transport and one Bloodhound squadron. The army is equipped with the most modern Chieftain MBTs, Scorpion tanks and Saladin armored cars. The air force is equipped with the interceptor Phantom aircraft, strike/attack Buccaneers and reconnaissance Jaguar aircraft. The Italian contribution to NATO is even greater because nominally all Italian ground forces as well as air forces come under the

Above:
A Hercules transport plane comes into land over a flight of RAF Jaguars.

Top:
A Jaguar tactical fighter bomber.

Right:
Mirage jet fighters have been widely sold and have proved themselves in many recent wars including the Falklands crisis.

Left:
The French Otomat missile B being fired.

Below:
The French nuclear missile submarine *Foudroyante* is capable of launching 16 M-20 nuclear missiles.

Bottom right:
The launch of a Pershing 2 tactical medium range nuclear missile. These will replace the Pershing 1s and together with the Cruise missile will provide a credible response to the Soviet SS-20.

southern command of NATO. The army fields 255,000 men organized in three army corps equipped with 550 M-47, 300 M-60A1, 900 Leopard tanks and 4,100 APCs. It also deploys 6 Lance missiles and 22 improved HAWK SAM missiles. The air forces consist of 69,000 men flying 310 combat aircraft, which include F-104s, G-91Rs, Tornado aircraft and 96 Nike Hercules SAM missiles. The most significant contribution to NATO strength comes naturally from West Germany. Nominally and in fact its entire army of 335,200 men comes under NATO command. It is organized into three army corps of four division each; of the latter six are armored, four are armored infantry, one mountain and one airborne divisions. Thus there are 67 tank, 62 armored infantry and 12 paratroop battalions in the field army. It disposes of 26 Lance missiles, over 4,000 tanks including Leopard 1 and 2s and 4,000 APCs. The best howitzers and various guns are also currently deployed as well as 100 Roland SAM missiles. The air force fields 106,000 men and tactical aviation consists of 479 aircraft, which include eight squadrons of F-104Gs and four squadrons of F-4Fs. The air force also controls 72 Pershing 1A IMBMs, 216 Nike Hercules SAM missiles, 216 HAWK launchers.

However, the most important factor for War

Far left center:
The British Sea Slug surface-to-air missile, with some surface-to-surface capability.

Far left bottom:
The Seacat surface-to-air missile has proved over 90 percent effective, although it relies heavily on radar to be operationally effective.

Far left top:
The Seawolf surface-to-air seaborne weapon, with anti-missile capability.

Left:
The HAWK missile is a low-medium altitude surface-to-air missile. It is transported by a self-propelled tracked launcher vehicle and has a range of 22 miles (35km).

Below:
A Nike Hercules surface-to-air missile.

Theater Europe lies outside NATO. Not only is the French army the largest on the European continent (504,630 men and women) but France is the only European country with a totally independent strategic deterrent. Its strategic forces amount to 21,000 and comprise ALBMs, IRBMs, and aircraft. Currently France deploys five nuclear-powered submarines each equipped with 16 M-20 missiles. The home base of these SSBNs is Isle Longue near Brest and the M-20 missiles have a range of 3,000 miles. The land-based missiles are located on Plateau d'Albion in Southern France and consist of one squadron of nine S-2 missiles and one squadron of nine S-3 missiles with a range of 3,000 miles. There are 33 Mirage IVA strategic bombers all capable of carrying AN-22 nuclear bombs. Compared to the strategic power, however, France's army, air force and navy, all equipped with the latest weapons, pale into insignificance. In the event of a limited nuclear conflict in Europe, France alone would be capable of nuclear response in order to prevent escalation, demonstrate resolve and affect termination.

Left:
An M-1 missile being launched from underwater with a range of 1,550 miles carrying a 500 kiloton nuclear warhead. In the search for further technical advance the French nuclear submarines have been provided with the M-2. M-20 and finally the M-4 with multiple warheads.

Inset center left:
A Super Etendard landing on an aircraft carrier.

Inset bottom:
French aircraft carrier *Foch* is the pride of the French Navy and part of the impressive equipment which the French armed forces possess.

Right:
NATO on alert. NATO ships patroling the Mediterranean Sea and Persian Gulf maintain a high level of alert. Here the USS *Nimitz* on exercises with ships from three other NATO countries.

Antisubmarine exercises continue. A helicopter dunks its sonar buoy while S2F and P2V submarine detection and attack aircraft fly past. Beyond the helicopters are the conventional submarines and antisumbarine destroyers.

North Atlantic Treaty Organization Command Structure

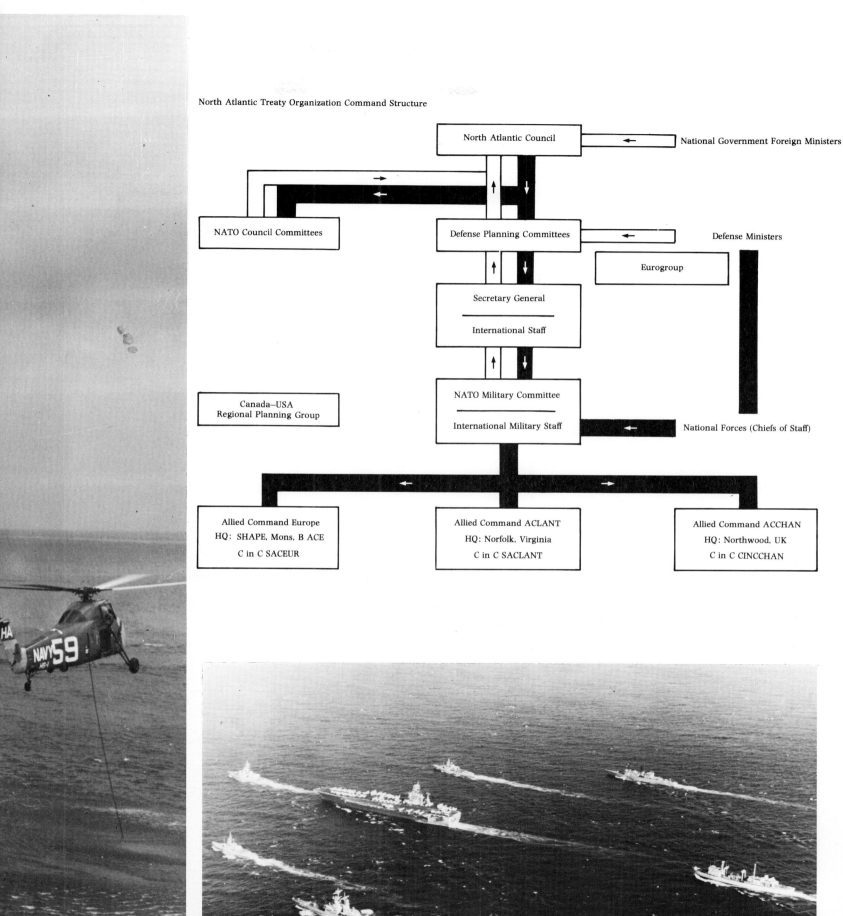

North Atlantic Council — National Government Foreign Ministers

NATO Council Committees

Defense Planning Committees — Defense Ministers

Eurogroup

Secretary General

International Staff

Canada–USA
Regional Planning Group

NATO Military Committee

International Military Staff — National Forces (Chiefs of Staff)

Allied Command Europe
HQ: SHAPE, Mons, B ACE
C in C SACEUR

Allied Command ACLANT
HQ: Norfolk, Virginia
C in C SACLANT

Allied Command ACCHAN
HQ: Northwood, UK
C in C CINCCHAN

FOR A THIRD WORLD WAR

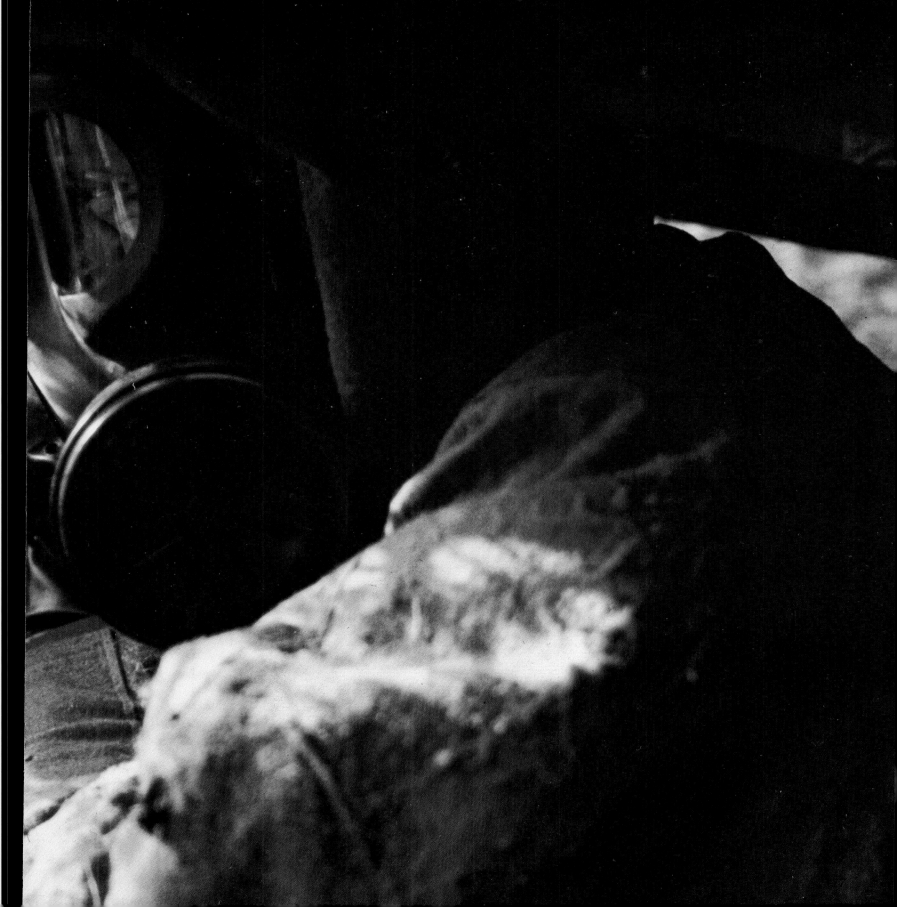

Both Super Powers have constructed broad general scenarios for a possible nuclear conflict; they also have contingency war plans. In America the principal concern of the largely academic strategic community has been deterrence. Nonetheless, many academic analysts have concerned themselves with the broad scenario for a strategic conflict and come to the conclusion that the causes of such a conflict would be complex political, economic, and military ones. Dr. Herman Kahn, in his *Thinking About the Unthinkable*, came to the conclusion that if the nuclear conflict did arise it would be most probably caused either by one major accident in a period of high international tension, or by several major accidents in sequence.

In the USSR, perhaps rather typically, nuclear war scenarios are part of military strategy and doctrine. The Soviet analysts (such as Marshal Sokolovsky) also conceive a nuclear conflict as arising out of a complex of political, economic,

A submarine-launched Cruise missile similar to the type that is suggested for basing in Western Europe. It has a range of 2,000 miles and assumes a low-level terrain matching missile.

and military factors. But once the point of a nuclear conflict is reached "doctrine recedes and strategy takes over"; as Sokolovsky put it "politics changes the pen for a sword." Henceforth the strategy of survival and victory takes over and that in Soviet strategic terms means (a) preemption, (b) mass in-depth strikes and (c) surprise use of nuclear weapons. Still even Sokolovsky admits that the decision to go to nuclear war would be political and that nuclear weapons and their direction would also be and remain under the top political authority. This means that primary objectives would be political and that allows for a possible limited nuclear conflict, though officially this concept does not exist.

Needless to say there exist many less realistic or purely speculative scenarios, particularly in the West. In the USSR such speculations are only possible in science fiction and outside that sphere such scenarios would be in conflict with a Soviet law on war propaganda. Thus one scenario elaborated by General Sir John Hackett invokes a massive Soviet invasion of Western Europe through Germany; Shelford Bidwell's invokes an invasion of Southern Europe through Yugoslavia. These invasions are sparked off by complex political causes: reunification of Germany; West German possession of nuclear weapons; serious disruption of NATO; the "trip wire" concept or "forward defense concept"; collapse of communist Poland. Necessarily these scenarios and causes as well as the sequence of the conflict itself are fictional, only loosely based on the facts of international politics and strategic studies. While the scenario that will be postulated here will also be fictional, its realistic basis is in the five preceding chapters.

The first problem with this scenario that has to be dealt with is the possibility of a full-scale strategic conflict. This would only be possible in conditions of deescalation of the strategic balance between the Super Powers, which no one postulates. However, as the graph on p 180 indicate there exists a balance of power between them both in strategic forces and their destructive power. This balance is therefore conducive to both declared US deterrence and undeclared Soviet deterrence. In fact the Soviet Union has the advantage in both the megatonnage and the so-called throw-weight of strategic weapons. However, considering that both Super Powers have accumulated so much destructive power as to achieve overkill, the MAD factor automatically operates and this mutually assured destruction element adds, if anything, to mutual deterrence. In the final analysis it seems unimportant whether the one Super Power is

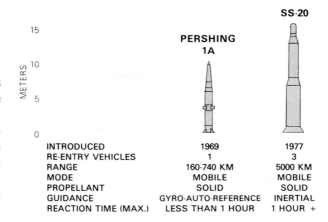

	PERSHING 1A	SS-20
INTRODUCED	1969	1977
RE-ENTRY VEHICLES	1	3
RANGE	160-740 KM	5000 KM
MODE	MOBILE	MOBILE
PROPELLANT	SOLID	SOLID
GUIDANCE	GYRO-AUTO-REFERENCE	INERTIAL
REACTION TIME (MAX.)	LESS THAN 1 HOUR	1 HOUR +

Characteristics of primary US and Soviet theater missiles.

capable of destroying planet Earth five times over, or the other 25 times. Thus a full-scale strategic conflict has to be eliminated.

Since there exists no probability of a full-scale strategic conflict all the strategic weapons likely to be employed in such a conflict can also be dismissed from our calculations: ICBMs, SLBMs and the strategic aviation of both the USA and USSR. As for the areas of a likely partial nuclear conflict the Far Eastern theater can also be eliminated: the USSR is roughly balanced in that area by communist China and US allies. In the Middle East the balance of power between the Super Powers is also established, especially after the US made it clear that the Gulf oil constitutes a vital interest, for which the Super Power would be prepared to go to war. In Africa neither Super Power has vital interests though confrontations in that continent do serve to increase international tension which is a pre-condition of any, however limited, conflict. The same condition pertains in so far as the rest of Asia is concerned; though Super Power confrontation in Southeast Asia, for example, considerably increases international tension. However, the most important factor behind the rise of any international tension lies in Latin America. Since the late 1950s the Super Powers have confronted each other over Cuba, which nonetheless remains a communist country, the only one so far in that continent. Historically the United States have been extremely sensitive about the continental sphere of influence and to put it mildly have always discouraged, particularly European powers, from "interfering" there. Cuba's adherence to communism and export of these ideas to other Latin American countries have been taken as examples of Soviet interference in American continental affairs. It is conceivable that the Super Powers could arrive at a similar strategic confrontation to that of 1962, but this now seems unlikely, since Cuba has renounced the possession of defensive nuclear weapons; also the Soviet Union has no need of Cuban silos, since it has fully developed its ICBMs. Therefore the political and strategic situation all over the world is not conducive to a strategic conflict.

It is, however, in Europe that political and military situations are most complex and most likely to lead to a conflict. The European situation is complex enough to enable us to discard from consideration the US strategic weapons based in the "forward positions": American SLBMs and strategic bombers based in Britain and Spain are thus eliminated. For similar reasons the British and French strategic deter-

rent forces can be excluded from consideration: they are four Resolution-class SSBNs each with 16 Polaris A3 missiles, each of which is in turn three-MIRVed; and five SSBNs each with 16 M-20 missiles. All these weapons are part of the Super Power balance of strategic power. However, the latest modernization of Soviet missile forces has brought a certain ambiguity and imbalance to Europe: since 1977 the Soviet Union has deployed in European Russia over 230 SS-20s, which are mobile missiles with three MIRVs and a range of 5,000km, which is far in excess of any NATO missile deployed in this area. Presently the only balancing factor in Europe (and for NATO) is the modernized French IRBM deterrent: nine SSBSs each carrying S-3 missile with a range of 3,000km.

Thus strategically speaking Europe is an unlikely cause of a full-scale nuclear confrontation between the Super Powers. However, it appears to be a veritable volcano in so far as theater nuclear forces and weapons are concerned. The imbalance in IRBMs between NATO and the Warsaw Pact appears most dangerous for an area known for unpredictability both politically and militarily. Thus, for example, the balancing factor on the Western side lies outside NATO and is in the hands of France, presently administered by a socialist-communist coalition. On the Soviet side it is clear that the use of SS-20s would be a political decision dictated by political developments within the Warsaw Pact. These two facts are therefore the most destabilizing factors in Europe and according to our scenario will have fatal consequences, when a conventional conflict breaks out as a result of political and military miscalculations on both sides.

In the 1980s the constatation of the nuclear imbalance in Europe produces an almost traumatic shock on the political leaders in Western Europe. After years of neglect, disregard of nuclear weapons and passive acceptance of the US nuclear umbrella NATO defense ministers agreed in December 1979 that this imbalance should be righted, and if by 1983 the Soviets continue deploying SS-20s NATO should deploy

COMPARATIVE NUCLEAR FORCES

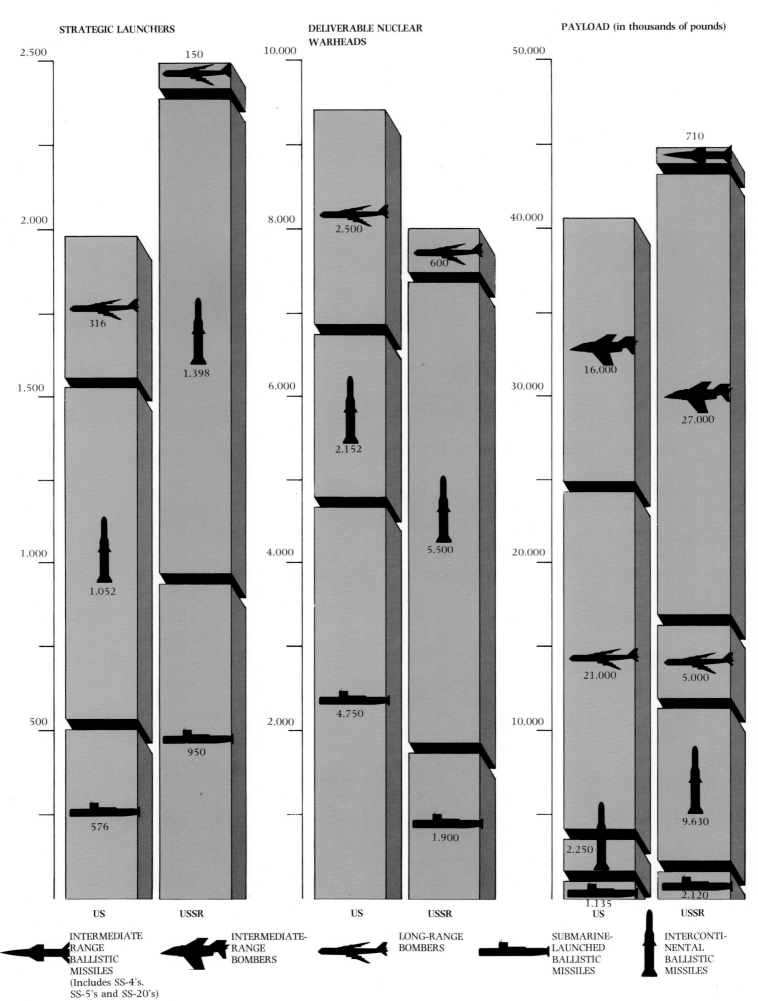

STRATEGIC LAUNCHERS

DELIVERABLE NUCLEAR WARHEADS

PAYLOAD (in thousands of pounds)

US · USSR

INTERMEDIATE RANGE BALLISTIC MISSILES (Includes SS-4's, SS-5's and SS-20's)

INTERMEDIATE-RANGE BOMBERS

LONG-RANGE BOMBERS

SUBMARINE-LAUNCHED BALLISTIC MISSILES

INTERCONTI-NENTAL BALLISTIC MISSILES

464 Tomahawk Cruise missiles and 108 Pershing 2 ballistic missiles in Europe. The Pershings which have a range of 1,288 miles would be deployed in West Germany and the Tomahawks with a range of 2,300 miles would be deployed in Britain (some 150 of them in US bases in East Anglia and Oxfordshire) as well as in Germany, Italy, Holland, and Belgium, if these countries agreed to the stationing of these weapons on their soil. However, almost immediately after these important stabilizing decisions were made, it became clear that a vast gap existed between Western political leadership and Western public opinion, which made the deployment of the balancing weapons problematic.

The peoples of Western Europe had become

Above:
An artist's impression of Pershing 2 being launched.

Below:
A nuclear-powered Polaris submarine.

Left:
A Tomahawk Cruise missile takes to the air.

Above:
CND Campaign for Nuclear Disarmament March in London, 1981. Over 100,000 joined in and a mass rally was held with several prominent politicians speaking.

Above right:
The SS-20 and SS-4 nuclear missiles are replacing the now aging SS-9 seen here.

failing, and under popular pressure perhaps falling apart.

In face of this mass European opposition the Americans tried to put a brave face on their military policies in NATO and Europe. At first they attempted to ignore these demonstrations or get round them by accusing the organizers of either being communists or naive fellow travelers. However, when senior churchmen backed the anti-nuclear movements, they were forced to change their attitudes. First they attempted to call the Soviet bluff by proposing not to deploy the new IRBMs in Europe, if the USSR dismantled the existing ones and deployed SS-20s and SS-4s and SS-5s. Since neither the USSR nor the NATO allies took these proposals seriously and rather dismissed them as "obvious propaganda," the US reaction became negative. Old isolationist ideas were voiced with increasing frequency. Thus the American ambassador in Bonn gave the West Germans a lecture on the tremendous utility of NATO over the past 35 years. US senators raised questions in Congress and some proposed to cut American commitments in Europe by half in order to force the missile issue. Many more Congressmen renewed their interest in the past policy of isolationism and Fortress America views had a new currency. Excitement over the nuclear issue seems to have affected even the President who declared with what appeared to many Europeans as malicious poignancy that there could be a limited nuclear war in Europe without it escalating to an exchange of strategic intercontinental ballistic missiles. Though the Soviet President immediately disclaimed this possibility both the Warsaw Pact and NATO were greatly confused, neither alliance being sure of the intentions of the Super Powers in Europe.

To the political confusion in the West and the virtual collapse of NATO must be added an even greater political confusion in the East. At first this was thought to be beneficial: it was argued that since NATO ceased to exist, it would be good for the peace in Europe if the Warsaw Pact fared likewise. Strong indications arrived from the East, particularly from Poland, Rumania, and the peripheral Yugoslavia, that the Eastern alliance was also dissolving as a result of political confusion. In Rumania economic failure forced the Rumanian communist leaders to look for scapegoats both from inside and outside the country. The Rumanian president, Ceaucescu, first blamed his fellow communists for failing to live up to the tasks that their leading positions demanded of them. He mercilessly purged them, but then gave their jobs not to newly discovered non-communist experts, but to mem-

deeply suspicious of American foreign policy and instead of thinking of their future security the nations of Europe shocked their political leadership by rejecting the nuclear plans. While in the 1970s only the extreme left had opposed nuclear missiles. The various peace movements and nuclear protest groups of the 1980s have attracted mass following. In Britain the Labour Party approved unilateral disarmament as its policy at its annual conferences. In London some 250,000 marched to support such policies as well as protesting against nuclear missiles. In Italy and France, anti-nuclear demonstrations organized by the communist parties in October 1981 attracted even larger numbers than in Britain. In Belgium and Holland churches and conservative elements were involved in such manifestations of opposition to nuclear arms in Europe. In West Germany over 250,000 people converged on Bonn, the capital, and made it abundantly clear that even the most faithful member of NATO had within it a mass opposition to nuclear weapons, be they in the West or the East. Curiously these anti-nuclear protests were also staged in Rumania, a member of the Warsaw Pact, thus indicating that not only NATO, but also the Warsaw Pact alliance, was

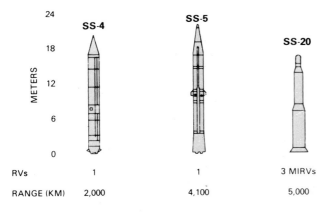

	SS-4	SS-5	SS-20
RVs	1	1	3 MIRVs
RANGE (KM)	2,000	4,100	5,000

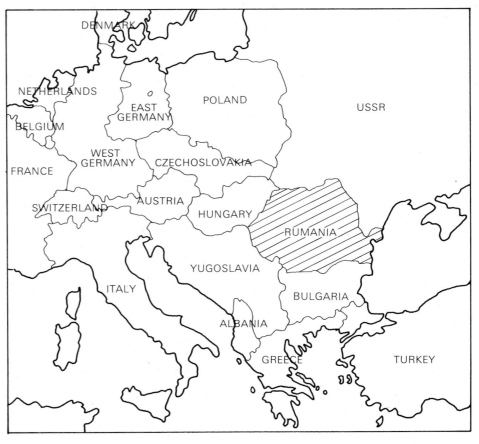

bers of his wide family circle. The Rumanian internal power struggle was exciting increasing hostility in the USSR, making it certain that allied communist countries of Eastern Europe would not help the Rumanian president with his internal difficulties. As if to avenge himself for the lack of allied support the President embarked on a totally independent course in foreign affairs. Rumania decided to refuse to spend any more money on defense and by mass demonstrations for a nuclear free zone in Europe politically confused other Warsaw Pact countries.

However, in the face of continuing bread and meat shortages and under the pretext that the Warsaw Pact had denied any help, Rumania refused to honor its economic obligations within Comecon, the Warsaw Pact's common market. This act set in motion a series of crises throughout Eastern Europe which aggravated the political, economic, and military confusion.

In the early 1980s the situation in Yugoslavia was similar to that in Rumania: the country felt itself isolated because it did not belong to either bloc and consequently neither side was keen to help politically or economically. The country's economy was failing, inflation increasing at an alarming pace; its barely concealed unemployment became more and more obvious. The economic crisis was more acute in the northern parts of the Yugoslav federation hitting hard the prosperous Croat and Slovene populations and economic difficulties were producing political discontent, for these nationalities had long been dissatisfied with the communist arrangement by which the prosperous north had been obliged to invest in the underdeveloped south. Open nationalist rioting in Kossovo was mercilessly repressed but mass nationalist demonstrations in the north could not be controlled even by the army and Yugoslavia slid into chaos similar to that of neighboring Rumania.

If the economic situation was better in East Germany, Czechoslovakia, and particularly in Hungary, it was far from satisfactory. East Germany also had its shortages which could be exploited and taken advantage of by the workers, who were more than willing to follow the example of the neighboring Polish workers.

Below:
The Gdansk Lenin Shipyard from which the independent Trade Union "Solidarity" emerged.

In Czechoslovakia, apart from economic confusion, provoked above all by the collapse of the Polish and Rumanian economies, a dissident communist group was causing anxiety among the communist leaders and confusion among the rank and file. The die-hard president insisted on rearmament, which, fanned by increases in energy prices, forced price rises and inflation in the country. In these circumstances this politically most reliable Warsaw Pact ally became a potential powder keg of destabilization. In Hungary though economically in the most strong position, dissident political rumblings boded no good for the Warsaw Pact, and the unpredictable Bulgaria remained in enigmatic stability.

However the dissolution of the bloc and the consequent Soviet reaction was in the final analysis the result of developments in Poland. In the early 1980s the communist leader, Stanislaw Kania, failed to arrest the demoralization and decomposition of the Polish communist party, not to mention solve the Polish economic crisis. General Jaruzelski, who succeeded Kania, then attempted to come to terms with the Solidarity trade union which represented the Polish workers and with the Roman Catholic Church which appeared to represent practically the entire Polish population. Negotiations which dragged over several months proved fruitless. The Communist Party was anxious to ameliorate, if not solve, the economic crisis into which it had led the Polish nation during 35 years of incompetent rule. It saw in its solution the only chance for itself to retain power, which it was most reluctant to relinquish to the new forces which the protracted crisis brought up. The Church acted, throughout crisis negotiations, as a mediator, now admonishing Solidarity, now warning the Communist Party. Even skillful negotiations proved incapable of resolving such deep economic conflicts and while negotiations lasted the Western allies, and particularly West Germany, were most willing to help Poland financially as well as with food and energy. Every time negotiations reached a turning point at which the Polish Communist Party would hand supreme power to Solidarity, the threat of Soviet military intervention was evoked and the hand over postponed. Solidarity aimed at a peaceful transition; it wanted to make the communists agree to a really free election so that the country could be ruled by a representative coalition, including the Communist Party. Such a government would not only attract massive Western aid but would also solve the internal political and economic crisis by the amount of confidence and good will it would

create in Poland. The communist leaders tried to postpone such a solution as long as they could, especially before their last instruments of power, the army and the police, melted away under their very eyes. However, after Poland was threatened by a famine coupled with energy shortage, the communist leaders finally gave up and prepared to hand over power.

Nothing in Poland could be done without Soviet approval and the Soviet Union had a long history of deciding everything that mattered in Poland by itself. At first it seemed that the Soviet Union would acquiesce to the Polish Communist Party submitting itself to the test of a free election. When, however, several leading Polish communists appealed to the fraternal Soviet Communist Party not to allow them to be "executed and buried by the Polish reactionaries," the Soviet politburo was forced into making unpalatable decisions. It was thought to be high time for such decisions, not only on Poland but also the entire Soviet hegemony. Whatever decisions were made and whatever actions taken, they would only affect the Soviet hegemony and therefore not cause a strategic confrontation or conflict; after all there were historical precedents for such Soviet intervention in its hegemony. In 1953 Soviet tanks had restored the German Democratic Republic, after the counterrevolutionaries had tried to seize power. In 1956 in a truly genocidal power act the Soviet armies had crushed the rebellious, national-communist régime in Hungary. In 1968 the mildly reformist Dubcek régime had been snuffed out of existence in Czechoslovakia by a massive invasion of some 250,000 Soviet and Warsaw Pact troops, including Polish troops. Since the developments in Poland violated Soviet ideological concepts on the irreversibility of communism, it had to be resolved, not by ideological, but power means.

Long discussions preceded the Soviet decision to intervene in Poland; more discussions followed as to the shape of the intervention. The virtual collapse of the Warsaw Pact appeared as an additional reason for the intervention: under the terms of the pact the Soviet armies, which were also stationed in Poland, had a legal right to intervene. But by the time the decision to intervene was reached this legal right was practically non-existent and would be resisted not only by the Poles, but also by other members of the Warsaw Pact, above all by Rumania. This consideration made the Soviet politburo realize that its intervention in Poland had to be extended to the whole Pact with Yugoslavia added for good measure. The Soviets reasoned that communism was in equal danger from im-

Russian tanks cross the Czechoslovak border during the 1968 invasion.

perialism in all these countries, albeit their communist parties have not yet started handing over power voluntarily to the domestic agents of Western imperialism. Thus ideological considerations led to political decisions which in turn had to be carried out by military means.

At this stage the Soviet politburo called in its military leaders. Marshal Ustinov, Defense Minister, had already participated in the discussions which led to the political decision to restore the power stability of the Soviet hegemony. He now directed his military chiefs to put before the politburo the military options for the intervention and also acquaint it with the existing contingency plans. It was obvious to both the political and military leaders that a military operation of such magnitude, with so many unforeseeable risks, had to be well planned and even better executed. In 1979 the political and military leaders had faced and resolved a

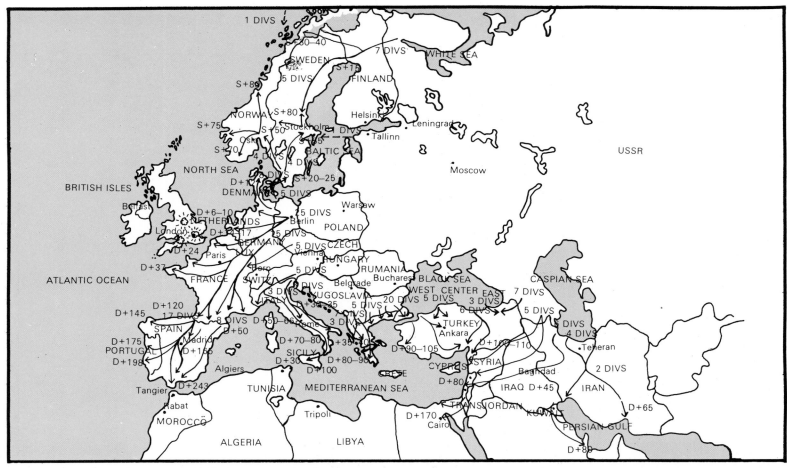

Map labels (as shown on the map):

1 DIVS · S+80-40 · 7 DIVS · WHITE SEA · SWEDEN · S+15 · FINLAND · 5 DIVS · S+80 · NORWAY · S+80 · Helsinki · Leningrad · USSR · S+75 · S+50 · Stockholm · 1 DIVS · Oslo · Tallinn · S+70 · BALTIC SEA · 4 DIVS · NORTH SEA · 4 DIVS · Moscow · BRITISH ISLES · D+10 · S+20-25 · Belfast · DENMARK · 5 DIVS · Warsaw · D+6-10 · NETHERLANDS · Berlin · 5 DIVS · London · POLAND · D+24 · GERMANY · 5 DIVS · CZECH · D+24 · Paris · Vienna · 5 DIVS · HUNGARY · D+37 · FRANCE · SWITZ · 5 DIVS · RUMANIA · ATLANTIC OCEAN · Bern · 5 DIVS · Belgrade · Bucharest · BLACK SEA · CASPIAN SEA · 3 DIVS · YUGOSLAVIA · WEST CENTER EAST · 7 DIVS · D+120 · ITALY · 5 DIVS · 20 DIVS 5 DIVS 3 DIVS · D+145 · 17 DIVS · 8 DIVS · D+34-35 · 6 DIVS · 5 DIVS · SPAIN · D+50 · 3 DIVS · TURKEY · 5 DIVS · D+175 · Madrid · D+70-80 · Ankara · 4 DIVS · PORTUGAL · D+155 · SICILY · D+35 · D+100-110 · Teheran · D+198 · Algiers · D+30 · D+80-90 · D+90-105 · CYPRUS · SYRIA · Baghdad · 2 DIVS · Tangier · D+243 · TUNISIA · MEDITERRANEAN SEA · CRETE · D+80 · IRAQ D+45 · IRAN · Rabat · Tripoli · D+170 · TRANSJORDAN · KUWAIT · D+65 · MOROCCO · Cairo · PERSIAN GULF · ALGERIA · LIBYA · D+80

Right:
A detailed view of the Soviet invasion plan for Western Europe.

Above:
An overview of the Soviet invasion plan for Western Europe.

similar situation in Afghanistan: the country was a self-proclaimed communist system, was not part of the Soviet buffer, was of no strategic significance — notwithstanding, after long deliberation and on military advice, the Soviet army was permitted to launch a brilliantly executed, armed intervention, which has since kept in power the communist faction of President Karmal. Nothing followed this invasion of a non-aligned country: detente with the United States was dead anyway; the Third World protests quickly petered out and only a few paper resolutions by mainly Eurocommunist parties disturbed this power takeover by the USSR.

However the Soviet military leaders were quick to point out that large-scale military operations conducted all over Eastern Europe would be a different problem, even if the political leaders guaranteed American political and strategic non-interference. First of all, the military operation against Poland had to be carried out by the troops from Soviet military districts, the Byelorussian and the Carpathian ones with the Baltic fleet cooperating (this operation had been rehearsed in the fall of 1980). Likewise the operations against Rumania and its extension to Yugoslavia, had to be undertaken by the Southwestern and Odessa military district forces. The most dangerous part of this operation codenamed *Warsaw Pact* was a preventative invasion of Western Germany and possibly parts of Western Europe beyond Germany, by Soviet forces in Eastern Germany

under the Warsaw Pact command. The Soviet military leaders claimed that without this preventative strike Operation Warsaw Pact would be impossible.

The politburo took a long time to consider the political implications of this military demand. It was convinced that the USA would not be provoked by an internal hegemonial affair. But it had to decide whether the US would get involved in a conventional conflict in Europe, when it flared up following the Soviet preemptive conventional strike. It was recognized that the situation was different from that in Afghanistan. Nonetheless it was thought that the risk involved in invading West Germany was justified: (1) Soviet invasion would follow an appeal launched by the West German communist party inviting the USSR's fraternal aid against German reactionaries and militarists; (2) the ostensible objectives of the Soviet intervention in West Germany would be the restoration of law and order and freedom in that country; (3) since the invasion was not directed against NATO forces in Germany they would be bidden to withdraw from Germany (mainly British, American, and Belgium troops) to avoid the fighting; (4) since NATO was virtually dead no military complication was expected from that quarter. Reassured by the politburo decision to proceed the military leaders agreed to carry out this politically-inspired operation, after due military preparation.

The Soviet Marshals and Army generals had no need for lengthy preparations for the operation within the Soviet hegemony in

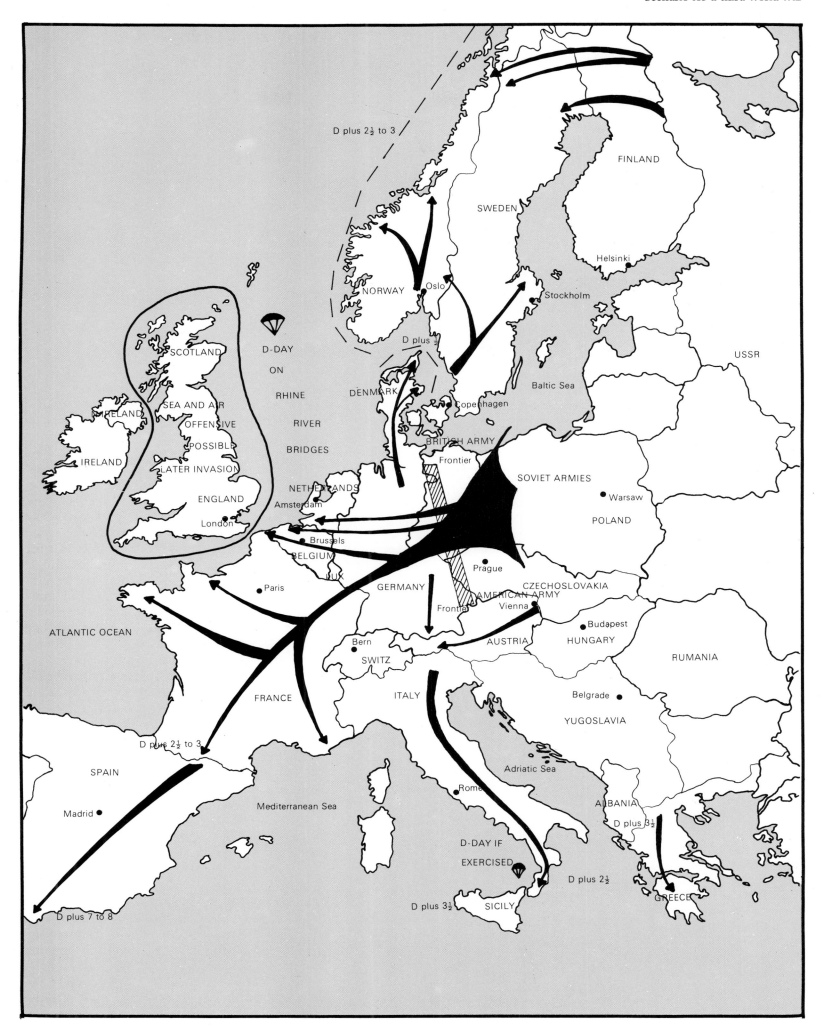

D plus 2½ to 3

D-DAY
ON
RHINE
RIVER
BRIDGES

SCOTLAND

N IRELAND

SEA AND AIR
OFFENSIVE

IRELAND

POSSIBLE
LATER INVASION

ENGLAND

London

NETHERLANDS

Amsterdam

Brussels

BELGIUM

LUX

NORWAY

Oslo

D plus ½

DENMARK

Copenhagen

BRITISH ARMY

Frontier

FINLAND

Helsinki

SWEDEN

Stockholm

Baltic Sea

USSR

SOVIET ARMIES

Warsaw

POLAND

Paris

GERMANY

Prague

CZECHOSLOVAKIA

AMERICAN ARMY

Vienna

Frontier

Budapest

HUNGARY

RUMANIA

ATLANTIC OCEAN

Bern

SWITZ

AUSTRIA

FRANCE

ITALY

Belgrade

YUGOSLAVIA

D plus 2½ to 3

SPAIN

Madrid

Mediterranean Sea

Adriatic Sea

Rome

ALBANIA

D plus 3½

D-DAY IF
EXERCISED

D plus 2½

GREECE

D plus 7 to 8

D plus 3½

SICILY

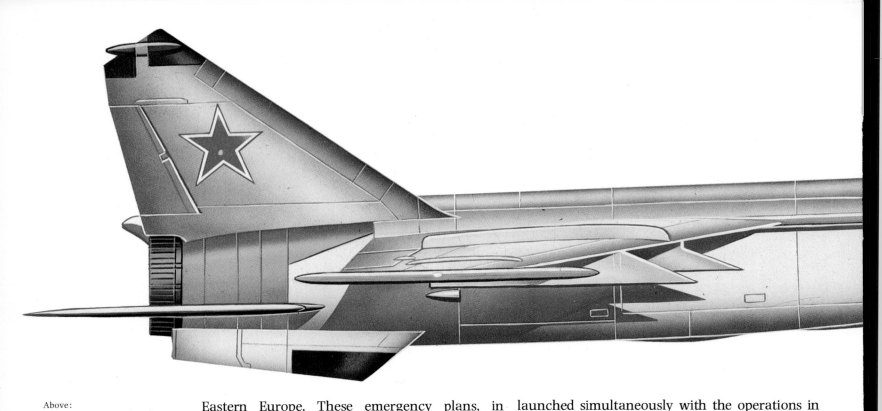

Eastern Europe. These emergency plans, in existence since the late 1940s and prepared on Premier Stalin's orders, were familiar even to the new Soviet commanders and had been rehearsed from time to time by Soviet troops. In the late 1960s an addendum was affixed to them concerning the restoration of Yugoslavia to orthodox communism; in 1979 this addition to the emergency plans was rehearsed by mobile Soviet troops on the plains of Hungary. With the exception of Poland no hard military resistance was anticipated by Soviet military leaders; even in Poland it was thought that initial resistance would rapidly collapse by doubly demoralized Polish troops. Rumania and Yugoslavia were obviously politically demoralized, but in addition their armies were no match for the Soviet forces largely because of the miserable state of training and equipment, which was not the case of Poland, hence the concentration on this part of the operation.

The invasion of West Germany was to be launched simultaneously with the operations in Eastern Europe. Though the Soviet command knew that the existing contingency plans for this invasion were known to the Americans and therefore to their German ally, they were forced to make use of them, for no alternatives existed. The Soviet command counted on the element of surprise to compensate for the Western pre-knowledge of such plans. This contingency plan was indeed grandiose and envisaged a three-pronged invasion of Northern, Central, and Southern Europe ultimately leading to the occupation of entire Europe, Britain including. Details of the Northern operation were well known in the West: "S-Day is considered to be the day hostilities commence against Norway and Sweden. (It is believed that S-Day will not be concurrent with D-Day). In the event that the Soviets deem it necessary to attack Norway and Sweden, it is estimated that the USSR has the capability of overrunning Norway and Sweden as indicated . . ." (S+70 and S+80 days). "Although Soviet capabilities against Norway and Sweden are of the magnitude as indicated (12 mechanized divisions) it is believed that the Soviets would make every effort to ensure the initial neutrality of both countries by diplomatic pressure and military threat. . . ." Both Soviet political and military leaders agreed to engage the latter variant of the plan.

In the south the plan involved the Soviets in very complex operations against Italy, Greece, and Turkey. However, the execution of the southern operation was thought indispensable both for the success of the central operation as well as the internal hegemony operations against Rumania and Yugoslavia. The southern thrust would be executed by 27 Soviet divisions, most of them coming from the Kiev and Odessa command, after accomplishing their hegemonial

mission. Although this operation was to start simultaneously with the central one, because of its subsidiary value its times of completion were over S + 100 by which time the central thrust was to have subdued most of France, complete the occupation of the Netherlands, Belgium, and Denmark. The delay in the completion of the southern operations was also caused by anticipated logistic difficulties and rough terrain conditions in Yugoslavia, Greece, and Turkey.

Soviet invasion of West Germany in the central sector was planned on an impressive scale, in the shape of a three-pronged thrust. In the northern sector, in the area of 2nd Guards Tank Army, five Soviet armored divisions, would thrust westward and when they reached Schleswig-Holstein would swing northward deep into Denmark. In the southern sector, in the area of Central Group and Czechoslovak army, the combined group of 15 armored and mechanized divisions would thrust southwesterly through Bavaria, in the general direction of Switzerland. In the central sector main forces for the Soviet invasion would be concentrated in East Germany and would include the elements of the 2nd Guard Tank Army, 1st Guard Tank Army and 20th, 3rd and 8th Guards and Shock Armies as well as the Volksarmee. The thrust of this mighty army group ran along the Berlin-Paris axis. Subsidiary thrusts would enable the Soviets to overrun Holland by D + 6–10, Belgium D + 14–17 and occupy Paris D + 24.

The Soviet contingency plan also contained, in supporting role, tactical aviation. Although Soviet tactical aviation consists of 195,000 men, 5,300 aircraft and 1,000 armed helicopters, only four tactical air armies with 2,000 aircraft were deployed in Eastern Europe; the 16th based in East Germany was the best trained and equipped. Soviet air armies are composed of air regiments each usually consisting of one type of

aircraft. Thus there were regiments flying Soviet fighters (ground attack): MiG-21s (code-word Fishbed), MiG-23 (Floggers), SU-7s (Fitter), Su-17 (Fitter C/D/H), Su-24s (Fencer), Yak-28s (Brewer) and the latest Su-RAM-Js which are being deployed. MiG-21 (Fishbed C/D/F) and MiG-23 (Flogger) fighters are complemented by helicopters of Mi-1/2/4/6/8 type with the latest Mi-24 (Hind) type also deployed in Eastern Europe. Two Czechoslovak air armies with 471 combat aircraft (mainly MiG-21s and MiG-23s), two East German air divisions with 359 combat aircraft (mainly MiG-17s and MiG-23s) and four Polish air divisions with 705 combat aircraft (mainly MiG-17s and MiG-21s) bolster the Warsaw Pact deployment in Eastern Europe to some 3,500 aircraft as compared to some 2,500 deployed by NATO. Tactical aviation is trained to support ground operations as well as attack the enemy. In this contingency plan tactical aviation was to enhance the surprise factor which was so much required for the successful

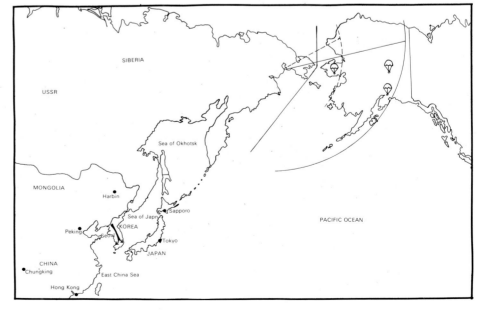

The Soviet plan for the invasion of the Far East. This is to take place at the same time as an invasion of Europe but is of less importance.

189

execution of the plan.

Soviet military leaders briefed the politburo in person and after further deliberation the politburo fixed the D-Day of Operation Warsaw Pact. It was further decided that the United States president would be informed of the outbreak of hostilities in Europe over the Hot Line after the Soviet attacks. Soviet ambassadors in Bonn, London, and Paris would warn these countries of Soviet actions and explain their causes: Western imperialism, particularly the West German one, has subverted Soviet Warsaw Pact allies, particularly Poland. The USSR has decided, in defense of communism, to strike against imperialist forces and destroy them for ever.

For several weeks prior to the Soviet invasion KGB's disinformation department was waging an intense propaganda war. Western European public was bombarded with gross overstatements of Soviet strategic power, while rumors were artificially circulated according to which the United States had definitely abandoned their "umbrella" responsibilities in Europe. Europe was left in the lurch by the US. Western European

defense was nought when compared to Soviet strategic power. Moreover European communist parties were exhorted to prepare for an early collapse of Western capitalism; when the state structures crashed down the communist élite groups were to take over the governments of Western Europe. Soviet propaganda reported that the French right was going to stage a coup against the socialist-communist coalition; in Britain widespread confusion ruled in consequence of violent demonstrations and armed clashes between extreme right and left; in West Germany the neo-nazis seized the control of the Bundeswehr, which constituted another provocation of the peaceloving forces in the USSR and East Germany. As a result of false rumors asserting that all immigrant workers would be forcibly transported back to their countries of origin widespread civil disorders broke out in Britain, France, and West Germany; in Belgium and Holland disorders broke out on a smaller scale. The whole of Western Europe was in an uproar and utterly confused, especially when some of the rumors turned out to be true.

Alongside this propaganda campaign a whole

series of border incidents took place. In East Germany along the border with West Germany the barbed wire fencing was dismantled, mine-fields cleared and numerous East German and Soviet motorized patrols strayed into West Germany. Such border incidents were occurring daily on such a scale, and not only in Germany but also on the Czechoslovak, Austrian, Yugo-slav, and even Finnish and Norwegian borders, as to cause complete muddle in national command as well as in NATO. The West was registering these incursions, but not even protesting; such was the state of confusion and lack of co-ordination. In outer space a whole series of mysterious accidents took place: usually Soviet and US communication and surveillance satel-lites colliding. The satellites relaying the Moscow-Washington Hot Line, equally mysteriously, avoided collision. Soviet aircraft were sighted all over the world, even in New Zealand, which all the same seemed highly improbable. But all of this was part of the Soviet war plans to confuse, demoralize and misinform the enemy.

In this atmosphere of total chaos the American president refused to believe his own intelligence service which reported to him that an un-specified military operation was being planned and prepared in the USSR, not directed against the US. Seeing the widespread disorders reported from Eastern Europe, especially from Poland, Rumania, and Yugoslavia, it was generally believed that if Soviet military moves did take place, they would be directed against these countries. Western European countries came to believe the same despite the growing numbers of reports by senior Warsaw Pact deserters asserting that the USSR was preparing an invasion of Western Europe. Moreover the US and Western Europe were in the grip of annual holidays, when virtually every one who mattered was away, especially from the defense establish-ments where only skeleton staffs were main-tained. Defense computer systems had not yet recovered fully from a recent government strike. To compound Western confusion Soviet leaders failed to deploy their Ocean fleets; they were not even put in a state of alert. The observed low-alert state of Soviet strategic forces was main-tained throughout and the few surveillance satellites, which were still circling the earth, after the spate of reported accidents, developed an inexplicable type of interference, and failed to alert the West to the mighty concentrations of Soviet conventional forces.

If total confusion reigned in Western Europe, the Warsaw Pact countries and Yugoslavia were possibly even more disoriented. In Poland it was not clear who was in power, who issued

orders and who was running the country. The bulk of the population in any case was enjoying summer holidays, despite food shortages. In Rumania party leaders were in their villas on the Black sea coast, while in Yugoslavia only the current president was in the country, while the rest of the political leaders were sampling holidays in capitalist countries. Populations were further confused, if not panicked, by several war scare campaigns, according to which the West German Wehrmacht had invaded Poland, Yugoslavia, and Rumania in that order, without declaring war, exactly as Hitler had done in 1941. Defense forces were badly demoralized by these false rumors, and also badly displaced, since military leaders acted on these rumors regrouping their national forces to face a Western invader. Under the pretext of man-euvers and "reacting" to the rumors of Western invasion, the Soviet high command launched the Operation Warsaw Pact at 6am of D-Day, fixed previously by the Soviet politburo.

On that day the forces of the Soviet military districts, Byelorussia and Carpathia, and South-western and Odessa, formed themselves into the northern and southern War Theater Command and launched their operations, the one against Poland, the other against Rumania and Yugo-slavia. The Byelorussian group, consisting of nine tank and two motor rifle divisions, was concentrated along the Eastern Polish border; its mission was to strike toward Warsaw, and on reaching a northern point near the city swing southward to take the Polish capital in the historical, Russian manner. The Carpathian group, consisting of two tank and nine motor rifle divisions, concentrated along the South-eastern Polish border, was to strike northwest-ward, across Southern Poland, with its objec-tives Cracow and Wrócaw. Both groups were supported by tactical air armies each flying over

Above:
Tourtine flight patrols are sent out from the USS *Nimitz*. Here F-14 Tomcats are launched to patrol the Iranian border.

500 aircraft. These meticulously rehearsed operations were carried out by enthusiastic command and men with the most ruthless efficiency witnessed in 1979 in Afghanistan, and now repeated in the country toward which the Byelorussian and Ukrainian troops felt historical hostility. This indeed was the repetition of Hitler's Blitzkrieg, except that its end was even swifter. The country was crushed and occupied within one week and only a few elements of Polish air force succeeded in escaping from Poland by flying West thus increasing confusion there even more. The Polish high command deserted the country and went over to the Soviet invading forces *en masse*, after it had lost control over the Polish armed forces. Resistance against the Soviet invader was unorganized, but some units, especially the Polish paratroopers, put up a spirited fight, only to disperse, but not surrender, after they had exhausted their ammunition. The surprise was such that even the free Polish trade unions

To confuse intelligence-gathering agencies the Soviet Fleet maintains routine levels of readiness. The *Kiev* even goes back to its home port in the Baltic.

had no time to call for a general strike; the Polish population was simply unable to resist. Soviet occupation authorities immediately put into power a new Polish government, consisting largely of the old discredited communist leaders.

In the south the Soviet forces' mission was not to restore a communist government, but rather occupy Rumania and Yugoslavia militarily, in order to insure the security of the Soviet hegemony. At 6am of D-Day the combined forces of the southern war theater, consisting of seven tank and 10 motor rifle divisions, burst into

Soviet APCs move troops forward to positions on the front.

Rumania from their concentrations along its Eastern border. The surprise was total and no armed resistance was offered by Rumanian armed forces, which in any case were confined to barracks or in holiday camp. The dash for Bucharest resembled a joy ride; the Soviet armies, however, did not halt there but continued their drive toward the Yugoslav border. Their objective was Belgrade: after overrunning Rumania only token troops were left behind and the rest was concentrated against Yugoslavia. This attack was launched on D+5, while that country was previously invaded from the north by two tank and two motor rifle divisions stationed in Hungary. Yugoslav armed forces disintegrated into national units which instead of fighting the invader withdrew to their respective province, dissolving in the process. A leading member of the Soviet politburo was dispatched to both countries to negotiate with the communist leadership the voluntary stationing of the Soviet troops there. As in Poland Soviet operations were carried out most efficiently and both countries were fully occupied

Soviet troops establish positions in Yugoslavia.

on D+7. As the Soviet military leaders had predicted these operations within the hegemony (though Yugoslavia was outside) were a complete success with hardly any blood spilled. All three countries were caught unaware and struck with such overwhelming force that they yielded without practical resistance.

There was great satisfaction in Moscow at the outcome of this part of Operation Warsaw Pact; in fact the developments in Germany seemed to be going well, according to the plans, at least up to D+7. At 6am D-Day Soviet, East German, and Czechoslovak forces attacked specially selected points all along the West German and Austrian borders. During the preceding night sabotage commando groups, consisting of local communists as well as infiltrated agents, went into action attacking military and communication centers, police stations, fire brigade headquarters, railroad points, as well as power stations. Surprise was fully effective as not even duty officers were often at their posts. However the wave of sabotage acts was so overwhelmingly effective that it completely isolated the Western military command. This was the first unexpected and unplanned result of Operation Warsaw Pact: the political masters of the NATO command could not issue orders for

midable weapons. South of this sector was the central sector, pivot of the Soviet offensive, where the 3rd Shock Army, 2nd Guard Tank Army, 8th Guard Army and 1st Guard Tank Army were concentrated to deliver the most withering strike attack against central Germany. The two tank and four motor rifle divisions of the Volksarmee were not deployed westward, but rather shielded the rear of these two sectors facing Poland. In the southern sector seven tank and six motor rifle divisions were concentrated in the Cheb area for a drive to Nuremberg and in general direction to Switzerland. Even this relatively minor sector disposed of over 3,000 tanks, most of them T-64s. All these forces launched their attacks simultaneously and only in the southern sector was there no striking initial success, largely because the terrain was too heavy for tanks and the Czechoslovak divisions fought without enthusiasm.

Soviet armored thrusts were preceded by bombing and artillery preparations. Since NATO and local German communications were hopelessly disrupted all the Allied commanders decided on their own to resist Soviet invasion most vigorously and with all means at their disposal, until such time when higher command might order otherwise. The first wave of assault was made up of the formidable T-64s and T-72s with a few T-80s scattered among them. Although the German border forces resisted valiantly they were overrun within hours and the second-wave troops, mainly motorized infantry supported by their tanks made penetrations up to 10 miles deep. It was some two hours after the outbreak of hostilities that all NATO forces in Germany were alerted and directed by local commanders to the three points of the Soviet invasion. It was thought that this confusion and lack of coordination would favor the attacking Soviet forces; soon however it transpired that it would also work the other way round. Thus, in the southern sector, Soviet tanks

German border forces offer useless resistance.

surrender, even if they wanted to, and it was part of the Soviet plan that this should be so.

Soviet forces in East Germany, which amounted to nine tank divisions (two tank divisions from Poland went to reinforce the southern sector which consisted of two tank and three motor rifle divisions stiffened with three Czechoslovak tank and motor rifle divisions) and 10 motor rifle divisions, were concentrated at three points for attack. In the north in the area of Eberswald was 20th Guards Army which was to attack in the direction of Hamburg and then swing northward. This army had only 1,100 tanks, but they were almost all the T-72s, most for-

blundered into the path of 1st and 4th German Bundeswehr divisions, which were being rushed into the sector to stem the Soviet breakthrough. After heavy fighting Soviet tank penetrations were temporarily blocked, but after suffering immense casualties the German divisions were obliged to withdraw from the battlefield and regroup. A similar situation arose in the central sector, where the armored penetration was deepest, and where British reinforcements, the 6th and 20th Brigade ran into the armored elements of the 3rd Shock army. Once again the shock of the unexpected British brigade blunted slightly Soviet tank penetration, but after several hours of hopeless fighting the brigade practically ceased to exist. Still by D+2 all three invading task forces had achieved their objectives and were deep in West German territory. The 20th Guard Army was the most successful of them all; its tanks went through the 6th Bundeswehr division like a knife through butter and the eastern suburbs of Hamburg were in sight toward the end of D+2.

NATO's tactical aviation was out of action throughout the first two days of the invasion.

Sabotage groups were particularly successful on the airfields where communications were completely destroyed and many aircraft disabled in hangars. It appears that a particularly important number of communist agents penetrated and infiltrated airfield security; most of the civilian employees were in fact communist agents. Miraculously a majority of the NATO ground-to-air missiles remained undamaged and were used against the tactical bombers at the start of hostilities. That was the apparent reason why Soviet tactical aviation appeared subsequently so inactive. On NATO's side communications in the area under attack were reestablished, more or less, and erratically at that, by the end of D+2. Henceforth both sides would try and fight regular battles. As for the political battles nothing was known of them on the battlefields. To all purposes Germany was cut off from the rest of the world. What, however, was fairly obvious was that the Soviet invasion was taken as a limited war, of local significance, a by-product of the forceful Soviet tidying up in Eastern Europe.

During the subsequent five days (up to D+7)

battles were raging all over Germany, both sides suffering heavy casualties. Thus, on D+3, the US 2nd division sent to meet the armored column of the 1st Tank Guards, stopped its advance, but when the bulk of the Soviet armor reached the battle area, they simply blasted the hapless 2nd division from the ground. Subsequently the US 8th division met a similar fate in a different sector. In the central sector Soviet advance still continued though not at the planned speed. Only in the southern sector were the Western allies more successful: the 1st and 10th Bundeswehr divisions were rushed to Nuremberg to bar the penetration of the weakest, mixed Soviet-Czechoslovak force. As if by miracle several air force bases in Baden-Würtemberg were preserved intact and after two days of confusion both American and German aircraft were launched on first reconnaissance missions and went up to Nuremberg in support of the Bundeswehr. After attacking several armored columns, Allied aircraft noticed that movements in this sector abruptly stopped. As the advance Soviet tanks reached the area of Nuremberg and made contact with the Bundes-

wehr it became clear that they would get no reinforcements. The Czechoslovak contingent, which went into action only reluctantly, decided that it had had enough. Since the Czech and Slovak troops found it impossible to desert to the West they simply fanned out into the German countryside, conducting a sort of war, but certainly not the one the Soviets planned. Soviet commanders before Nuremberg, on finding out this Czechoslovak "treachery," refused to engage the Bundeswehr in battle and instead called for armor reinforcements from the central sector. Soviet tactical aviation was also called in, not to attack the Western positions, but to hunt and mop up the dissident Czechoslovak divisions.

Although now under control NATO forces were still reacting rather slowly and were ignorant of Soviet movements and penetrations. Thus the reinforcements to the southern sector were sent there by the 8th Guard Army whose penetration was considerably farther west of Nuremberg. When on D+6 the Bundeswehr noticed these armored columns from the north on the line which would have cut them from the west, local German commanders, who had

A Chaparral ground-to-air missile is launched against a Soviet tactical bomber.

The French offer some resistance.

again lost contact with CENTAG ordered withdrawal. By D+6 French divisions, though not part of NATO, stationed in Germany, and equally effectively cut off from their HQ, began to move up against the Soviet invader on local command initiative. They found movements eastward extremely difficult, for all roads from the east were blocked by masses of refugees. The refugee problem loomed large in all sectors and there was no civil authority left in Germany to attempt to solve it. In fact under the impact of the first victories by the invading Soviet forces the West German government thought it safer to evacuate the West German capital and transfer its seat to Paris. This move was approved and welcomed by the socialist government of France; the same government ordered its forces stationed in Germany to aid the Bundeswehr. However, this order never reached the French command. At the very onset of the Soviet invasion the governments of Belgium, Holland, and Denmark, though not directly threatened, decided to transfer to London. While the military command was hopelessly confused, politically Western Europe was non-existent. On the one hand there was the Franco-German Axis centered on Paris, but so far silent, and inoperative; on the

other hand there was Britain and the minor allies who also remained curiously quiet. Still by D+7 with communications and control reestablished and the military situation in the flux, the combatants launched political initiatives.

It was on D+7 that the Soviet president pronounced Operation Warsaw Pact as successfully concluded, reiterated his initial assertion that this was a purely European conflict and described the invasion of Germany as a punishment expedition "which would soon come to an end." Both the USA and China had accepted this Soviet declaration and their acceptance of the Soviet explanation was confirmed by the fact that there was no strategic conflict. The US president, however, was facing a terrible dilemma: he did not want to declare war on the USSR, but since his forces were decimated in the European conflict, he had to react somehow. Hence he had to make two announcements very rapidly: (1) issue a political ultimatum to the Soviets to stop their military operations in Europe and withdraw as soon as possible to the old hegemonial line; and (2) seeing NATO forces defeated and to prevent their complete annihilation order the use of tactical nuclear weapons,

the Warsaw Pact forces would break through NATO's forward defense positions. If tactical nuclear weapons were not used at this point, the games suggested that NATO's conventional forces could resist until D+19, when the Soviet forces would break through NATO's rear defensive lines and would start moving rapidly westward. On D+24 NATO would be unable to maintain a cohesive defense and would collapse. In addition to these game predictions all the NATO allies were also familiar with the Soviet contingency plan according to which Paris would be taken on D+24.

The Soviets subsequently suggested that the United Nations should be brought in to supervise an eventual agreement between the US and USSR in Europe. Without the slightest reference to the Europeans the Super Powers engaged in political negotiations over the Hot Line. The Americans wanted a rapid peaceful resolution of the European conflict, so that the use of nuclear weapons be avoided. The Soviets also wanted a peaceful solution, especially since they had already achieved their objectives by force: their hegemony in Eastern Europe was restored and "German imperialism rooted out" so that it would never again undermine Soviet security. However, with the military situation in Western Germany still very obscure, Soviet reluctance to withdraw from Western Germany before negotiations and given the slowness of US-Soviet and US-NATO communications, the peaceful resolution of the European conventional conflict, before tactical nuclear weapons were used seemed unlikely.

D+12 now appeared as the culminating point of the European conflict. Thus it became clear that a political solution could not possibly be found in such a short time, and the US

so far unused. Without consulting the European allies the president issued the political ultimatum to the Soviets on the Hot Line. Only afterward did the Americans transmit to their European allies the president's order to use tactical nuclear weapons on D+12 so that Soviet advance could be halted and reversed.

While the London-based allies welcomed American political and military initiatives, the Franco-German political leaders appeared stunned. Their worst political fears were thus confirmed: as they suspected in a European conflict the USA would refuse to engage their strategic forces. Now the US was prepared to start political negotiations with the Soviet aggressor but only after devastating continental Europe with tactical nuclear weapons. They immediately recognized that a US-Soviet "deal" over their heads would be the worst solution, but they themselves had no alternative proposals nor solutions. However, they were united in opposition to the tactical nuclear decision, and informed the London allies accordingly. Both the US and NATO allies (France including) were familiar with the secret war games conducted in the Pentagon for the year 1986. According to the games D+5 was in fact the day on which

Below:
Abandoned NATO equipment.

Above:
The X-2 rises from a silo in the Plateau d'Albion. This rocket has a 150 kiloton nuclear warhead.

negotiations. They came quickly to the conclusions that whatever their outcome West Germany would at best remain under Soviet military occupation for years to come before a negotiated settlement was concluded (the Soviets were notoriously slow at coming to negotiated agreements). At worst the country might be sacrificed altogether for the sake of US-Soviet peace and might be incorporated permanently into the Soviet hegemony "to avoid future conflicts." France obviously disliked such prospects, especially since they were formulated by the Super Powers, without the slightest reference to the interested European powers. If Germany was prepared to contemplate such a solution, France was not prepared even to consider it. Furthermore the reports from Germany alarmed the French leaders considerably: these reports spoke of grandiose movements of the Soviet forces, and though sometimes contradictory, they also reported the arrival of huge armored groups in the area of the Black Forest. Although at the outbreak of hostilities the French mobilized and transferred all their available troops to their borders with Germany, they could not dream of successfully opposing Soviet armor at this point. The probability of a Soviet breakthrough into Alsace was strong; and Paris was in such circumstances only one day away from Strasbourg.

On D+11 German leaders raised with their French counterparts the question of the French strategic deterrent. Though this was done formally for the first time, the French president had already considered proposals from his military leaders concerning the deterrent: they suggested that a warning shot should be fired at a Soviet target to show political and military determination. The president rejected the proposal at this stage, but after the formal German proposals the two allied governments met to consider it again. At the end of day-long considerations the Franco-German leaders agreed that if on the following day there was no US-Soviet peace agreement, and before the US orders to use tactical nuclear weapons could be implemented, France would use her strategic deterrent as envisaged by her strategic military specialists, without further consultations.

Immediately after the Franco-German meeting, the French president adjourned to the Elysées palace, his own residence as well as the Jupiter strategic HQ. At first he was briefed by the military on the capability of the French nuclear strike: the entire squadron of the ground missiles would have to be fired at a Soviet target to insure penetration and strike. Since only one squadron was in the range to reach a Soviet

president once again facing agonizing decisions. Was he to continue political negotiations and postpone the date set for the use of tactical nuclear weapons? After all the Soviets made it clear that they had finished with the "chastizing of German imperialism" and did not wish for the escalation of the conventional conflict. But could they be relied on? On the one hand they proclaimed their aims at the beginning of the conflict: they were strictly defined and did not involve the use of any nuclear weapons; therefore they had to be believed. On the other hand the reports filtering out of Germany both to the US and Paris and London still spoke of Soviet military activity: Soviet armor was still on the move and NATO forces still unable to check them. In view of these ambiguities the president therefore decided to attempt to find a peaceful political formula by D+12; however, if this attempt failed US and NATO forces would be ordered to make use of tactical nuclear weapons. In Paris the Franco-German leaders were kept in relative ignorance of US-Soviet

French missile explodes over Kiev.

target, this target had to be the city of Kiev; the city was without an anti-missile system. The French military further maintained that though penetration and strike could not be guaranteed, the Soviet retaliatory strike was a certainty. The president and his government continued their deliberations throughout the night. Occasionally German leaders were consulted, but no attempt was made to consult either the American leaders or the Soviets. In the early hours of D+12 the French president held his last meeting with his government to which the German leaders were invited. The decision to use the nuclear deterrent was confirmed and immediately after the meeting the president transmitted his order to the general on duty in the strategic HQ.

Within half an hour the whole world knew of the French nuclear strike against Kiev. Within an hour the Soviet retaliatory strike from SS-20 missile force hit Lyons.

Even before the retaliatory strike a joint Franco-German communique offered the Soviets and Americans Rome as a place where peace negotiations should immediately commence. The shock of the strike and counterstrike brought about immediate acceptance of the proposals by all concerned. Thus the world was spared a strategic conflict and the European conflict was brought to a swift end but at a price: the effects of the French and Soviet nuclear strikes were truly devastating.

CHAPTER EIGHT

CONSEQUENCES
OF A NUCLEAR CONFLICT

From the analysis so far it is clear that the simulated limited nuclear exchange would have escalated into a full-scale strategic one, had it not been for the Moscow-Washington Hot Line, Moline. It has proved imperative to maintain a continuous communication link between the Super Power NCAs; the Soviet leaders were able to describe precisely and meticulously the limited nature of their actions, including the desire to avoid being involved in a full-scale strategic conflict. Thus political leaders on both sides were under powerful pressures to avoid strategic involvement. Therefore the Hot Line communications enabled both sides to explain and clarify confusing events, provided a channel for negotiations, precluded escalation and finally made possible the negotiations of war termination.

Paradoxically the Hot Line communication system could only be really useful, because the nuclear conflict was of a limited character. As soon as a strategic exchange occurred the system would have been destroyed, for the satellites the Hot Line relies on, become exceedingly vulnerable after a certain stage of nuclear conflict. However, even in a limited nuclear conflict the Moline would not have functioned, were it not for US improvements in 1981. The great bulk of the development of inter-communication systems has been concerned with the beginning and the early stages of a limited conflict; beyond that only the process of escalation was of interest to the communication experts. Only in 1981 did the US Secretary of Defense request that the C3 strategic system "facilitates termination of nuclear strikes." It was fortunate that no full-scale strategic exchange did take place, for even this improved system was not specially protected from the collateral effects of such an exchange.

Below:
A nuclear-powered Polaris submarine.

The limited nature of the Franco-Soviet nuclear strikes therefore miraculously avoided escalation and subsequently led to global war termination. To explain it fully the strategic causes of the limited conflict have to be considered first, before the consequences are dealt with. The root cause for the French nuclear initiative lay in the Super Powers' inability to appreciate fully the implications of the medium powers' nuclear deterrent. The Americans failed to include the French and British deterrents in their contingency plans. The Soviets were so convinced that the Americans had the European deterrents under their control as to practically ignore them. This was the basic Soviet miscalculation, when embarking on a conventional conflict: while the French deterrent was acknowledged it was not sufficiently considered.

Both Super Powers have known of the development of French strategic doctrines which differed from those of the Super Powers. The United States should have been warned by the French refusal to have an integrated operational conventional command formed within NATO in peacetime. The French also refused to have a common military infrastructure. While France was participating in the military structures of NATO it disliked the fact that modern (above all nuclear) armament was manufactured by the United States; even if the individual allies were permitted to determine the numbers and types of armed forces for their individual country. Within this framework there was no place for French nuclear development. As General Ailleret put it "French forces would be common sharpshooters in American armies, while the noble command would be in American hands." Instead of taking these utterances at their face value, the Americans explained them by an inferiority feeling of the French brought about by the lost war, and lack of political and economic stability thereafter.

However the United States did try to appease the French, keep them in NATO and prevent them from developing nuclear weapons unilaterally. One way of satisfying the French was the doctrine of collective management in NATO. During the Algerian crisis the French quickly found out that even this doctrine did not suit them; it limited the use of their armed forces for their own purposes and they therefore removed many units from NATO. Furthermore the French disliked the placement of military bases on their territory. They reasoned that if any of the NATO ally was involved in a war which was not the result of Soviet aggression French troops could get enmeshed in such conflicts where no French interests would be served.

Above all the French repeatedly asked themselves as to how dependable their NATO allies really were and whether they would always be willing to defend them. They came to the conclusion that with the receding danger of Soviet aggression, with the various forms of cooperation, detente and technological exchanges, the balance of terror operated to perfection and there was no need for France to be a member of the military side of NATO. In 1966 the French President, after his attempt at reforming NATO had failed, took France out of the military structures of the alliance, asked for NATO bases and HQs to be taken out of France and transferred elsewhere, and above all came to rely exclusively on the French nuclear deterrent.

Although the decision to build an independent deterrent was taken before General de Gaulle came to power, he gave it a renewed impetus, especially after the Americans had rejected his nuclear proposals for NATO in 1958. In 1960 France tested its first atomic device and in 1968 she was in possession of a hydrogen bomb. By 1972 France had some 92 strategic delivery systems and figured fifth in the strategic table, after the USSR, USA, China, and Britain. In the 1980s France's was the only national, independent deterrent in Western Europe: all three strategic systems, IRBMs, SLBMs and strategic aircraft capable of striking against the only possible aggressor in Europe, the USSR. Its 18 nuclear warheads had a maximum yield of 150 kilotons each (the Hiroshima bomb yielded 20 KT) and were therefore, buttressed by SLBMs and bombers, of a considerable deterrent value. In 1963 France concluded a treaty with West Germany which gave the French deterrent double political significance: if ever the American nuclear umbrella became defective, was withdrawn or evaporated for all sorts of reasons, the French deterrent would take its place. Only in the 1980s did this become a reality as the French developed the three-fold deterrence forces, NATO became weakened and the US became interested in bilateral agreements with the USSR. Thus both Super Powers miscalculated when they failed, each for different reasons, to take the French nuclear deterrent sufficiently seriously.

The impact of the nuclear strikes has been studied and the results have been used in various computer war games to give us a reasonably clear picture of devastation, though many side effects, the collateral damage, still cannot be calculated. Albeit a limited strike would have a devastating impact and the numbers of death casualties might reach 20 million people, the consequences might still be endurable: rather like in the past wars and major epidemics. However the nations surviving a nuclear strike would live in unprecedented conditions and these would subsequently deteriorate before improvement could be envisaged. It is clear that overall damage would be greater than that anticipated by the military commands. National economies of nuclearly afflicted nations would continue to decline for years after the nuclear impact. And as a result of the strike a long-term ecological damage would ensue. Even civil defense in a limited nuclear conflict cannot be expected to be conclusively effective.

As for the targets of the French and Soviet nuclear strikes they were preselected with meticulous care so as not to excite further retaliation. Kiev is the capital of the Ukraine, the second largest and most populated republic after Russia. It is a historical city with some 2,000,000 inhabitants whose center consists of high density old buildings with masonry load-bearing walls. It is an industrialized city with industrial suburbs where there are new buildings with steel frames and precast concrete walls. The Soviet retaliatory strike for the destruction of Kiev had to be targetted on Lyons, France's second largest connurbation. It is also an ancient capital of Gaul peopled by some 2,000,000 inhabitants: again there is a historical center and modern suburbs in this highly developed industrial metropolis.

Neither side could ascertain how many of their warheads reached the two cities and it has to be assumed that Kiev was struck by 1MT warheads and the Soviet counterblast was of the same magnitude. In neither case was there any warning given and the populations of the two cities could not be evacuated. As the strikes occurred in the early hours of the morning most people were still at home in their houses and apartment blocks, and no one was in nuclear shelters. Weather was clear and visibility 10 miles: the detonation took place one mile from the center of Kiev on the surface.

Within seconds of the detonation a huge fireball was observed above the city from the neighboring countryside. The 1MT explosion on the surface left a crater 300m in diameter and 61m deep; all around the crater, up to about twice the diameter, was a rim of highly radioactive soil. In a one kilometer elliptical ring from the epicenter of the explosion nothing recognizable was left standing, except massive bridge foundations on the banks of the river Dniepr and foundations of some buildings. Up to this distance only the twisted remains of the railroad bridge was left standing; up to 2km a few of the most solidly built buildings survived. However, all interiors were totally destroyed by blast penetrating through the windows. Only at a distance of 2.7km were there any significant buildings left standing.

Of the 600,000 population in the area of the epicenter (up to 1.7km) there were virtually no survivors. In the zone between 1.7km and 2.7km, where there lived some 250,000 people, 130,000 were fatal casualties; 100,000 injured and only 20,000 uninjured. In the outer districts, between 2.7km and 4.7km, where some 400,000 people lived, there occurred 20,000 fatalities and 180,000 people suffered injuries. Only in the distant suburbs, between 4.7km and 7.4km where some 70,000 people lived, were there no fatalities and only some 17,000 suffered injury.

In the band between 1.7km and 2.7km commercial, industrial and residential multistorey buildings had their walls completely blown down, but as distance from the epicenter increased the massive skeletal structures remained standing. Individual houses in this zone were completely destroyed with foundations and basements remaining only; the debris was curiously evenly distributed over the whole area. Heavy industrial buildings were completely destroyed within the inner ring, but toward the outer ring some remained standing. The debris cluttering up the streets in this band depended on the height of the building and their spacing. All the vehicles parked in the streets were destroyed either by blast or by debris. Most of the deaths among the population in this ring occurred from collapsing buildings. Many fires were started but only a few buildings continued to burn after the passing of the blast wave. The spread of fire was slow and no firestorms occurred. Up to 2.7km the initial nuclear radiation's effect on people was lethal, but outside that band was insignificant. In the area up to 1.7km it was impossible to determine the

cause of fatalities: blast, debris, or radiation or all three. On this clear summer morning some 25 percent of the population were exposed and suffered from thermal radiation, while second-degree burns were produced up to the distance of 10km. Thus some 190,000 deaths were caused by thermal radiation, 75,000 injuries by the same.

In the outer ring, between 2.7km and 4.7km large buildings lost their windows, interior partitions and frames; those of light walled construction lost their upper floors which were blown into streets. Load-bearing walls were severely cracked, while low houses were totally destroyed or severely damaged. Substantial amounts of debris was scattered in the streets, but a significant number of vehicles in the street remained usable. The heavy industrial plants were damaged and most of the aircraft and hangars at Kiev airport, which is situated within this zone, were destroyed. In this band only about five percent of population was killed, but nearly one half were injured; casualties were mainly caused by fires which spread in this zone more easily than in the completely flattened inner areas. Some five percent of buildings were initially ignited and as fire spread it burned over the next 24 hours. Dry weather made the spread of fire easy and the injured population proved apathetic to firefighting. In this zone 95,000 additional deaths were caused by thermal radiation; 11,000 were severely injured by the same and many of these died subsequently because they could not be adequately treated.

In the outermost ring only light damage was done to commercial structures and moderate damage to housing. Human casualties were 25 percent and only an insignificant number of people were killed. Additional injuries, amounting to 5,000, were caused by burns, but fires were rare and they were brought under control by survivors.

Finally the city suffered from the fallout coming from the stem and the cap of the nuclear mushroom which affected both the population and also the emergency services subsequently. Fallout from the stem built up after some 10 minutes and since it affected an area of 10.5km radius it represented prime-radiation threat to the emergency services which survived in the outermost suburbs. Though fortunately there was no significant wind that morning, the main fallout from the cap of the mushroom enlarged the contaminated area considerably, when it descended upon the stricken city after an hour interval. The effect of this fallout on the population lasted for one week, though it had no effect on the emergency services, which within 24 hours procured protective clothing and could operate within the blast area.

Within an area of 20km people were blistered; trees were singed and their leaves crisped as if fall had set in; haystacks burned spontaneously; paint on houses and fences blistered; in some cases curtains burned, in others just smoldered. The shockwave of the detonation was heard all round the Ukraine and reached Moscow, though by then muffled. The psychological shock in the Ukraine was such that Moscow had to take over organizing emergency services and aid. The 500,000 injured presented an incredible medical problem and the central authorities addressed themselves to it immediately. Since there were only some 65 hospitals with 20,000 beds in the vicinity of Kiev the entire army medical corps from the surrounding military districts was ordered to Kiev. Even then the problem appeared insoluble given its magnitude. In the first days transport of injured from the blast area of Kiev was severely limited by debris clogging up the streets. However, the response of the population which survived helped to save many lives which would have been lost because of transport and hospitalization difficulties. However, even after the transportation problem was solved medical services throughout the Soviet Union were grossly overburdened, especially with the tens of thousands of burn cases.

The secondary damage to all public service in Kiev and the Ukraine was inevitable. The electric power network was totally destroyed in the blast area, but the collapse of buildings, toppling of trees and pylons as well as the discharge of thousands of volts into broken wires inflicted almost irreparable damage to the whole national power grid. Since the Soviet power grid was suffering from underproduction the damage caused by the nuclear blast took months to be made good and a semblance of power normality returned to the Kiev area shortly before winter.

Fortunately the water system remained almost intact with the exception of one or two pumping stations. The waterworks were outside the blast area; however, the loss of power to the pumping stations as well as many services connected with the distribution of water caused the loss of water pressure, hence the water service also collapsed. The most immediate task of the water service people was to cut damaged valves and pipes as well as turn off supply pipes leading to the damaged areas. In the undamaged sections, where the mains were undisturbed, emergency water pipes were put up at all cross-roads so

A victim of the nuclear holocaust.

that the remaining surviving population could be approvisioned.

The gas system was in a similar condition as the water system. There occurred loss of gas pressure because of the many broken service connections, mains and raging fires. This service took longest to reestablish; Kiev was already in a privileged position in so far as the gas system was concerned and the USSR simply had no spare capacity to restore it in the city. Only the gasoline supplies, well outside the city limits, were undamaged, although many gasoline tanks were destroyed in the blast. However, the use of gasoline as energy depended much on the clearing of street and roads in the damaged area, which was too slow; thus this useful commodity and energy source was underutilized.

Rescue and recovery depended heavy on the reestablishment of transportation; the Soviet army and its fleet of personnel cars and lorries performed their tasks with energy, efficiency and as soon as it became possible. The greatest problem was the removal of debris; however, to clear it took the soldiers weeks rather than the months anticipated. The Kiev airport was essentially destroyed, its aircraft and facilities going overboard. Clearing the runways was not a difficult task and they were clear of smaller and heavier debris within two days. Most unfortunately the airport became the center of intensive fallout and the cleaning efforts lasted over two weeks. In any case the airport could not have been opened to traffic, as emergency power lines were established after two weeks' delay. All the railroad stations were totally destroyed, but the tram depots suffered relatively small damage. Transportation within the city took several months to reestablish, because of the immense amount of debris which had to be cleaned from the streets.

The last but not least effect the Kiev area had to suffer from the nuclear blast was radioactive fallout, which continued to come down for several weeks. As there is always in the summer a southerly breeze in the area the fallout in fact drifted toward the north where there is a sparsely populated agricultural area. During the first few days the fallout density in the north was most dangerous, but on the second day, when the army arrived, the civilian population was evacuated from this area. Nonetheless because of the initial confusion many people living in the direct path of fallout received a fatal dose of radiation within the first week. People living in the adjoining areas of fallout contracted severe radiation sickness when they stayed at home; those who spent much time outdoors received fatal doses of radiation. However, even people who lived at some considerable distance from the fallout path contracted mild radiation sickness and with it increased the risk of death from other diseases. Moreover these people's life expectancy decreased and the risk of contracting cancer increased. Fortunately the decay of fallout radiation in these areas was accelerated by natural decontamination: in the second week several rainstorms came down and washed the contaminating particles into the soil which attenuated the radiation. All the same the area in the direct path of the radioactive fallout had to be evacuated as soon as the decontamination experts reached it in week three: not only was it estimated that the natural processes and food chain would be affected by the fallout, but it was also established that the natural decontamination process would take between eight to 10 years on the inside path and three to four years in the outlying areas as to achieve safe radiation levels for people to return.

To summarize the effect of the surface blast in Kiev the following salient features stand out: (1) 70 square miles of property destroyed; (2) over 750,000 deaths and 500,000 wounded; (3) additional damage from widespread fires; (4) casualties could have been much reduced if the population was war alerted and civil defense in a state of preparedness; (5) rescue and recovery operations had to be organized and carried out from outside.

Lyons is an important industrial and transport center and was built on the river Rhône. The old center is largely the seat of commerce and administration. Industry surrounds the city while the new residential areas are to the south and east. In the older parts of Lyons the buildings have masonry load-bearing walls and do not exceed six floors. The postwar housing constructions are 10–12 floor apartment blocks with steel frames and pre-cast concrete walls. All these data are important, for the retaliatory Soviet nuclear strike was detonated in the air, 300m above the city.

Even though the Soviet strike was equivalent to the French one and was detonated over the city the 1MT blasted the solid inner city structures and blew down their walls although some steel skeletons withstood the pressures created by the 1MT detonation, they were all twisted beyond safety definition. Otherwise the damage and human casualties were similar to those in Kiev. Buildings, except in the old part of the city, did not burn, especially the suburban apartment blocks which were so widely spaced as to make it practically impossible for the fire to spread. Because of the wide spacing, again excepting the old city, which was only thinly inhabited, there was much less debris preventing access to the damaged areas. Rail and road transport and the new subway suffered much less damage than in Kiev and the radio and television aerials outside the city limits were in fact intact.

Thus though the damage and casualties inflicted on Lyons were almost identical to those of Kiev, there were striking differences. Lyons lies in the Rhône valley and in the proximity of the Alps and Massif Central mountains. The mountains cause frequent precipitations in the summer and the rains, lack of visibility and the prevailing winds cushioned the city against certain effects of the blast. The radioactive fallout drifted into the mountainous region lying southeast from the city, and its effects were minimal. Rescue and recovery efforts were also much swifter than in Kiev. Without waiting for instructions from Paris the neighboring cities of Grenoble and St Etienne sent over to Lyons their emergency services, while the French army medical services were rushed into the damaged area from the southwestern and southern regions. Casualties were evacuated relatively quickly because the city was not isolated by the blast from the rest of the country, but train and road connections were reestablished within hours rather than days as in Kiev. Numerous voluntary organizations, such as the Red Cross, charity groups responded immediately to the emergency; international aid, particularly from the United States started to arrive within days.

Relatively speaking both nuclear strikes

caused less material destruction and smaller loss of life than the conventional war in West Germany. There the vast tank battles devastated numerous German cities and caused heavy casualties on both sides, which exceeded those inflicted by the nuclear strikes. Civilian casualties were in fact higher in Germany than both in Kiev and Lyons. This was mainly due to the wave of panic which seized the German civilian population after the Soviet invasion. As previously, in 1941, the German Panzer formations did not take kindly to Russian refugees clogging up their roads in Russia, so now, in the 1980s, did Soviet armor manifest its discontent by firing indiscriminately into or simply crushing the masses of terrified German refugees. The massive dislocation of population brought with it the usual epidemics and steeply increased casualties. The horrors of conventional war seemed to have outweighed those of the nuclear one.

If the conventional war unleashed by the Soviets in West Germany proved more terrible in facts and figures, its psychological effects on mankind were nowhere near those of the nuclear strikes. In 1945 the US atomic bombs dropped on Hiroshima and Nagasaki were greeted even by the enlightened public as just another technical innovation to end the war without major casualties. It was only much later that the horror wrought by this new weapon dawned on mankind. Anti-nuclear marches only slightly blunted this feeling of repulsion that the public all over the world began to experience when learning the real facts of these first atomic explosions. World political leaders were also affected by this repulsion, and were appaled by the spectacle of one Super Power trying to exploit these justified emotions to its own advantage. Nonetheless, when the Super Powers had faced each other in a nuclear confrontation over Cuba, which could have turned into a nuclear conflict, they were able to withdraw from the precipice by compromising: neither leadership was prepared to unleash the nuclear holocaust then. However, the shock of this confrontation soon wore off and all the nuclear powers began once again to bandy about these terrible weapons in international politics with increasing frequency, until in the 1980s these noises turned into the real thing. This time the limited nuclear strikes have dumbfounded everyone.

Profiting from the Moline the Soviet Union made known her conditions of peace to the USA and the world. The Soviets proposed an immediate cessation of hostilities in West Germany; as soon as an armistice was arranged

A nuclear explosion. The most destructive force known to man.

Soviet forces would begin their withdrawal to the former boundaries of the Warsaw Pact. Consequent on this a political summit of all the powers involved in the conflict, namely the USA, France, Germany, and Britain, should meet in Rome to hammer out a political agreement. The summit then should transform itself into a general disarmament conference, which should remain in session until all essential points of disarmament were agreed to. The American President relayed these proposals to Europe and the European leaders immediately agreed to this Soviet initiative. The United Nations were then asked to send negotiators to Germany to arrange an armistice and teams of UN observers were made ready to supervise Soviet withdrawal. The Rome summit was fixed to take place three days after the armistice.

Thus it took mankind a limited nuclear holocaust to put its affairs in order. Prior to this nuclear shock all disarmament and peace moves seemed predestined to failure. Undoubtedly the nearness of a full-scale strategic conflict had the desired effect on the Super Powers in this direction; still the terrible spectacle of nuclear devastation was decisive in making the whole world more reasonable, and shrink from overstepping the ' line of self-destruction. All the same, immediately after the catastrophe people began to ask the question: how soon would mankind forget the destruction of the martyr cities of Kiev and Lyons?

ARMED CONFLICT

A MILITARY PICTURE ESSAY

The Battle for Europe begins

The Soviets aim to occupy Western Europe, while avoiding the eruption of a nuclear holocaust. Their secondary objective is the final subjugation of the Central European states, especially Poland. The first move is the placing of all front-line troops in a state of readiness. The Central Front is the most important area and has the largest concentration of men and equipment: some six armies and 3,500 aircraft. Officers and men are briefed for combat and support elements are brought forward. Although the Warsaw Pact armies are well equipped, the sight of a 122mm rocket launcher which saw action in the closing stages of World War II, next to a FROG-Tactical Missile, bears out the fact that numbers rather than quality is the essential factor in this war.

Invasion

A series of local troops and armor penetrations take place confusing the NATO command and giving Warsaw Pact forces valuable information for the initial stages of the invasion. Tank officers are given their objectives and the invasion begins. Tank and motorized infantry elements of the 1st, 2nd, and 8th Guards Armies and the 3rd Shock Army move forward along the Berlin–Paris axis. The time is 6am and the invasion of Western Europe has commenced. Never before has so great a number of men been moved with such precision. The plains of Europe rumbled with the sound of tank engines. The Soviet War Machine had moved.

Forward strategic positions are seized

Paratroopers are sent in. Deep penetrations are achieved in the initial moments by paratroop drops. Supported by ASU-85 tanks which have been brought forward by glider, the paratroopers seize strategic objectives before calling the main forces to consolidate their terrain. Regular troops move forward supported by both tactical and strategic air strikes. The initial phase of the invasion has gone exceedingly well, with NATO forces being flung back in total confusion and the armored steamroller presses on, virtually unopposed.

NATO'S response

Once the NATO command realized that the invasion was really taking place, it also knew there was little likelihood of repulsing the attack. It believed that if the advance could be delayed, then negotiations would be started. This became NATO's primary objective and as many troops as possible were flung into the fray. There were pitiably few. All NATO avaiation had been mysteriously grounded and there was severe shortage of troop transport owing to recent cuts in military backup systems, imposed for financial reasons. Despite this as many men and as much equipment as possible were sent to the front.

Total destruction of forward forces

After the total annihilation of the West German Bundeswehr divisions the British 6th 20th Armored Brigade bore the brunt of the fighting. Chieftain tanks, the main weapon of this formation, went forward and a series of intense tank battles ensued, both sides inflicting heavy casualties on the other. In the closing stages of the first day of fighting the Warsaw Pact forces used shells filled with noxious gas. The effect was instantaneous with men dropping like flies but the officers soon got the situation under control and fighting gained in intensity throughout the night.

British tank forces are forced to withdraw

The British 6th 20th Armored Brigade despite being heavily outnumbered continues to fight. With the number of effective fighting units decreasing with every encounter and ammunition running dangerously low, the decision is taken to effect a rapid withdrawal. With great speed the Royal Engineers construct a system of bridges over the Weser River, thus making good their escape and regrouping to face the enemy once more. The 3rd Shock Army finally catches up with the Brigade and one of the most bloody encounters of the whole conflict ensues.

Determined resistance by ground forces

Following the virtual decimation of NATO armored forces, infantry and antitank forces bear the full weight of the advance. Wave upon wave of T-64 and T-72s come forward. The fighting is fierce but unequal. NATO headquarters realizing the risk of a general collapse, order the gradual withdrawal of all units. Light reconnaissance tanks of the Dutch and Belgian armies are brought forward to provide information and if necessary covering fire. Warsaw Pact forces oblivious of the state of their opponents become worried by the sight of these large numbers of tanks and troop movements and so continue cautiously forward thus missing their chance.

Warsaw Pact Air Force poses a threat to NATO forces' withdrawal

NATO aviation being temporarily out of action due to enemy sabotage, means that the Pact Air Force had virtual control of the skies. This fact might have made the NATO withdrawal impossible but for the protection that massed batteries of surface-to-air missiles provided. Helicopters which had not been affected by sabotage proved invaluable in transporting troops and providing a measure of ground support. Although the NATO troops had received a heavy battering in the last 48 hours they had unified front and communications began operating normally. As communications improved more support units are sent up to the combat zone.

Warsaw Pact forces are worried by intensity of NATO resistance

Toward the end of day two of fighting, after the successful repletion of forward forces, NATO artillery and surface-to-surface missiles began a powerful barrage which inflicted horrific losses on Warsaw Pact forces. The American T-22 Corps Support System was especially effective with its ability to disperse a large number of guided submunitions. So the second day of war ended in a blaze of high explosive and a slackening in the speed of the advance. By next morning NATO fighter and tactical aircraft are once more in the air and Warsaw Pact forces are forced to move within a time-consuming network of surface-to-air missiles and ground-support fighters.

Warsaw Pact problems

It is following the partial reorganization of NATO forces in defensive positions, and the heavy casualties that surface bombardments cause to Warsaw Pact forces, that the attack begins to develop problems. Although American units had been overcome in the southern sector near Nuremberg, it is noted with considerable amazement by NATO command that the enemy had halted. It appears that while American and East German forces had been fighting intensely in very bad conditions, Czech troops had mutinied and begun to disperse. So the East German forces were ordered to discontinue the advance and destroy the mutinous troops.

American reinforcements stem the tide in the Southern Sector

In the Southern Sector the advance is contained by a massive injection of American fighting units. A mobile command post is set up to co-ordinate the organization of interconnecting transverse positions serviced by armored and air support units. This means that a unified front is available against any renewed Warsaw Pact advance in this area. The US who had up to this moment had very little part in the action now become the major element in the NATO defense forces. All along the front US troops take over from heavily depleted Allied forces.

American troops save the day at last moment

Although huge casualties had been inflicted by Day 5 of the Invasion, the question of numbers is such that by this time British, Belgian and Dutch forces in the Northern Sector are at breaking point having been continually on the move since the start of hostilities. When the US troops arrive at the front, they are not only essential to maintain the front line but also for reasons of morale. However, although the line is preserved and the orderly withdrawal of NATO forces continues, American casualties are so high that American politicians began to question whether the defense of Europe is really necessary.

Land based Cruise Missile launch.

AFTERWORD

"If you gaze long into an abyss,
the abyss will gaze back into you."

Friedrich Nietzche

The author of an afterword of a futuristic symposium has two options: either to summarize systematically and synthesize clearly the main arguments of the preceding chapters, or to challenge them lock, stock, and barrel. Believing that the issues at stake would be best clarified in the heat of a vigorous debate, the present author chooses the second alternative. Assuming the role of a devil's advocate, he is going to argue that the bunch of near-senile senior citizens deliberating twice a week at the Kremlin and known as the Politburo, is far from eager to launch a third world war, quite the contrary, that it is bent on avoiding such a clash at least as much as we are.

In adopting a defensive attitude, the gnomes of the Kremlin are motivated by two sets of reasons. The first is the most basic instinct common to all living creatures, namely, the instinct of self-preservation. The second is the awareness of the political, economic, and strategic weaknesses of the Soviet Union. I propose to argue that the Soviet leaders are as afraid of the inevitable cosmic

Right:
A launch of a nuclear test missile.

Below:
Missile Silos in the Nevada desert.

catastrophe as anybody else of sane mind; they realize perfectly well that they share with the rest of humanity the same natural environment, especially the supplies of air and water; they know that epidemics, unleashed by lack of medical care and inadequate shelter recognize no national borders and blow across the continents like winds. They are equally aware that our globe would be utterly devastated as a result of a nuclear holocaust: the surfaces of the earth would cool; the vegetation would wither away; the waters would become contaminated; and, most importantly, the ozone layer, which protects living creatures from the harsher rays of the sun, would gradually evaporate and disappear. The detonation of even a small part of the world's fast-mounting supply of megatons would mean the end of human life on earth.

War is the agency by which nation-states protect what they consider to be their "vital interests." Our present predicament is that recourse to all-out warfare on the part of any of the nuclear powers would be so devastating that no conceivable interest, national or international, vital or otherwise, could possibly be served by it. Although for domestic consumption the Soviet leaders continue to reiterate Stalin's old slogan that only the capitalistic countries would be decisively affected by a nuclear war, they are aware that atomic and hydrogen missiles make no ideological distinctions, and that the war of the future will know no victors.

The machinery of destruction is complete, poised on a hair trigger. The Americans and the Russians are like two gamblers sitting across a table, each with a gun pointed at the other's head and each gun on a hair trigger. The size of the guns does not make much difference: if either gambler uses his nuclear guns both of them are dead. They and most of the people around them together with the fruit of four to five billion years of evolution would be destroyed.

Contrary to Ian Fleming's formula, each of us lives only once. This does not exclude the Soviet leaders who also share with us planet Earth. That is why I refuse to believe that even the leaders at the Kremlin, as unscrupulous as they are, would venture in cold blood a premeditated first strike. In my opinion no person in his right mind would ever do it. Only a deranged, insane creature could push the critical button, only a faulty computer chip could send out the instruction to fire the first nuclear, intercontinental salvo. If a Soviet first strike against the US were powerful enough to destroy American retaliatory capacity, its ecological after-effect would be so awesome as to damage the Soviet Union as well. The sheer quantity of nuclear weapons now in existence is sufficient to do it. Nobelist Linus Pauling has calculated that the total stockpile amounts to 500,000 megatons, which is about 100,000 times the total of explosives used during the whole of World War II.

History teaches us that there has never been an arms race which did not end in war. Is there any reason to believe that this pattern would suddenly change? The present writer, as a student of history, doubts it. But the absolute finality of a nuclear war may change the character of future wars. Nuclear weaponry cannot be uninvented. The genie cannot be driven back into the bottle, but it can be tamed so as not to destroy us all. Do we really have any doubts that the senior citizens at the Kremlin would prefer to end their days comfortably in their own beds and not incinerated or asphyxiated in the bomb shelters?

Not moral considerations, therefore, but a healthy impulse toward self-preservation may compel the Super Powers to shift the nuclear weapons as the last resort instruments and tacitly agree to conduct their confrontations either by strictly conventional means or by tactical and/or theater nuclear weapons only. Consequently, I propose that the strategic missiles may never be

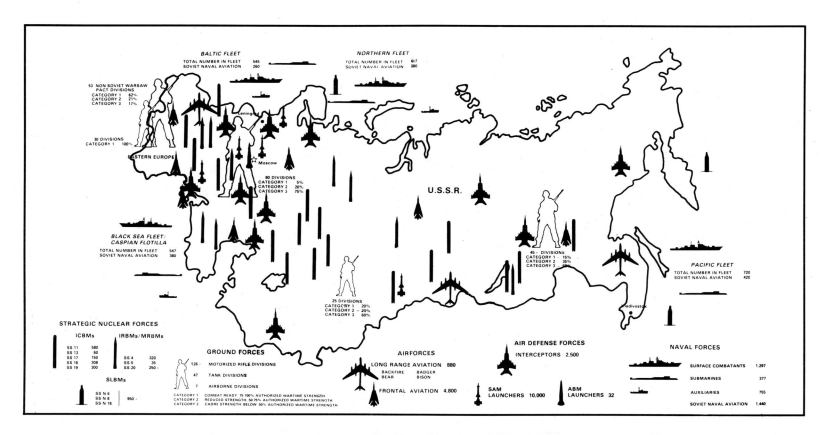

BALTIC FLEET
TOTAL NUMBER IN FLEET   545
SOVIET NAVAL AVIATION   260

NORTHERN FLEET
TOTAL NUMBER IN FLEET   617
SOVIET NAVAL AVIATION   380

53 NON SOVIET WARSAW
PACT DIVISIONS
CATEGORY 1   62%
CATEGORY 2   21%
CATEGORY 3   17%

30 DIVISIONS
CATEGORY 1   100%

EASTERN EUROPE

Leningrad

Moscow

80 DIVISIONS
CATEGORY 1   5%
CATEGORY 2   20%
CATEGORY 3   75%

U.S.S.R.

BLACK SEA FLEET/
CASPIAN FLOTILLA
TOTAL NUMBER IN FLEET   547
SOVIET NAVAL AVIATION   380

45 · DIVISIONS
CATEGORY 1   15%
CATEGORY 2   35%
CATEGORY 3   35%

PACIFIC FLEET
TOTAL NUMBER IN FLEET   720
SOVIET NAVAL AVIATION   420

25 DIVISIONS
CATEGORY 1 — 20%
CATEGORY 2 — 20%
CATEGORY 3   60%

Vladivostok

STRATEGIC NUCLEAR FORCES

ICBMs
SS 11   580
SS 13   60
SS 17   150
SS 18   308
SS 19   300

IRBMs/MRBMs
SS 4   320
SS 5   35
SS 20   250 ·

SLBMs
SS N 6
SS N 8   950 ·
SS N 18

GROUND FORCES
126 · MOTORIZED RIFLE DIVISIONS
47   TANK DIVISIONS
7   AIRBORNE DIVISIONS
CATEGORY 1   COMBAT READY 75 100% AUTHORIZED WARTIME STRENGTH
CATEGORY 2   REDUCED STRENGTH 50 75% AUTHORIZED WARTIME STRENGTH
CATEGORY 3   CADRE STRENGTH BELOW 50% AUTHORIZED WARTIME STRENGTH

AIRFORCES
LONG RANGE AVIATION   880
BACKFIRE   BADGER
BEAR   BISON
FRONTAL AVIATION   4,800

AIR DEFENSE FORCES
INTERCEPTORS   2,500
SAM LAUNCHERS   10,000
ABM LAUNCHERS   32

NAVAL FORCES
SURFACE COMBATANTS   1,297
SUBMARINES   377
AUXILIARIES   755
SOVIET NAVAL AVIATION   1,440

used at all just as poison gas was never used in World War II: each is too double-edged a weapon.

The second reason why the Soviet leaders, while often making boisterous, bellicose propagandistic pronouncements, are actually more afraid of an armed showdown, is their awareness of their empire's multifaceted vulnerability. The greatest Soviet weakness is its geopolitical situation. Since the consummation of the Sino-Soviet split some 20 years ago, the USSR has been for all practical purposes encircled by potential adversaries. It is enough to glance at a north polar projection of the map to see how precarious the Soviet strategic position is. In any global conflict the USSR would almost inevitably wage a war along at least two distant fronts separated by 5–6,000 miles with all the logistic implications of such a predicament. Since the Soviet ambitions seem to be focusing recently in the direction of the Middle East and the Indian Ocean, there is a good chance that, in case of an armed clash, the USSR would have a third front as well.

Despite the arguments of the previous chapters, even if the Kremlin leaders were mad enough to unleash a war, there is no reason to believe it would start in Europe. The present author believes that it is not the European approaches, but the Middle and Far Eastern approaches which are the main Soviet preoccupation these days. China is probably considered at the Kremlin as the greatest threat to the USSR. The Chinese, rather than the US, are seen as "the enemy" and the sense of inevitable conflict with China is pervasive. A study made in 1981 by the US International Communication Agency concluded that while the Russians apparently do not fear direct nuclear attack by the US, they suffer their own kind of phobia about the United States as a power that can overwhelm them by superior military technology. In the popular Soviet view, the United States is seen as capable of changing the military balance in its favor overnight by a series of technological inventions that will leave the Soviet Union far behind in the arms race. The Soviet governing elite, according to the study, harbors doubts "about the competence, reliability, and effectiveness of their own forces," as well as those of their vassals. The events of 1980–82 in Poland are a warning to the Kremlin.

Thus, in the middle of their seventh decade, the Soviets live in a friendless environment. In case of a global conflict, the Soviets are in danger of having to fight at least a two-front war against a combination of powers which far outweighs them in population and resources, and even in weapons, while their economy is shaky and lags far behind the West, and is actually dependent on the West in many respects, especially food. In the slow-motion economy and repressive system a quarter of the Soviet workforce remains on the farm compared with less than four percent in the United States. Yet the Russians cannot feed themselves, they import grain from us, their factories are inefficient, and their immense war machine puts a terrible burden on the people.

To this one should add the shortcomings of the rigidly centralized, overbureaucratized industry. Much of the Soviet economic weakness is a result of the growing rigidity of the system desperately clinging to obsolete 19th-century Marxist concepts. This has steadily widened the gap between the fast-progressing Western world and the USSR. Much of the world — headed by the United States, Western Europe, and Japan — has participated in

Chinese soldiers have clashed several times over the last 15 years with Russian border guards.

the technological revolution of the last 30 years. Its impact has been tremendous. The technological upheaval has scarcely yet hit the Soviet Union, where only the space program, some military industries, and few branches of science are automated and computerized. As a consequence of this scientific retardation the Russians are not only missing an important stage in man's intellectual evolution, but are hampering the progress of the entire economy on which, ultimately, their military potential also depends.

Another major source of Soviet weakness is the ethnic structure of their heterogenous empire composed of well over 100 ethnic groups. These nationalities have been conquered and kept together largely by naked force. Since the end of the 18th century the empire-building Muscovite-Russians never amounted to more than half of the entire population and for the last two decades or so the great Russian component has been shrinking rapidly. While the Russians still dominate smaller ethnic groups, this domination is threatened by the rapidly declining birthrate of the Great Russian stock. In the USSR the decline

severely affects all the Slavic-populated, industrialized areas of the country but is most dramatic among the Great Russians. The Muslim population of Central Asia, on the other hand, has been

Below:
American scientists have an extensive system of military research facilities which has maintained US technical superiority in the nuclear field.

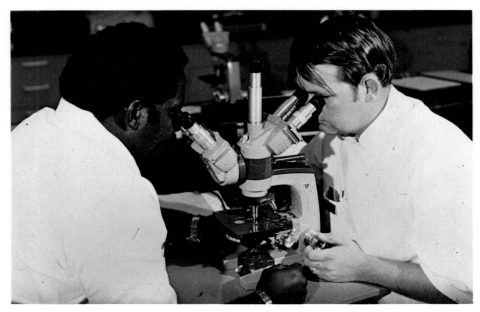

growing quite rapidly. The Muslims, less affected
by secularization, consumerism, and the spread
of contraception, have retained their traditional
high fertility rate. The Muslim people, who by
now number over 40 million people, are relatively
young: in 1980 some 55 percent of them were
under 15 years of age, while the corresponding
figure for the Russians was only 26 percent.

Other Asian ethnic groups also rapidly increased in numbers. While the yearly contingent
of military recruits contains an ever higher per-
centage of Muslims from Central Asia, and Asians
in general, it counts a decreasing number of
Russians. The declining manpower pool, which
will reach a low point in 1987, will stretch manpower needs very thin and create sharp internal
conflicts over whether to send young scientists
and technicians into industry or the armed forces.
According to most estimates, Soviet economic

growth rate is bound to decline — from a current
annual level of three percent down to as low as
one percent in the 1980s, largely because of a
sharp decline in the growth of the labor force
because of a slump in births in the 1960s.

The present demographic trend, if unchecked
(and there is no indication that it could be in the
near future), is bound to have a far-reaching impact on the ethnic makeup of the USSR, including
the Party, the governmental bureaucracy, and,
last but not least, on the structure of the Armed
Forces, including its top echelons. Can the Russian
leadership rely on the soldiers who are increasingly non-Russian? The behavior of the Muslim
soldiers during the Afghan adventure is here
another warning.

The Soviet Empire, like the planet Saturn, is
composed of two segments: the inner core; that
is, the prewar USSR, and the outer ring; that is,

its vassal states. After World War II, Stalin added to the old imperial structure well over 100 million East Germans, Poles, Czechs, Slovaks, Hungarians, Rumanians, Serbs, Croats, Slovenians, and Albanians as his vassals. Instead of being a source of strength, the Soviet domination of East–Central Europe has been for the Kremlin a constant sore spot. Since Yugoslavia's expulsion from the Cominform in 1948, the Soviet hegemonial sphere in Europe has been shaken by a series of revolts: the East German in 1953, the Polish and Hungarian in 1956, the Albanian in 1960, the Rumanian in 1963, and the Czechoslovak in 1968. The recent events in Poland, the crisis of 1980–82, have demonstrated once more that the East Europeans are a volcano and that in case of an international crisis, Moscow can hardly rely on their satellites.

Strategically, the most important of them is Poland. The Solidarity crisis of 1980–82 has, for all practical purposes, paralyzed that country. Nominally it is still a fully-fledged member of the Warsaw Pact, but the Soviet lines of communication running through Poland are most precarious, especially in case of an aggressive war against the West. No sober Soviet military planner would rely these days on Polish loyal cooperation in case of a serious clash with the NATO powers. Now, to the old political problems must be added the economic ones, including that of oil. The East Europeans must pay increasingly higher prices for Soviet oil; although they are still below world prices they are quickly catching up with them. Moreover, the Soviet vassals must look for alternative sources of oil supply and pay for them through the nose in hard currency which is difficult to come by in a world hit by recession. This is unlikely to strengthen one of the major props of the Soviet hegemonial system in Eastern Europe: the economic dependence of the client states on the Center, symbolized by the Council of Mutual Economic Assistance, or CMEA.

Thus, there is no end to the Soviet troubles in their hegemonial sphere. A prominent American scholar, Professor Robert F. Burnes, rightly called the Soviet domination of Eastern Europe "hegemony without security." It would not be an exaggeration to say that, in its seventh decade, the USSR is surrounded on both its Eastern and Western frontiers by communist nations that are either hostile, like China, or captive nations, like those of Eastern Europe. Until recently Moscow dominated the World Communist Movement, a potential source of both intelligence and diversion, but now a growing number of communist parties are attempting to shrug off the old stereotyped image of subservience to Moscow by stressing more the primary responsibility of each communist party toward its own country and working

class, and by emphasizing the paramount importance of basic human rights. Soviet relations with most European communists, Japan, and the non-aligned movement have never been worse. What we are witnessing is a further spread of ideological and organizational diversity. "Polycentrism" is the order of the day and the wave of the future. Until 1953 the Moscow Party line, defined by a single man, was decisive wherever the writ of communism ran. Since Stalin's death, especially since the Sino-Soviet split of the 1960s, things have begun to change. Moscow's bitter competition with Peking is here one of the major factors.

The Soviet position in the Third World is also shaky. Despite Soviet claims, it is not the Soviet Union but the West that stands as the model for economic progress. Moscow is no more "the Rome of the proletariat" of the world, as Andre Gide once put it. While theoretical Marxism seems to hold a strange fascination for many leaders of developing nations; the tools of press that these nations desperately need are more frequently than not provided by the West. The Soviet leaders realize better than anybody else that they are losing the ideological and geopolitical momentum. For them the global balance-sheet of the last

Above:
The Polish leadership affirm their membership and role within the Warsaw Pact. Following the imposition of martial law in Poland the Party leadership was taken over by the commander of the armed forces General Jaruzelski.

Below:
Soviet trucks lie abandoned in an Indonesian street due to a shortage of spare parts. This inability to meet commitments has meant that the Soviet image in the Third World, as an economic model, has suffered.

instance, the much-advertised Soviet naval forces. Here undoubtedly their progress has been most spectacular and has caused a great deal of serious apprehension in the West. But are we not too much mesmerized by sheer magic of large numbers? Does quantity really mean quality? And what about the geopolitical framework within which the Soviet Navy would have to operate in case of an armed conflict with the NATO forces? The editors of *Jane's Fighting Ships*, for example, claim that the Russians have achieved superiority in a variety of ships — submarines and heavy cruisers, for instance — and have challenged the US in a number of other naval weapons. Leaving aside for a while the issue that Western ships are on average much larger, technologically more advanced and hence much more effective than the Russian ones, it is worth focusing on the geopolitical aspects of Soviet naval power. The amazingly fast expansion of the Soviet Navy, as well as the merchant marine, has overshadowed the fact that the USSR is suffering from several handicaps that hamper its maritime potentialities. One of the disadvantages is a relatively short non-freezing and easily accessible coastline.

decade is negative. In the last 10 years, the USSR has bolstered its position in Afghanistan, Vietnam, Cambodia, Laos, Mozambique, Grenada, Libya, Chad, South Yemen, Angola, Cape Verde, Ethiopia, and Nicaragua. The total population of their new friends amounts to 136 million while the total GNP is $35 billion. On the other hand the Soviets have definitely lost ground in China, Egypt, Sudan, Indonesia, Somalia, Iraq, Guinea, Equatorial Guinea, Zimbabwe, and Jamaica. The total population of their losses reaches at least 1.25 billion while the GNP is $450 billion.

The gnomes of the Kremlin also realize that, despite their numerical superiority in conventional weapons and their theoretical nuclear parity, they suffer from such a large number of basic shortcomings that they are actually weaker even in purely military terms. Let us consider, for

Although it has some 35,000 miles of coastline (the largest in the world), the USSR is the most landlocked country on the globe. The farthest point from the ocean, Semirechye in Kazakhstan,

is about 1,600 miles from the seacoast. Moreover, most of the USSR lies as far north as Canada. Moscow is situated north of Edmonton, Alberta; Leningrad lies as far north as Anchorage, Alaska; the Crimean port of Sevastopol is as far north as Bangor, Maine. It is a severe strategic and economic handicap that most of the Russian ports are icebound for a considerable part of the year. Paradoxically, Murmansk, the northern-most Soviet harbor, is an exception, being usually accessible throughout the year because of the gulf stream.

On the other hand, the Gulf of Finland, with its ports of Leningrad, Kronstadt, and Reval, is frozen around the shores from November to April. The harbors of the Black Sea are as a rule iceblocked throughout January and February. Vladivostok in the Far East is icebound for four months in the winter, is precariously suspended at the end of a long line of communications, and is situated in a region claimed by China.

The stretches where Russia has access to the moderate Baltic and Black Seas are inhabited by non-Russian and highly restless people: the Finns, Estonians, Latvians, and Ukrainians. The outlet of the Black Sea is held by the Turks, while the outlets from the Baltic are held by the Danes and the Germans. The access to the Atlantic leads through the remote and desolate Murmansk and the Kola peninsula. The Pacific coast is separated from the

main centers by a formidable distance of up to 4,000 miles.

One has also to bear in mind that the sea coast of the Soviet Union is split into four main sectors: the Black Sea; the Baltic; the Arctic, with its subsidiary, the White Sea; and the Pacific Ocean. Maritime communications between the Black Sea

Above:
The prestige ship *Kiev* which is one of the most modern in the fleet shows the importance that the Soviets see in having a presence all over the world.

Below:
The Russian Navy has grown over the last 20 years yet is still inferior in number and quality to that of the United States.

and the Baltic are difficult enough, much less the journey from either the Black or Baltic Seas to the Pacific. The Imperial Fleet learned this fact first-hand in 1905 during the war against Japan, when its Baltic squadron tried to rush to the Far East to rescue its comrades-in-arms in the Pacific.

Even the canal routes between the Baltic and the White Seas, painstakingly built by Stalin with forced labor, do not permit the passage of sea-faring craft. The route from the White Sea to the Far Eastern waters along the northern shores of Siberia, some 4,000 miles long, also involves considerable hardship, despite the new technological developments, including the atomic icebreakers.

One of the main handicaps of the Soviet naval position is the distance separating the two inland seas, the Baltic and the Black Seas, from the three oceans. This compels the Soviet Union to maintain four separate fleets: the Baltic, the Black, the Arctic, and the Pacific.

Only in the Far East does the USSR enjoy true ''blue water capabilities.'' One has to remember, however, that the access to its bases there is precarious both geographically and politically because of the Sino-Soviet split. It is enough to look at the map to realize that, in the case of a Sino-Soviet war, Vladivostok would be the first target of Chinese missiles and bombs, as well as of a land attack.

Adding to this the fact that the Soviet Black Sea bases are situated on the southern fringe of the volatile Ukraine, ''the soft underbelly'' of the Soviet empire, one realizes that the geopolitical factors underlying Moscow's actual naval position are not too solid.

This should be compared with the broad and varied ''blue water'' capabilities of the Western navies, able to deploy easily relatively large and highly experienced forces throughout the world. The gnomes of the Kremlin realize all this very well. They are also well aware of the shortcomings of their conventional forces, including their tanks which need some 40 minutes of warming-up before their turrets can operate properly.

Another argument against a Soviet nuclear first strike is the awareness of their weakness, both on the ground and in the air. The Kremlin realizes that although the Warsaw Pact leads NATO in numbers of most weapons, the quality of the Western weapons mitigate the picture considerably. The Soviet leaders realize that their advantage in conventional forces is more than balanced by the Western superiority in intercontinental nuclear forces and Cruise missiles. They know that there is no ''definite margin of superiority'' on the Soviet side. The US alone has some 9,000 deliverable nuclear warheads against about 7,000 for the Soviets. To this one should add the nuclear arsenal of Great Britain and France. The West also has qualitative superiority in several areas such as accuracy, survivability and, in nuclear submarines, superior ability both to keep the seas and to escape detection. The US B-1 bomber also promises to be a formidable weapon.

The Soviet leaders also realize that the NATO forces are greatly superior to theirs in one category of weapons which may be of crucial importance during the next few years, namely in MX and Cruise missiles. Because the Cruise missile is only about 20 feet long, it can be easily hidden from satellite surveillance and other existing means, by which each Super Power successfully counts the other's missiles and launch silos, bombers, and submarines.

Cruise missiles could be hidden in internally modified commercial aircraft, or in almost any vehicle, for example an aircraft carrier or a truck. A single commercial jet could carry and launch several such missiles. The size and mobility of the Cruise missiles make the assessment of the location and numbers of these weapons virtually im-

possible. The United States plans to deploy more than 3,000 of a new version of vastly improved air-launched Cruise missiles both on B-52s beginning in 1982 and on B-1s in subsequent years; several 100 sea-launched Cruise missiles on submarines beginning in 1984; and 464 ground-launched Cruise missiles in Europe beginning in 1983.

All three types of Cruise missiles are small, mobile, self-guided in flight, and highly accurate. What is also important, the MX missiles are very inexpensive. Their launch equipment and operating costs are far less than those of bombers or land-and-sea-based intercontinental ballistic missiles. While ballistic missiles follow a parabolic trajectory similar to that of an artillery shell, the Cruise missile can maneuver and hug the terrain much closer than a manned aircraft.

Thus, NATO has not only stolen the march on the USSR in Cruise missiles, but thanks to the

Below:
The Cruise missile is of vital importance in American nuclear strategy. It is a low-level intermediate nuclear missile with a large variety of launch modes.

American superiority in electronics it has progressed in this category of weapons so far that, in the foreseeable future, it would be very unlikely to be overtaken by the Soviets. The US already has a new generation of highly sophisticated Cruise missiles on the drawing board. This generation includes multiple warheads, terminal supersonic speeds, and the Advanced Strategic Air-Launched Missile. Consequently, the Soviet military analysts look beyond first strikes to second and third attacks, in which numerous air- or sea-launched Cruise missiles, with warheads up to 300 kilotons apiece, would be devastatingly destructive of their residual capacity to continue the struggle, if ever unleashed. For all these reasons Cruise missile technology represents a quantum jump over the Soviets.

There is only one bright spot in the Soviet–Western technological race: it is the space program. So far, the Soviets have maintained momentum across the board in their space program, which has given them leadership positions in this decade in such diverse fields as planetary research and permanently manned space stations. For instance, on March 1 and 5, 1982, Soviet Veneras

13 and 14 respectively, landed on Venus. They returned a stunning array of color photos while reporting the first-ever chemical analyses of that planet's surface. These Veneras are to be followed by four others in 1984. These successes may be of crucial importance during World War IV. If there is ever such a conflict, it is most likely to be waged predominantly in outer space, but a conflict we are likely to witness will probably still be dominated by terrestrial realities. Even in space the West has some assets up its sleeve. One forgets that the space shuttle is being tested as a possible bomber operation in outer space.

Another point which the present writer would like to argue is the most likely area in which another global conflict may begin. Despite the opinions of my mostly Western-oriented colleagues, I believe that Moscow's strategy focuses more and more on the Middle East. The Afghan invasion appears as a deliberate act of policy which forms part of a grand design to encircle, subvert and eventually dominate the key areas of Arabia and the Persian Gulf. Just as the Near East is the treasure house of oil, so Africa is the treasure house of all sorts of mineral wealth, including oil.

Left:
President Anwar Sadat of Egypt, President Carter and Israeli Prime Minister Menachem Begin sign the Camp David agreement in 1978.

In 1979, when President Sadat and Prime Minister Begin signed the Egypt–Israel peace treaty, many in the West hoped that decades of Mideast strife were coming to an end. President Carter said he hoped the treaty would lead to "permanent peace in the Mideast." As we see now, these hopes have been dispelled. It seems that the Middle East is the main tinderbox of the world. There the Arab–Israeli conflict is the most highly explosive issue of our day, although, alas, not the only one. There are various other possible scenarios for the Middle East providing the fuse. When Ayatollah Khomeini goes, the Soviet Union may be tempted to take advantage of the ensuing chaos and intervene, thus triggering an armed response on the part of the US. (Or, for instance, Israel may decide to go to war with Syria, with Moscow deciding not to let its old client down for fear of losing credibility as a protector of the Arabs. After all, Syria's support is indispensable to bolster the already acquired Soviet strategic position in the Middle East.)

Military analysts in Washington and at the North Atlantic Treaty Organization's headquarters in Brussels tend to agree that there are no indications of an immediate Soviet move into Iran at the present moment. The Soviet Union is now too tied down in Afghanistan, where the Russians are reportedly continuing to build new airfields, barracks, and depots. But, in case of a crisis-situation in Teheran, Moscow could probably use the Tudeh party to destabilize Iran further and then make three Soviet proxies – Southern Yemen, Ethiopia, and Libya – intervene in a possible civil war. Late last year the three governments signed a treaty of mutual support. This could result in another scenario; for example, an attack on Saudi Arabia by Southern Yemeni and Ethiopian troops, possibly backed by Cuban pilots and commandos. In such an event, instant American assistance would be required. Such

assistance could come from the airborne battalion with the multi-national force in Sinai or from another airborne battalion stationed in Northern Italy. It seems beyond doubt that any serious

Below:
The Columbia space shuttle thunders away from the launch pad. The military potential of this space vehicle is enormous.

Soviet move in the Middle East would promptly create a major confrontation in that region with complications difficult to forecast at the present moment.

Another highly explosive scenario could be triggered, for instance, by a radical, pro-Soviet revolt in Saudi Arabia. There have been numerous speculations as to what the US is planning to do about the possible need to occupy Saudi and other gulf oilfields in the event of an Iranian-type upheaval there, whether executed with or without Soviet assistance. The Rapid Deployment Force and the base facilities it is acquiring in Kenya, Somalia, Egypt, and Oman are certainly tailored to that contingency.

What then are the conclusions of my speculations? To sum up, I would like to reiterate the following three main points:

(1) A premeditated nuclear war is unlikely. The Soviet leaders are as much afraid of a full-scale nuclear war as anybody else out of a sense of self-preservation. The Soviet leaders know that even the survivors of a nuclear war would envy the dead because the planet Earth would beomce uninhabitable. A deliberate first-strike gamble on either side is the least likely possibility.

(2) The present writer believes that outright Soviet aggression, especially in Western Europe, is unlikely in the near future and only a catastrophic politico-economic breakdown of the region, bordering on civil war or complete anarchy, could induce Moscow to intervene. So far our deterrence there has been credible enough and the Soviet strategists are unlikely to attack along the line of strongest resistance. They are like hotel thieves who try all the door handles and enter only unlocked rooms.

(3) Should a third world war break out after all, it is more likely to start in the Third World, but not as a result of a premeditated plan, but rather as a result of local or interregional conflicts, which the Kremlin would be tempted to exploit for its purposes. Such an intervention may or may not escalate the crisis and result in global catastrophe.

This leaves us with a scenario of a conflict conducted essentially with conventional weapons, with the nuclear missiles kept in reserve as was the case with poison gas during World War II. Since even the present-day conventional weapons are devastating enough and are available in terrifying quantities throughout the world, the future war would probably be much more ruinous and exhausting than the previous one.

After all, the arms race has not been limited to the Super Powers, but has covered most of the globe. This has been reflected in the phenomenon

of the enormous growth in both the quantity and quality of arms transfer, mostly to the countries of the Third World. In 1969 worldwide arms sales amounted to $9.4 billion; at the beginning of 1980 they had more than doubled, totaling $21 billion a year. The US arms sales abroad, which stood at $1.1 billion in 1970, rose in 10 years to a yearly average of $10 billion. From 1969 to 1978, arms exports by developing countries increased from $250 million to $837 million. Even more significant is the growing sophistication of the weaponry. In 1960 only four developing nations had supersonic combat aircraft; by 1977, 47 had them. Long-range surface-to-air missile owners rose from two nations in 1960 to 27 by mid-1975.

A protracted war of attrition may leave both sides so exhausted and so short of sophisticated hardware that we may retrogress to more primitive, long discarded methods of warfare. In November 1967, on the 50th anniversary of the Bolshevik revolution, an American journalist interviewed one of the organizers of the Red Army, Marshal Semyon Budyonny, then 84 years old. Toward the end the interviewer asked the old leader what, in his opinion, would be the role of the cavalry in a war of the future, Budyonny answered without hesitation: "Decisive!" Is this a truly realistic vision of the agonizing stage of a third world war if fought with non-nuclear weapons?

University of Wisconsin   M. K. Dziewanowski

Below:
Cuban commandos are called on to further Soviet interests around the world.

ACKNOWLEDGMENTS

The picture researcher would like to thank the following libraries for supplying the photographs:

Marcel Dassault: p 154 top right.
Hughes: pp 150, 196.
PAN-AM/DNA Photo: pp 8–9.
McDonald Douglas: p 149 top.
Ministere de la Défense, Paris: pp 56–7, 152–3, 168.
Ministry of Defence, London:

pp 48–9, 155 bottom, 162 inset, 164, 166–7, 170–1, 176–7, 192 bottom, 204, 218–9, 220–1, 222–3, 224–5, 226–7 top, 228.
John Moore: pp 15, 17 top, 32, 36, 39 top, 78, 91 top right, 98, 116–7, 126–7, 128–9, 130–1, 132–3, 134, 137, 139, 140 top, 140–1, 142–3, 144 top, 145 bottom, 146, 168 inset left, 173, 174, 178, 181, 183, 200, 202–3.

209, 238, 247, 249, 250
National Archives: pp 14 top, 37 top, 38 top, 39, 60–1, 96–7 center, 103 top, 104–5, 122–3, 141 inset top right, 145 top right, 148 bottom, 149 bottom, 156–7, 160–1, 185, 210–1, 229, 232–3, 234–5, 240, 243 below, 245, 248.
NATO: pp 50–1, 147, 148 top, 151 bottom, 154, 155 top left, 159 top, 162–3, 165 top

center right, 175, 190–1, 226–7 bottom.
Orbis: pp 29 top, 30 right, 84.
Panavia Tornado: pp 155 center right, 158–9.
Popperfoto: pp 11, 12–13, 16, 18–19, 72–3 inset, 74–5, 122 top left, 182, 184, 201.
Robert Hunt Library: pp 17 bottom, 22–23, 24, 26–7, 28–9, 31 bottom right, 41, 42–3, 44–5, 54–5, 58, 65, 67, 85, 96–7 top, 100–1 top, 101,

118–9, 120–1, 122–3, 124 top, 125 bottom, 135, 188–9 top, 243 top, 244, 245 top, 246, 251, 252.
TASS: pp 34–5, 38 top left, 52–3, 59, 62, 70–1, 72–3, 76–7, 80, 87–8, 88–9, 90–1 top, center right and bottom right, 92–3, 94–5, 99, 100–1 bottom, 102, 108–9, 110, 188 bottom, 193, 194–5, 205, 207, 212–3, 214–5, 216–7, 230–1, 241.